AFRICAN ISSUES

From the Pit
to the Market

AFRICAN ISSUES

AFRICAN ISSUES

From the Pit to the Market

Politics & the Diamond Economy in Sierra Leone

DIANE FROST
Department of Sociology,
Social Policy & Criminology,
University of Liverpool

JC JAMES CURREY

James Currey
is an imprint of
Boydell & Brewer Ltd
PO Box 9, Woodbridge
Suffolk IP12 3DF (GB)
www.jamescurrey.com
and of
Boydell & Brewer Inc.
668 Mt Hope Avenue
Rochester, NY 14620-2731 (US)
www.boydellandbrewer.com

First published 2012

1 2 3 4 5 15 14 13 12

The right of Diane Frost to be identified as
the author of this work has been asserted in accordance with
sections 77 and 78 of the Copyright, Designs and Patents Act 1988

British Library Cataloguing in Publication Data
A catalogue record for this book is available on request from the British Library

ISBN 978-1-84701-060-5 (James Currey paper)

The publisher has no responsibility for the continued existence or accuracy of URLs for external or third-party internet websites referred to in this book, and does not guarantee that any content on such websites is, or will remain, accurate or appropriate.

Papers used by Boydell & Brewer are natural, recycled products
made from wood grown from sustainable forests.

Typeset in 9/11 Melior with Optima display
by Avocet Typeset, Chilton, Aylesbury, Bucks
Printed and bound in Great Britain
by CPI Group (UK) Ltd, Croydon, CR0 4YY

This book is dedicated to the youth of Sierra Leone,
my partner Mel Walker and our children Ellie and Beth

CONTENTS

LIST OF ILLUSTRATIONS

Tables

ACRONYMS & ABBREVIATIONS

ADMS	Alluvial Diamond Mining Scheme
AFRC	The Armed Forces Revolutionary Council
APC	All Peoples Congress
CAST	Consolidated African Selection Trust
CDC	Chiefdom Development Committees
CDFs	Civilian Defence Forces
CSO	Central Selling Organisation
DCSL	Diamond Corporation Sierra Leone
DIFID	Department for International Development (UK)
DIMINCO	The National Diamond Mining Company (Sierra Leone) Ltd, jointly owned between the Government and the SLST
DTC	Diamond Trading Company
ECOMOMG	Economic Community of West African States Monitoring Group
ECOWAS	Economic Community of West African States
FAWE	Forum for African Women Educationalists
GDP	Gross domestic product
EO	Executive Outcomes
KPM	Kono Progressive Movement
GGDO	Government Gold and Diamond Office
ILO	International Labour Organisation
IFI	International financial institutions
IMF	International Monetary Fund
MOCKY	Movement of Concerned Kono Youth
MOPP	Movement for Progress Party
NDMC	National Diamond Mining Company
NGO	Non-governmental organisation
NPFL	National Patriotic Front of Liberia
NPRC	National Provisional Ruling Council
PMC	Private military company
PNP	People National Party

PSC	Private Security Company
SLA	Sierra Leonean Army
SLGR	Sierra Leone Government Railway
SLPP	Sierra Leone Peoples Party
SLST	Sierra Leone Selection Trust (became NDMC also known as DIMINCO)
RUF	Revolutionary United Front
UN	United Nations
UNAMSIL	United Nations Mission in Sierra Leone
UNDP	United Nations Development Programme
UNHCR	United Nations High Commissioner for Refugees
UNICEF	United Nations Children's Fund
UNOMSIL	United Nations Observer Mission to Sierra Leone
USAID	United States Agency for International Development
UPP	United Progressive Party
WHO	World Health Organisation

GLOSSARY

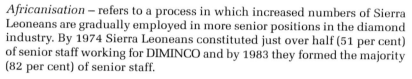

Africanisation – refers to a process in which increased numbers of Sierra Leoneans are gradually employed in more senior positions in the diamond industry. By 1974 Sierra Leoneans constituted just over half (51 per cent) of senior staff working for DIMINCO and by 1983 they formed the majority (82 per cent) of senior staff.

alluvial – diamonds found close to the surface in gravels and river beds. These can be mined using mechanised or non-mechanised artisanal techniques.

blood diamonds – has been used inter-changeably with conflict diamonds. This is also the name given to a Hollywood film, a book by Greg Campbell and a Kanye West song. All three are based on the conflict in Sierra Leone.

carat – unit of measurement of a diamond

colour – diamonds can be described as whitish, yellowish, greenish, brownish and pinkish.

conflict diamonds – diamonds that originate from areas controlled by groups opposed to the legitimate government and which are used to fund opposition to that government through armed conflict. Many such conflicts relate to Africa.

foreigners – from overseas, non-African

four Cs – colour, clarity, cut, carat that are taken into to account when valuing a stone

gems – the highest quality of diamond used in jewellery

Kamajor – A hunting sect/society of the Mende ethnic group that formed one of the Civilian Defence Forces (CDF) during the civil war.

Kimberlite – diamonds found in deep underground volcanic pipes that require deep mining technology to extract.

Marakas/Maracchas – Mandingo and Senegalese traders

Mixed parcel – a parcel of rough diamonds from more than one country

native foreigners – Africans from neighbouring countries

parcel – A package of diamonds containing varying amounts of carats from 10 to up to thousands of carats

polished – the skilled working of stones where as much as fifty per cent of the diamond can be lost.

resource curse – also referred to as the paradox of plenty in which large parts of Africa remain poor and underdeveloped despite an abundance of natural resource wealth.

rough – diamonds in their natural state and before cutting and polishing

shadow state – a theory created by Reno (1999) in which state officials of weak states acquire power through alliances and deals with corporations, warlords, local chieftaincy structures and arms dealers.

shell companies – companies that offer services to other companies without having any independent assets or active business operations themselves. Some shell companies have been used for money laundering purposes.

sobels – government soldiers by day, rebels by night

sights – around ten 'sights' a year are held by the CSO in which 'sightholders' are allocated a quota of diamonds for purchase (price determined by De Beers).

sightholders – are those chosen by De Beers to purchase a diamond quota (also determined by De Beers). Numbers are limited with less than 200 sightholders worldwide.

strangers – Sierra Leoneans who were 'non-Konos'. This was formalised under the 1954 Diamond Industry Protection Ordinance.

supporter – licensed investors who seek access to mining plots and who hire gangs of labourers (tributors) to work these plots in return for the use of tools and 'payment' in food. The proceeds of any 'winnings' (diamonds) are shared with the tributor.

tributor – a gang of labourers who work the gravels under a *supporter*

ACKNOWLEDGEMENTS

I wish to thank and acknowledge all those who have given me so much support during the research and writing of this work. They include first and foremost my long time friend Albert Moore, Chief Archivist, Government Archive, Freetown who as well as his friendship provided me with the luxury of transport to get around Freetown and arranged additional transport to do fieldwork in the Eastern province. Thank you also for providing the necessary letters for my Visa; introducing me to some important people and for helping to smooth my stay. I must also give a massive thank you to my other good friend Mr Sahr Bendu – a real fighter with guts and conviction who shared with me his anger and determination to change things in Sierra Leone and for introducing me to likeminded people and other contacts in the Kono area. Thank you for opening my eyes more widely to the hardships and suffering your people have endured. Keep up the struggle. I also wish to thank all those people I interviewed (some of whom wish to remain anonymous). The conversations I had with you all not only impressed me with your wealth and depth of political knowledge and understanding of the world but you inspired me with your enthusiasm for the future of your country in spite of what you have endured and continue to face. I also wish to thank the Town Chief who provided me with somewhere to stay in Koidu Town and for 'the driver' (and 'mechanic' – country style) of that very old Mercedes Benz that loyally got us back to Freetown despite the leaking sump.... I also wish to thank Mr Usman Kamara, Deputy Director of Mines (Ministry of Mineral Resources) for agreeing to be interviewed and Mr Lawrence Ndola-Myers (Manager of the Government Gold and Diamond Office) for giving me access to this closely guarded office and allowing me to observe the process of diamond evaluations. I have a huge debt of gratitude to my partner Mel Walker for the unconditional encouragement, patience and support you have provided in the course of my work over many years. Thank you for the extra care and love given to our daughters Ellie and Beth when things were sometimes difficult for them during my time away in Sierra Leone and elsewhere. A special thank you to Ellie, (a whizz kid on the computer) for the technical help with illustrations. I also acknowledge the financial support given by the University of Liverpool Research Development Fund which funded the fieldwork to Sierra Leone in 2003 and the Department of Sociology for a semester free of teaching in the autumn of 2004. Other people I wish to acknowledge and thank include Geoff Wilson (University of Natal) and my work colleagues, Dr Nicole Vitellone, Professor Sandra Walklate and Dr David Whyte, all in the Department of Sociology, Social Policy and Criminology, University of Liverpool. I would also like to thank the anonymous reviewers for the helpful suggestions and feedback. Finally, I acknowledge the assistance of various institutions including SOAS Library, the Public Record Office, Kew, John Rylands Library and Department of Geography Library, both at the University of Manchester; the Government Gold and Diamond Office and the Ministry of Mineral Resources, both in Freetown.

Diane Frost

PREFACE

In 2002 Sierra Leone emerged from a decade long brutal civil conflict. Since then renewed interest in this tiny West African state emerged as 'conflict diamonds' globally came to be the subject of much controversy and attempts to combat this trade continued to prove problematic. Indeed the concern over conflict diamonds even managed to penetrate aspects of popular culture seen in the Steven Speilberg film *Blood Diamonds* (2006) loosely based on the conflict in Sierra Leone. These diamonds also became the subject of a Kanye West single *Diamonds from Sierra Leone in* 2005. Such efforts have without a doubt contributed to raising awareness of conflict diamonds in Africa and have perhaps enlightened a few to this previously little known country. Today, blood diamonds continue to provoke controversy, whether this involves allegations against a certain supermodel said to have accepted 'blood diamonds' from a former Liberian war lord or whether this relates to concerns surrounding the human rights of those working in the mining of these stones. Sierra Leone continues to occupy an uneasy position as one of the world's poorest nations and at the same time the provider of millions of dollars worth of mineral wealth. So whilst Sierra Leone has provided high quality gem diamonds since the 1930s for the luxury markets of the West, as a nation it appears to have benefitted very little in return. Sierra Leone today continues to be an area of 'peripheral capitalism' and like many other developing nations that have come to rely on extractive industries this has brought a multitude of problems that will continue to afflict these countries in the future.

In attempting to explain how and why Sierra Leone occupies the position it does today, a number of complex contributory and inter-related factors will be examined throughout this work that acknowledge short-term and long-term factors, internal-external players, socio-economic and political factors and historical-contemporary issues. Within this broad nexus, we can further distinguish between wider structural factors on the one hand and the role of human agency on the other. Today, it would appear that Sierra Leone has become trapped in a system of corporate neo-colonialism, characterised by a reliance on external capital that translates into a huge debt burden, and aid to keep it afloat. Sierra Leone's political position not only in the global South, but more significantly as part of the African continent is significant particularly as this relates to the role of Western socio-economic and political policy here and the part played by foreign corporate business interests (often with the collusion of national elites). Only by acknowledging this can we begin to see the exploitation of Sierra Leone as part of this broader pattern of global inequality that continues to be perpetuated by the developed world on the developing world and sustains inequality *within* Sierra Leone. At the same time, the emergence of a 'shadow state' (Reno 1995) in the immediate post-independence period that runs parallel to the official state, continues to support an internal and corrupt elite at the expense of the poor. The shadow state perpetuates poverty and inequality here. Such factors contributed to the recent conflict and produced and sustained an economy of blood diamonds. Whilst conflict has ended and the diamonds coming out of Sierra Leone today can no longer be classed as blood or conflict diamonds, nevertheless evidence suggests that illicit activity in this industry continues and is doing little to tackle the gross and obscene poverty and inequality that many Sierra Leoneans endure. Moreover, while a process of reconstruction, reconciliation and integration have begun in Sierra Leone and the deep wounds of civil conflict have started to heal, inevitably the scars left will be a constant reminder of a dark period in this nation's history. This legacy will continue to impact on its future development to a greater or lesser degree.

Finally we need to acknowledge that there have been signs of improvements (albeit limited) in recent years. For example, Sierra Leone's Gross Domestic Product (GDP)[1] rose in 2007 by an estimated 6.4 per cent based on expatriate remittances and investments in mining (mainly rutile and bauxite) but also less positively through a reliance on foreign aid. Indeed debt relief under the *Enhanced Heavily Indebted Poor Countries* (HIPC) initiative will see Sierra Leone's total relief amounting to approximately US\$1.6 billion over 30 years (World Bank, October 2008). However, the country's GDP has been on a downward spiral since the end of the civil war as the figures opposite in Table 0.1 show.

At the same time, under the presidency of Ernest Bai Koroma (elected in 2007) a number of socio-political improvements have been implemented in terms of increased electricity supplies, strengthening legal protection for women and children and reform of the Anti-Corruption

[1] GDP is defined by The World Bank (2012) as 'the sum of gross value added by all resident producers in the economy plus any product taxes and minus any subsidies not included in the value of the products. It is calculated without making deductions for depreciation of fabricated assets or for depletion and degradation of natural resources'. See World Development Indicators, The World Bank http://data.worldbank.org/indicator/NY.GDP.MKTP.KD.ZG/countries/1W-SL?display=default. Accessed February 2012

Commission. However, such improvements are tempered by deeper and more widespread problems.

Sustained economic growth that is sufficient to create employment has not occurred. Large-scale, capital intensive mining almost ceased in recent years (*Africa Confidential* May 2009) and this sector continues to remain volatile. In 2006, large-scale mechanised mining accounted for 10 per cent of Sierra Leone's diamond exports by value (Fanthorpe and Maconachie 2010). Alluvial mining that relies on artisanal and small-scale mining (ASM) still forms the majority of Sierra Leone's production. According to a recent World Bank *Country Brief* document (2008) there is still a long way to go in terms of sustained development. As a result, real economic growth in Sierra Leone has declined from 27 per cent in 2002, to 9 per cent in 2003 to just over 7 per cent for 2004–2007. Health and Nutrition outcomes were among the worst in the world. Infant mortality (defined as the number of deaths under one year of age per 1000 live births) for example, was 160 in 2006 for Sierra Leone (World Bank 2008) in contrast to the United Kingdom that stood at 5 in the same year (UNECE 2008). Maternal mortality (defined by the World Health Organisation as the death of a woman while pregnant or within 42 days of termination of pregnancy) stood at 900 per 100,000 live births in 2005 in Sub-Saharan Africa as a whole (the highest regional rate). Of these, Sierra Leone had 2100 maternal deaths compared to Rwanda 1300, Liberia 1200 and Nigeria 1100. For the UK as a whole this stood at 8 in the same year, whilst the figure for Ireland was one (WHO 2007).

Moreover, the incidence of tuberculosis – a well known disease of the poor is high with an estimated 628 cases per 100,000 compared to 495 cases for the region as a whole. Figures for 2004, estimate that 66 per cent of the population live below the poverty line with a higher concentration (79 per cent) in rural areas. The 2007 UNDP Human Development Index Report ranked Sierra Leone at the very bottom at 177 out of 177 countries (based on 2005 data). Moreover, underemployment (particularly in urban

Table 0.1 GDP Annual Growth Figures for Sierra Leone (%)

2002	27.5
2003	9.3
2004	7.5
2005	7.2
2006	7.3
2007	6.4
2008	5.5
2009	3.2
2010	4.9

Source: GDP Growth (annual %) World Development Indicators, *World Bank* 2012

areas) continues to present problems. In 2006, three out of ten men aged 20–24 were neither formally employed nor in education (World Bank 2008). Recent research has highlighted the continuing issue of a 'youth crisis' that has become concentrated in urban areas where problems of crime and security have become an issue (Fanthorpe and Maconachie 2010). In general terms, youth unemployment can have cataclysmic effects on future conflict, can create problems of inter-generational poverty and is associated with high levels of crime, violence and in some cases political extremism (ILO 2003). Such youth proved ripe for enlistment into the recent civil conflict.[2]

It was the former British Prime Minister Tony Blair who described Africa more generally as being a 'scar on the conscience of the world' (BBC News 2001) giving some indication of Africa's troubled history and its continuing problems. Africa it would seem continues to be a continent 'disarticulated' from the global economy. According to Castells:

> Africa is not external to the global economy. Instead, it is disarticulated by its fragmented incorporation to the global economy through linkages such as a limited amount of commodity exports, speculative appropriation of valuable resources, financial transfers abroad, and parasitic consumption of imported goods. (Castells 1998: 91)

In 2005 the *Commission for Africa Report* (Chaired by the then Prime Minister Tony Blair), made a number of Recommendations at the G8 Gleneagles Summit (July 2005). This included a commitment to action that would generate a 'strong and prosperous Africa'. Reporting five years later at the UN New York Summit (September 2010) the Commissioners reported (my emphasis):

> There is much to celebrate. African governments have done more than ever before to promote business and investment. Donors have supported this by boosting their support to infrastructure and providing the aid and debt relief that has allowed African governments to increase their expenditure in key areas such as health, education and agriculture.
>
> But there remains much to be done. Progress on reforming international trade rules has been dismal; donors are still providing less in aid than their commitments; and African governments are still not investing as much as they promised in key areas. That is why we believe this review is timely, and why we believe it is right to renew a number of the recommendations we made in 2005 – because they have yet to be fully implemented – as well as make new recommendations.
>
> Africa's development requires a range of measures, with African governments in the lead supported by the international community. For example, *harnessing international demand for Africa's natural*

---

[2] See Fanthorpe and Maconachie (2010), and Peters (2011) for a comprehensive review of the literature on the role of youth in the civil war

resources to benefit ordinary Africans will depend on the commitment of African governments to passing on the benefits to their citizens, but also them having access to the best legal advice and a system of international trade that does not disadvantage Africa's products. (*Still Our Common Interest* September 2010)

The Commission concedes that whilst some progress has been made, this is not enough to meet the Millennium Development Goals (MDG). Indeed: 'sub-Saharan Africa as a whole will not achieve any of the MDGs on time and the vast majority of Africans have yet to benefit from the economic success of recent years' (*Still Our Common Interest*, 2010, Executive Summary).

Outline

The book is divided into two parts. Part I (Chapters 1–4) focuses on Sierra Leone as a nation endowed with natural resources. It looks at the way diamonds became embroiled in its social, economic and political history. Part II (Chapters 5–7) positions Sierra Leone in the wider context of global capitalism and examines its position through the lens of the international diamond trade. The chapters are organised along the following lines. Chapter 1 focuses on the broader historical context of Sierra Leone as a British colony and looks at the discovery and mining of alluvial diamonds from the 1930s onwards. It will look at developments in the diamond areas during British colonial rule and later under post-colonial governments and examine these developments in the broader context of theories of colonialism and peripheral capitalism. Chapter 2 will examine some of the debates that have emerged to account for the civil war there and will look at the role of private security firms who were paid for their services in diamond concessions. Chapters 3 and 4 are based on oral testimonies of those active in a number of organisations that have emerged in Kono since the conflict. These include discussions of the ongoing issue of smuggling of illicit diamonds despite recent developments such as the Kimberley Process, devised to ensure that diamonds being traded are 'clean'. Chapter 5 looks at Castells' concept of 'global criminal networks' and examines how far this concept can be applied to Sierra Leone. Chapter 6 examines the notion of parallel global economies in relation to diamonds – of the way the 'legitimate' diamond trade runs parallel to, and often overlaps with, the illicit trade in diamonds involving global criminal networks. Chapter 7 concludes by looking at Sierra Leonean diamonds in the broader context of recent developments in global resource predation, and in particular the dominance of corporate neo-colonialism. It will ask whether diamonds have been a blessing or a curse for Sierra Leone.

Introduction

This work examines the social, economic and political role that diamonds have played in Sierra Leone's development since they were first discovered during British colonial rule in the 1930s. While Sierra Leone gained political independence in the early 1960s its economic independence remained problematic. Moreover, issues of governance that have plagued many African nations and the continued problems of poverty and inequality have remained a prominent part of that history. These factors have ultimately fed into the decade long civil conflict that dominated much of the 1990s. This book argues that although this conflict became synonymous with *blood diamonds*, it actually had its roots in more complex and deep-rooted historical, socio-economic and political factors. In addition, continuing social and economic deprivations in Sierra Leone today occur in the context of an ever developing and ever wealthier global economy, in which poor nations like Sierra Leone are excluded and marginalised. This work will argue that Sierra Leone has become the victim of resource predation as far as diamonds are concerned as the search for valuable minerals or scarce resources continues unabated. Indeed, it would appear that a form of neo-colonial corporatism has emerged in which international business interests are exercising increasing economic and political control over Sierra Leone. Such developments appear to perpetuate existing underdevelopment in the diamond industry and involve both global criminal networks and international terror groups that operate alongside 'legitimate'mining and trading companies. The question one may ask is why and how do pieces of carbon rocks that have the same atoms as coal make them the focus of conflict, destruction and desire? What is it about diamonds that makes them valuable and why does their value continue to be fought over, contested and controlled in an industry that remains highly secretive and guarded?

Diamonds as objects

In order to understand why diamonds have the ability to provoke such powerful responses perhaps we need to have some understanding of diamonds as objects. Objects like diamonds are created in the context of specific but prevailing socio-economic and political conditions. They are not objective in the sense that they have uniformity of value or desirability; rather they are subjective creations that carry with them a story that is revealing of wider political economies and cultural norms and tastes. Objects have a biography or life in Kopytoff's (1986) words that is both revealing of the lives of those who have some connection with such objects, as well as revealing broader socio-economic, political and historical structures that reflect power relationships and cultural and historical desires. Diamonds, like other objects, have been subject to commoditisation – that is, they have acquired exchange value to be used to acquire other things. In most cases diamonds are exchanged for money, but they have also been exchanged at particular points in time for other objects or services.

We have seen in recent years the way diamonds have been responsible for funding civil wars, including those in Africa, (Sierra Leone, Angola, and Liberia) and played a more minor role in conflicts like that in the Democratic Republic of Congo. These *conflict diamonds* are particularly attractive to rebel forces for a number of reasons. These include the ease with which alluvials[1] can be mined using basic equipment; the difficulty of governments trying to enforce controls (even in peacetime) because of their scattering over large remote areas; their small size but high value making smuggling easy, and the lack of will in developing technologies that make identification easier. During the conflict in Sierra Leone, diamonds were exchanged for weapons by those on all sides of the war and had long been used in the system of patronage to acquire power and influence. More recently, such diamonds became embroiled in illegal drug trading and money laundering by international criminal networks. Terror groups like al-Qaeda for example have been implicated in such illegal dealings.

The biography of objects like diamonds then naturally leads us into the human relationships associated with these stones. Human relations with such objects are not necessarily based on need. If we consider for a moment the intrinsic value of objects like diamonds, we can say that there are some stones that do actually possess use value, and have what Mumford (1934 in Dant 1999) calls a 'life-function'. To this extent, industrial diamonds (as opposed to gems) do serve a useful purpose in industry and have always been in demand because of their versatility and their properties of toughness and hardness. Such diamonds have been used to

---

[1] Alluvials are defined briefly as diamonds found close to the surface in gravels and river beds.

penetrate steel, resist acid and provide the best thermal conductivity of any material. As a result they have become invaluable in industry and have been used in grinding, grooving, polishing, etching and sharpening tools. They have also been used in the drilling of oil wells and were used on the blades of knives used to cut cataracts from eyes. In this way, the value of industrial diamonds is in their ability to enrich life through their use in technology, rather than their rarity or aesthetic value. Indeed, the majority of the world's diamonds are industrials with only around 20 per cent of diamonds considered as gems and of sufficiently high quality to be used in jewellery. Industrial diamonds then have not been the focus of conflict nor have they attracted the level of desire and aesthetic value that gem diamonds have. Gem diamonds on the other hand serve no life function as such. Their value lies in their aesthetic qualities; their rarity and in the subsequent demand created through their use in jewellery. It is this that attracts high prices.

The life of a diamond begins millions of years ago when these stones were formed deep in the earth from compressed carbon at extreme temperatures. Igneous pipes of rock formed during volcanic activity hold diamond deposits called Kimberlite. These pipes exist on all the world's continents but not all contain diamonds. However, the concentration of Kimberlite pipes in Africa, can perhaps explain why around twelve African countries produce 75 per cent of the world's gem diamonds.[2] Over millions of years, the protruding pipes have become weathered, eroded and washed away with the surrounding land so that any diamonds present have been scattered over large areas. This explains why some can be found relatively close to the surface and in river beds, like those in Sierra Leone, Angola and Zaire. These alluvial diamonds compose around a third of the world's diamonds. The pipes from which these alluvials have been released can continue many miles deep into the earth's surface and require the use of explosives and machinery to extract them (as in the Kimberlite deposits in South Africa and Botswana), whilst in other cases erosion has exposed and broken down much of the original pipe. Evidence of alluvial stones can sometimes be a clue to richer deeper Kimberlite deposits, though not always (Green 1984).

Since the 1930s, Sierra Leone's diamond production has been dominated by alluvial stones, though in recent years deeper Kimberlite pipes have been found and exploited by mining companies like Branch Energy and Koidu Holdings Ltd. The demand for high quality Sierra Leonean gem diamonds has consistently increased since their discovery in the 1930s. This demand forms an important part of their life history since there is a very clear demarcation between those involved in the digging and extraction of these stones in Africa (many of whom will rarely see the finished product), and those in the West who consume these stones in the form of

---

[2] These are Angola, Botswana, Democratic Republic of Congo, Ghana, Guinea, Lesotho, Liberia, Namibia, Sierra Leone, South Africa, Tanzania and Zaire. See Green, T. (1981) *The World of Diamonds*, Weidenfeld & Nicolson London.

jewellery, but who have little idea of the conditions in which they have been exploited. In sub-Saharan Africa, many of these stones are extracted from the earth manually (artisanal mining) by young men and children. Apart from a few places, like South Africa and Botswana, there exists little industrial mining in Africa.[3] Indeed, globally there are estimated to be around 13 million people in 30 countries involved in small-scale/artisan mining, with around 80 to 100 million people dependent on the mining of gold and precious stones for their livelihood (Global Witness 2006).

It has been estimated that up to 120,000[4] Sierra Leoneans, possibly more, are engaged in some form of artisanal diamond mining. Diggers live a precarious existence receiving only a fraction of the value of the diamonds they recover (Goreux 2001). Moreover, the conditions in which artisanal/small-scale miners extract diamonds in Sierra Leone are feudal. Basic tools, like hand shovels are used to dig trenches and panning sieves are utilised to wash the extracted gravels. Often the work is carried out in several feet of murky water in the baking sun. This alluvial production which continues to dominate Sierra Leone today is typically artisanal or small-scale rudimentary production. It is often undertaken by poor unskilled labour (including child labour[5]) with little education and few employment prospects and usually takes place in remote rural areas where working conditions are dangerous, precarious, poorly paid and unhealthy. Moreover, where regulatory structures are weak or non-existent, a degree of illegal activity is often present (ibid.). In addition, the industry's global magnitude underlines the stark division between where the diamonds are found (developing nations) and where they are processed and sold (developed nations). There is also a gender divide since it is men and boys who toil, often in appalling conditions to dig these precious stones from the earth so that they can be worn by all classes of women in the developed world (although the biggest and most expensive are reserved for the rich and famous).

There are a number of general points that can be made with reference to commodities and their consumption, as well as more specific points. First, one issue that affects all commodities throughout their life history is that of knowledge, in particular knowledge of how commodities are produced (the technical and aesthetic), as well as consumed. A second kind of knowledge is that which characterises the space between the producers and consumers during the movement of commodities and the relative distance between these. Accordingly, the distance in knowledge between those involved in artisanal type digging of alluvial diamond deposits in Sierra Leone and those who consume diamond jewellery is

---

[3] Global Witness (2006) 'The Truth About Diamonds: Conflict and Development' November.

[4] Diamond Development Initiative website: www.ddiglobal.org. Accessed February 2012.

[5] The Child Rights Act (November 2008) criminalizes child labour in Sierra Leone defined as work that deprives children of their health, education or development opportunities. Full-time education is required for all those under 13 years. See 'Sierra Leone: Whether to criminalize child labour' IRIN – the UN Office for the Coordination of Humanitarian Affairs 4 September 2009. Accessed 18 September 2009.

huge. As already stated, those who consume diamonds often have little knowledge or understanding of where these stones come from nor the price paid throughout the *diamond chain* (from the small remuneration paid to diggers to the massive profits made by retail outlets). There is a clear relationship between the various stages in the process and the amount of profits made here. As a result, at the beginning of the stage when the stones are found and lifted from the earth, remuneration paid to the individual digger or to the government (where large mining companies are involved) is a fraction of the eventual value these stones will fetch. Similarly, those involved in the digging of these stones have limited knowledge of those who consume these diamonds and may erroneously assume this is confined to the wealthy.

In Western societies, diamonds have an appeal that has been cultivated amongst both mass consumers as well as the elite. The demand for gem diamonds for use in jewellery has remained steady over the years in large part because of the success of advertising campaigns like those crafted by mining and retail giant De Beers as well as others. Much of the marketing strategy used to sell diamonds by De Beers continues to be rooted in the constructed and symbolic association of diamonds (with their natural qualities of endurance and toughness) with that of eternal love. To this extent we are informed that 'the only thing stronger than a diamond is love itself'. The De Beers Group's success in selling diamonds can in part be explained by the construction of this symbolism as well as their trading on catchy and memorable slogans like 'A diamond is forever' based on the Ian Fleming book *Diamonds are Forever* (1956) later made into the film with the same title. The establishment of diamonds as a symbol of eternal love has helped fuel their commodification especially in the developed world. Market research conducted by De Beers in June 2009 gives some indication of the success of its marketing strategy in Europe. According to the company, seven out of 10 women think 'diamond jewellery is the most romantic gift a man can give a woman' (De Beers Press Release 2009). Clearly, De Beers has been highly successful over the years in selling a powerful image equating eternal love and romance, with the enduring qualities of diamonds.

Where the knowledge distance between consumers and producers is largest (this is especially so in the case of artisanal diggers at the bottom end), the social and economic consequences are greater. For Appadurai:

> ...such large gaps in knowledge of the ultimate market by the producer are usually conducive to high profits in trade and to the relative deprivation of the producing country or class in relation to the consumers and the traders. (Appadurai 1986: 43)

During the arduous journey diamonds make from being mined and eventually sold in jewellers shops they must pass through various hands. Rough gems have to be skilfully cut in established cutting industries like those based in Belgium, Israel and India before going on to be polished in

New York, Hong Kong or Tokyo and finally manufactured into jewellery. At each stage a percentage is taken with the retailer usually doubling the price paid when selling it on. The mark up of rough diamonds once cut and polished is as much as 50 per cent (*The Economist* 2007). The eventual mark up can reach up to 600 per cent (Green 1984). The largest profits then are made by the retailers including large monopolistic companies like the De Beers Group who have historically dominated the mining of African diamonds as well as controlling much of the international diamond supply to retailers (in which they also have interests).

A third area worthy of note relating to knowledge, involves the way diamonds are authenticated and distributed to potential buyers once they have left Sierra Leone in their *rough* state. The processes involved in diamond dealing and buying takes us into the 'bazaar' type scenario that Spooner (cited in Appadurai 1986) has written about with reference to oriental carpets. Spooner (1986) argues that in the oriental carpet business, as the relationship between producers and consumers of these commodities has changed over time, (with middle-class consumers having greater powers of direct negotiation with Central Asian weavers), this raises issues not just of the negotiation of price, but also of substance and in particular, the negotiation of authenticity – what constitutes a genuine oriental rug and what is a cheap replica (see Baudrillard 1981 and Bourdieu 1984 cited in Appadurai 1986).

Collaboration and negotiation between those in the know or the so called experts, and the consumer over value, authenticity and markets sees the qualitative transformation of the object that is now no longer just a commodity, but also a symbol or what Baudrillard (1981) terms a system of 'signs of status'. Similarly, in the diamond trade prices paid by dealers to licence holders (those who employ diggers) involves negotiation of price and authenticity. As the stones travel up the diamond chain (see Appendix A), the actual value dramatically increases as each stage of the journey involves a process of sorting, cutting, polishing, manufacturing and finally retailing as jewellery. During this process, a qualitative transformation occurs from a dull and unattractive *rough* into a highly sought after object of beauty and uniqueness that is marketed as a symbol of 'love' but which can also be symbolic of wealth, status and aspiration (seen through the culture of bling that initially began, we could argue, with the conspicuous consumption habits of the sixteenth-century European aristocracy). To illustrate how markets link into a system of signs of status we might consider the cultivation of demand for a particular piece of jewellery – the diamond engagement ring. Consumer demand for diamonds in the West became tied into the need to shift surplus stock of smaller stones during the 1940s. Here, consumption patterns were cultivated in response to production processes, and in particular the overproduction of smaller stones that would be used to create and invent the phenomena known as the engagement ring. This piece of jewellery was and still is marketed as a symbol of authentic love, so that engagement rings could not be anything other than diamonds. Diamonds and engagement have become synonymous.

The marketing of objects then like diamonds (particularly mass produced ones) has increasingly utilised a strategy that cultivates desirability whilst at the same time retaining reach-ability (Simmel cited in Appadurai 1986). The smaller stones used in less expensive engagement rings makes these affordable luxuries (though these are still beyond the reach of the majority of Africans). By attaching symbolism and significance to commodities, (love in this case, but also kudos, power, uniqueness and status in the case of larger diamonds and certain other commodities), this encourages the consumer to buy into a particular lifestyle or image that renders the object itself secondary to its social message. For Appadurai (1986) this represents an important cultural development of advanced capitalist societies. Commodities like diamonds then are objects that are cultural markers, they signify something that is beyond immediate usefulness, and their classification is indicative of the social and cultural structures and resources of societies. The way objects then are culturally defined and marked is more significant than the act of marking itself.

Colonialism and resource predation

Sierra Leone was colonised[6] long before diamonds were discovered and as with many forms of colonialism, the socio-economic and political interests of this country were geared towards serving the colonial power. Patterns of uneven economic development saw lucrative sectors like diamonds being 'developed' whilst other areas of the economy remained undeveloped. At independence, Sierra Leone emerged from colonial rule with an economy tarnished and restrained by the distorting influence of British rule here. Such patterns of economic development continued in post-colonial Sierra Leone as the elite[7] (an earlier creation of British involvement here) not only inherited this legacy but failed to challenge it. Colonial Sierra Leone had developed into an area of 'peripheral capitalism'[8] that was sustained and reinforced post independence.

Closely intertwined with Sierra Leone's economic characteristics was its political development. Patterns of rule and governance laid down during the colonial era had a profound impact on post-colonial Sierra

[6] Sierra Leone has a chequered history of colonisation. In 1787 the British colonised and created 'Freetown' as a settlement for freed African slaves (see S. Braidwood (1994) *Black Poor and White Philanthropists: London's Blacks and the Foundation of the Sierra Leone Settlement 1786–1791*, Liverpool: Liverpool University Press). In 1808, the coastal region became a British colony and this was later extended in 1896 to the interior. Independence was achieved in 1961.
[7] Sierra Leone's elite was dominated by the Creoles for several decades. This was a group made up of various strands of freed-slaves that were settled by the British in the late eighteenth century. Creoles were encouraged to be Christian, Western educated and to adopt British values.
[8] See Zack-Williams (1995) for a fuller discussion of this.

Leonean politics. For Reno (1995) the seeds of a parallel shadow state were sewn during colonialism. Indirect rule led to key individuals in diamond rich areas like Kono acquiring personal authority and paved the way for the emergence of an informal diamond market whilst simultaneously undermining state control over this. Various competing and conflicting interests emerged that formed part of this shadow state where a powerful predatory elite were able to use a proportion of the nations resources for both personal aggrandisement and as a means to buy political power. There is little doubt that poor governance and particularly corruption would come to have a huge bearing on Sierra Leone's development problems. Castells (1998) aptly describes the characteristics of such national groups and the economic impact of their activities in the following terms:

> The small, but affluent, bureaucratic class in many countries displays a high level of consumption of expensive imported goods, including Western food products and international fashion wear [Ekholm-Friedman 1993]. Capital flows from African countries to personal accounts and profitable international investment throughout the world, for the exclusive benefit of a few wealthy individuals, provide evidence of substantial private accumulation that is not reinvested in the country where the wealth is generated [Jackson and Rosberg 1994; Collier 1995]. So, there is a selective integration of small segments of African capital, affluent markets, and profitable exports into the global networks of capital, goods and services, while most of the economy, and the overwhelming majority of the population, are left to their own fate, between bare subsistence and violent pillage [Blomstrom and Lundhal 1993; Simon et al 1995] [....]. (Castells 1998: 91)

During British rule in Sierra Leone the development of mineral resources came to be dependent on direct foreign investment. Economic policies reflected this. Whilst it was illegal for Sierra Leoneans to be in possession of diamonds until the introduction of the Alluvial Diamond Mining Scheme (ADMS) in the 1950s, foreign mining companies like the Sierra Leone Selection Trust (SLST) continued to enjoy monopoly rights over such mining. Moreover, when Milton Margai became Sierra Leone's first prime minister in 1961 (under the Sierra Leone's Peoples Party - SLPP) he gave assurances to foreign mining companies that he would not nationalise these.

Colonialism had two faces. On the one hand it could display more nuanced and covert aspects that Fanon (1966) and others have perceptively observed. On the other hand, colonialism could unleash pillage and more naked violence. Both worked to render colonial subjects powerless. For Mbembe, colonial subjects: "had no rights against the state. He or she was bound to the power structure like a slave to the master" (Mbembe 2002:31). Bush (1999) also explains that:

Violence was integral to the creation of colonial Africa and, although administration became more complex and subtle, during the inter-war years, force remained a defining feature of colonial rule [...] Colonial rule was also sustained by the racist structures of colonial society, and consent was secured through the more subtle workings of cultural imperialism – what Franz Fanon (1966) has termed the 'colonisation of the personality'. (Bush 1999: 71)

A major preoccupation that has dominated diamond production in Sierra Leone both past and present is that of policing. A number of factors meant that control over the diamond areas has been a thorn in the side of the flesh of both government and mining companies. This can in part be explained by the type of diamonds found. The alluvial nature of these diamonds means they are relatively easy to access and notoriously difficult to police. Their high quality but small remuneration if working for a licence holder provides an added incentive to dig for these illegally or pocket any found whilst working for a licence holder. Moreover, in a nation where there are few employment opportunities and no welfare state, the temptation to pocket any diamonds recovered is extremely high. A final incentive for illicit digging or failure to hand over all diamonds recovered is that diamonds can fetch far more by selling directly to a dealer than the current system of working for a licence holder. Indeed, there is much emotional investment in digging for diamonds that resembles a form of gambling since it is propelled by both desperation in the face of poverty and the conviction that one could be lucky in finding a stone that could change one's life. And as with all gambling, the winners are seldom the one's doing the gambling. This is certainly true of diamond diggers. Nevertheless, in the absence of equitable and decent remuneration for artisanal diggers, poverty and desperation has encouraged illicit digging and dealing throughout this history. This meant the issue of security was dominant.

During the colonial period, a number of measures were taken to try and get a grip on illicit diamond activity. In the early 1950s when there was an illegal rush to tap into new deposits, the Freetown based police force was first extended to the diamond rich area of Kono District. The police were invested with powers to arrest anyone caught carrying tools that could be used to dig for diamonds. This was before Sierra Leoneans were allowed to dig for diamonds under the Alluvial Diamond Mining Scheme (ADMS). Also in the early 1950s, immigration controls were imposed on Lebanese and Africans from neighbouring countries and it became illegal for *strangers* (non-Kono Sierra Leoneans) or foreigners to be in the designated 'Diamond Protection Area' without a licence. However, the problem of illicit activity continued even though mining companies like the SLST had their own security and the support of the colonial authorities through the Sierra Leone Police Force. Accordingly, it was not uncommon for illicit digging to take place inside SLST concessions and on one occasion it was estimated that there were around 12,000 illicit diggers on SLST leased land in 1957. Huge efforts were made by the colonial government to protect the interests of this mining company as there were on occasion's major confrontations between illicit diggers who attacked SLST plant and the police. Illicit diggers began to form their own 'protection squads' against the actions of the police. Much of this was fuelled by anger and resentment that the land leased to the SLST had been cherry picked by the company, leaving the land outside these areas depleted of diamond stocks. It was not uncommon during the 1950s for violent confrontations to break out between the police and illicit diggers that led eventually to the police being issued with firearms to be used against illegal diggers. Diggers had begun to arm themselves with sticks and cutlasses.

A number of adjectives can be used with reference to the history of the diamond industry in Sierra Leone that include terms like exploitation, pillage, violence, secrecy, illicit dealings, control and policing, bondage, injustice and force. More controversially we might also draw an analogy between what has happened to Sierra Leone and its mineral wealth and the act of rape. Rape derives from the Latin *rapere* meaning to seize. The Oxford English Dictionary (2010) defines *rape* as 'violent assault'; 'forcible interference'; 'violation' and pillage. Indeed, such terms speak forcibly to the experience of Sierra Leone particularly during the recent civil conflict there with widespread atrocities committed by those on all sides of the conflict. Moreover, during British colonial rule here it is also true to say that Sierra Leone was subjected to violent and overt colonial power, particularly when resistance was employed that led to damaging long term consequences. Additionally, the political and economic power exercised during this period continues to have a stranglehold on both Sierra Leone and on the continent as a whole. This can be seen in subsequent unequal terms of trade, structural adjustment policies, the huge profits made by global mining corporations (and other business interests that bring few benefits to the majority), and the operation of criminal and corrupt networks (that include elements of the nation's elite). Moreover, like victims of rape, Africa has been blamed and seen to be responsible for those acts committed against it and for the position it finds itself in today. Whilst the act of rape affects individual victims, such acts are also part of wider structural problems in society that is reflective of unequal power relationships (between men and women; the colonised and the colonisers; the developed and the developing world). In addition, the way rape victims are dealt with by the judiciary (with victims themselves often treated as though they are on trial) is indicative of this disempowerment. Moreover, the relatively small number of perpetrators of rape who are actually convicted can be likened to the number of Western corporations, private military firms and national elites (in Africa) who also escape conviction of what can only be described as the raping and pillaging of resources in the developing world today.

Sierra Leone has endured unequal power relationships that continue to exist between the developed and the developing world. Its people were violated during the recent civil conflict with few willing to lend support and with many quick to blame this conflict and others in Africa on factors internal to that continent. The violation and brutality endured by civilians during colonial rule, the eruption of civil conflicts in places like Sierra Leone, Liberia and Rwanda and the subsequent abandonment of these victims by the international community says much about the unequal position of Africa in the world today and of the perceived cheapness of life on that continent.

When Sierra Leone gained its independence in the early 1960s it was clear to see that the economic patterns laid during colonialism continued as the needs of overseas markets dominated primary production (Cleeve 1997). Newly independent and cash-strapped nations like Sierra Leone continued to depend on private enterprise to finance, manage and provide technical expertise. For Bangura and Dumbuya (1993) large-scale corporations have been able to monopolise mineral production in Sierra Leone since its independence in 1961 through to 1992 for a number of reasons. These relate to Sierra Leone's government failure to nationalise a major share of mining operations allowing corporate giants to both dominate and benefit from the country's mineral resources. To this extent, the All Peoples Congress (APC) government under Siaka Stevens in 1968, resisted calls dating back to the 1960s, for the nationalisation of key industries (including diamonds). It would not be until the end of 1969 that Stevens buckled under pressure and gave in to calls to nationalise the diamond industry that came about in 1971 under the National Diamond Mining Company (NDMC). The grounds given for this action included the need to quicken *Africanisation* so that the government could more tightly control illicit mining. Since then, diamond mining in Sierra Leone continued to be dominated by small-scale artisanal alluvial mining with a smaller industrial mechanised sector.

Where mining corporations have been involved in the mining of raw materials more generally in Sierra Leone, this has been facilitated by their access to technology, their sheer size and their financial clout. As a result, subsequent economic growth in Sierra Leone was thwarted by the employment of expatriate rather than indigenous managers who implemented policies that were on the whole dictated by the parent companies overseas. This is particularly so with reference to long-term planning, capital investment and the location of production and processing (Bangura and Dumbuya 1993). Moreover, what was and still is particularly pertinent with reference to Sierra Leone's diamond industry is the remuneration or price paid for rough artisanal exports. So whilst mining companies' involvement in the actual mining of diamonds has been intermittent over the decades, at the same time their involvement in buying up rough stones from Sierra Leone has been important.

The colonial policy of producing commodities for export continued to dominate diamond production in Sierra Leone post independence. At the same time, mining giants like De Beers have wielded immense control over prices paid for artisanal export production here and have been monopolistic in their control over rough diamond stock supplies and distribution in the global diamond market. In the early 1990s whilst De Beers only produced around 45 per cent of the world's rough diamonds, at the same time it was able to keep a tight grip on regulating global diamond sales through the control it had over the selling of rough stones. In this way, De Beers controlled around 80 per cent of total global supplies (*The Economist* 2007). Today there are signs that this is changing as De Beers Diamond Trading Corporation (DTC – the distribution part of the De Beers Company) that once resided in London has relinquished centralised control here and invested some of this control in the producing countries themselves. The DTC now controls around half of the world's rough diamonds (by value) through its supply to 74 *sightholders* based around the world. The company's share of production continues to hold around the 40 percent mark (*The Economist* 2007; *The Economic Times* 2010).

Resource predation

Resource rich but economically marginal nations like Sierra Leone provide us with a good illustration of the way 'resources' and the influence of corporate neo-colonialism have brought misery and poverty for the mass of Sierra Leoneans. Long standing and deeply entrenched issues surrounding development (or lack of) were thrown into sharp relief as a result of the war. This includes the legacy of colonial exploitation, post-independence political mismanagement and the part played by global business interests in resource predation. All have contributed in one way or another to what some would argue is a *resource curse*.[9] Sierra Leone's diamond wealth has the potential to make this country rich yet as will be shown, a combination of complex historical and contemporary factors have worked together to halt this.

This dichotomy continues to dominate resource rich but economically marginalised nations like Sierra Leone who endure massive contradictions of on the one hand being endowed with large deposits of rich natural resources, including gold, diamonds, bauxite, rutile, and more recently oil (found off the coast[10]), and on the other is characterised by huge social and economic impoverishment, making it one of the poorest countries in the world.[11] In terms of GNP per capita, out of 206 countries covered in a

---

[9] See Alao, A. (2007) *The Tragedy of Endowment*, New York: University of Rochester Press for a more general discussion of this.
[10] See BBC 'Oil discovered off Sierra Leone' 16 September 2009.
[11] Sierra Leone is 183rd of the 183 nations listed in the UN Human Development Index. See I. Smillie, L.Gberie & R. Hazleton, (2000) *The Heart of the Matter, Sierra Leone, Diamonds and Human Security*, Partnership Africa Canada.

World Development Report 2000/01, Sierra Leone ranked 203, followed by DRC at 205 (Goreux 2001). Since the civil war and reconstruction efforts, Sierra Leone still remains fragile with half of government revenue coming from aid efforts. Moreover, this nation remains at the bottom of the UN Human Development Index with life expectancy rates of 39 years for men and 42 years for women (WHO 2008) compared with the UK of 77 years and 82 years respectively (UNECE 2008). Evidence suggest that in Sierra Leone in 2010 there existed approximately three doctors per 100,000 people (IRIN March 2010).

While there is a growing body of evidence that supports the notion of a 'resource curse', there is less agreement as to why this occurs. Economic explanations focus on unstable international commodity markets, declining terms of trade for primary resources and separation of resources from other sectors of the economy. Political explanations focus on kleptomanic elites and other groups whose looting of state assets empower these groups through the proceeds. The theft of resources both weakens the state and creates dependence on resource wealth booms and external aid. If taken together, such explanations link broader structural factors (economic) with the role of human agency (political).

There are many issues raised by the reliance of African countries on extractive industries and particularly luxury extractive industries like diamonds. Many of these industries do not have a local market (many Sierra Leoneans will never see a finished diamond). This means general infrastructures (like an educated workforce, distribution networks, consumer demand and even national energy supplies) often associated with market economies are not always necessary for such industries to operate. As Duffield states:

> On the contrary, extractive and niche export industries are relatively self-contained and insulated in relation to the rest of the society. That they are able to exist even in environments that are insecure also attests to their adaptability and resilience. Their main concern is to be able to extract commodities and realise them in the global marketplace with as few local commitments and difficulties as possible. In many respects, such industries complement the logic of liberal economic reform and its preference for privatised and debureaucratised facilitator states. (Duffield 2001: 183)

Whilst mineral exploitation has been seen as a catalyst for future economic growth in Africa as a whole this has not resulted in poverty reduction. Many mineral rich nations have the poorest people in the world; are heavily indebted (Angola had an external debt of \$10.45bn and Sierra Leone \$1.5bn [50% of GDP] in 2005) and have a poor history of political stability. Despite Sierra Leone's mineral deposits (diamonds, titanium, ore and bauxite) 89 per cent of its population was deemed to live in 'extreme poverty' in 2005 (*The Guardian* June 2005).

Of course there are many beneficiaries of Africa's resource wealth.

Alongside national elites we can include global corporations and criminal networks all of whom have benefitted and continue to reap rewards from Africa's resource wealth often through illegal and corrupt practices. Increasingly, predatory struggles for resource wealth around the world by Western multinationals has seen the violation of human rights and had devastating consequences on those communities affected (oil in Nigeria and Iraq, diamonds in Sierra Leone and Angola). A lack of political will to tackle corruption money entering the UK from Africa is still a problem as time and energy have been prioritised into investigating drugs and terrorism funds. Major loopholes remain in the realm of money laundering in Britain where the use of *shell companies* with nominee directors, numbered accounts and the use of trusts allow companies to keep one step ahead of existing (but outdated and inconsistent) anti-corruption law (Royal African Society 2005). At the same time, we need to be mindful not only of Western governments involvement in corrupt practices in Africa (and their unwitting encouragement of corruption through the privatisation of public services) but also of the hypocrisy of such governments in their own corruption scandals.[12]

The African Union estimated that Africa loses around $148 billion a year to corruption (not all of this domestically driven) and that much of this ends up in the international banking system, including Western banks (Royal African Society 2005). Such practices have been defined as a 'crime against humanity' because of the damaging impact on ordinary Africans (Hassan 2004). Accordingly:

> ...corruption may actually kill more people and wreck more lives than both drugs and terrorism. When a country's health budget is stolen clinics are left without drugs, hospitals without equipment, doctors are left unpaid and babies are not immunised. Corruption is a threat to the economic stability of countries whose resources have been stolen or diverted. (Royal African Society 2005: 3)

Indeed, the role played by overseas companies, financial institutions and Western governments must also be taken into account since these too have been complicit in the business of African corruption. In a report 'The Other Side of the Coin: The UK and Corruption in Africa' (AAPPG 2005: 20) it is argued that:

> We have to understand supply as well as the demand side of corruption. Who is offering the bribe and who is laundering the proceeds of corruption? In many cases western companies and western agents have been guilty of offering and paying bribes to government officials to secure contracts and other advantages. Western banks have been implicated in laundering the proceeds of corruption and western shell companies

---

[12] This includes MPs expenses in Britain in addition to the devastation wrought by other illegal actions (by their own standards) such as the military invasion of Iraq in contravention of international law.

and trusts have been set up to facilitate this. Western financial experts have also been accused of assisting corrupt officials to launder their illicit funds. And the international community, both donors and the private sector, have been guilty of turning a blind eye to rampant kleptomania [...]. Fear of detection means that the proceeds of corruption, like other 'dirty money', need to be laundered. The international financial system is riddled with loopholes. Poor enforcement of laundering regulations lead some experts to suggest there is as much as $1 trillion of illicit cross border flows annually [including proceeds from crime, corruption and commercial dirty money]. Unfortunately the UK, including the City of London and Overseas Territories and Crown Dependencies, has been implicated in this practice. (AAPPG 2005: 20)

The lack of transparency and scrutiny involved in such transactions not only increases the potential for corruption, a concern raised by both the World Bank and the IMF (*The Guardian* June 2005), but further encourages 'parallel economic systems'. This work shows (see Chapter 6) how close links have been found to exist between foreign extractive industries that operate in parts of the developing world and criminal dealings, including the funding of conflicts, terrorism, illegal arms trading and money laundering. Campaign groups such as Global Witness and Human Rights Watch have done much over the years to alert the public and governments to the links between natural resource exploitation and human rights abuses and have raised questions concerning the role of corporate social responsibility (Global Witness 2002, 2003; Human Rights Watch 2000).

Moreover, the use of natural resources as contraband trade (like drugs and diamonds) tends to prolong civil wars (Fearon 2004 cited in Maconachie and Binns 2007b). Diamonds have funded devastating wars in Africa (Sierra Leone, Angola, Liberia and Democratic Republic of Congo). This has not been helped by the fact that large parts of the continent were inundated with Soviet stockpiles of weapons in the 1990s left over from Cold War rivalries. This was in addition to illegal and corrupt arms trading from Britain and other Western countries and the deployment of private military companies (PMC) paid for in some cases with blood diamond or other valuable resources. Africa has paid a high price in terms of the loss of life, the unleashing of violence and other atrocities on innocent civilians and in terms of future independent and sustainable development. Whilst natural resources have been a curse[13] for many parts of Africa, causing devastation to nations like Sierra Leone, for the West, such resources have helped it grow richer and have helped widen the gap between the North and the South. Undoubtedly, some diamond deposits such as Kimberlite reserves (that rely on deep mining technology) have

---

[13] See Ross, M.L. (1999) 'The Political Economy of the Resource Curse' *World Politics*: 51. The term is used to explain the position of countries rich in mineral resources yet afflicted by extreme poverty and underdevelopment.

created wealth in countries like South Africa and Botswana where reserves have been easier to control. Diamonds of the alluvial variety however, that sit close to the surface and are more accessible have caused or fuelled conflicts, notably in Sierra Leone, Angola and Congo. In July 2000 in an attempt to identify and control *conflict diamonds* the International Diamond Manufacturers' Association and the World Federation of Diamond Bourses agreed at a meeting of the World Diamond Congress in Antwerp, a global certification scheme for rough diamonds (The Kimberley Process). It was also agreed that all rough diamonds be shipped in sealed packages certified by exporting nations and verified by a new international diamond council. However, continued smuggling and regulatory loopholes have undermined the Kimberley process that was introduced to combat illicit diamond activity. By the end of 2006, six years after the scheme was introduced, there were signs that this was being flouted. Not only have conflict diamonds come out of rebel-held territories in Ivory Coast (despite a UN embargo on all diamond from here), but it would seem the Kimberley certification scheme is being violated through the smuggling of diamonds from Zimbabwe into South Africa and through the illegal smuggling of Venezuelan rough diamonds into the US, Belgium, Guyana and elsewhere (Amnesty International & Global Witness May 2007).

Despite the country's mineral wealth (as well as diamonds, gold, rutile, bauxite and iron ore are also mined), Sierra Leone and the bulk of its people have been afflicted by a growing disparity between the relatively well off elite and the bulk of ordinary Sierra Leoneans. Crippling poverty, lack of social and economic opportunities, disempowerment and injustice continue to affect many. Whilst politicians, powerful chiefs in the diamond areas, diamond traders, arms dealers and mining companies have benefited, the political economy of diamonds has brought misery and poverty to the bulk of Sierra Leoneans.[14] In the context of state collapse and where the poor and disempowered have to survive through whatever means is available, the illicit informal economy of survival is strengthened (Mitchell 2005: 9). At the same time, such conditions are conducive to more organised forms of criminal and unethical business activities.

---

[14] Whilst alluvial diamond deposits in Sierra Leone have the potential to make this country rich, in reality diamond digging has led to many negative effects for the country as a whole. This includes soil erosion resulting in a decline of land for agriculture use, destruction of wildlife habitats, and disruption to drainage patterns (surface and subsurface). In addition the major beneficiaries of diamond production are multinational corporations that do not contribute to the national growth of Sierra Leones economy at present because the final product (and thus the bulk of the profits) is processed and marketed outside. What occurs through the trade in diamonds is an advanced export sector that does little to further the development of the rest of the economy and actually hinders and distorts this by diverting resources, including human resources. See Bangura, A.K. & Dumbuya, M.S. 'The Political Economy of Sierra Leone's Mineral Industry since Independence', *Sierra Leone Review*, Vol. 2 Winter 1993.

Debating the civil war

Various explanations[15] have been put forward to explain the civil conflict in Sierra Leone. These range from the racist and reactionary that point to an alleged inherent 'primitivism' in African culture to account for conflict (Kaplan 1994), to those that more convincingly examine a combination of internal and external explanations (Abdullah 2004, Keen 2005, Kandeh 1999, Richards 1996, Zack-Williams 1999). The former explanation was very much indicative of a pro-Washington perspective towards Africa that would be used to justify US withdrawal from the continent in the 1990s. The latter on the other hand emphasised the political role of the Sierra Leone elite that led to eventual economic crisis and subsequent alienation of large swathes of Sierra Leone's society, particularly its youth. Within this Reno (1995) identifies the shadow state to account for a parallel political authority of which many were excluded from and whose roots lay in the former colonial structure of British rule here. These latter explanations emphasise to one degree or another the integral relationship between self-serving political interests based on patrimonialism and the damaging economic consequences that led to the eventual involvement of international financial institutions (IFI) and subsequent austerity measures through structural adjustment policies (SAP). In such circumstances, it was the poor who bore the brunt of the corruption and misrule of post-independence governments and who continued to be squeezed the hardest under the austerity of SAP. When the RUF entered Sierra Leone, supported by Liberian Special Forces in the early 1990s, there were many willing recruits who appeared to have nothing to lose. For others they became the victims of a reign of terror and paid heavily through the loss of limbs, the killing of family and friends or the loss of their own life. Others too suffered from the psychological trauma of being witnesses to or victims of an array of other atrocities. As the conflict gathered momentum, Sierra Leone's mineral wealth in the form of diamonds diminished year on year due to a number of factors that ranged from pillaging by rebels to buy arms, to financing imports of foodstuffs like rice (which were then used to buy more diamonds from diggers and their agents); to the surrendering of control of diamond assets by the government to mining/security companies like Executive Outcomes to buy protection.

The mayhem of civil war provided a conduit for what can only be described as an anarchic global trade in illicit diamonds, where anyone and everyone with an interest appeared to have their snouts in the trough. If diamonds were not the cause of this conflict, they quickly

---

[15] See amongst others Richards, P. (1996) *Fighting for the Rainforest: War, Youth & Resources in Sierra Leone*, Oxford: James Currey; I. Abdullah (ed) (2004) *Between Democracy and Terror: the Sierra Leone Civil War*, Dakar: Council for the Development of Social Science Research in Africa; D. Keen (2005) *Conflict & Collusion in Sierra Leone*, Oxford: James Currey.

became embroiled as they were used not only as currency to buy arms and power by rebels and other military groups inside Sierra Leone and Liberia, but also by those whose influence extend beyond the borders of West Africa (including global criminal networks from the US and Russia, and more recently al Qaeda). In addition, large transnational mining companies like the world famous De Beers who whilst anxious to disassociate themselves from conflict diamonds, nevertheless became involved in the purchasing of rough diamonds from Sierra Leone during the conflict there (as they did in other conflict areas in Africa like Democratic Republic of Congo and Angola). De Beers has continued in recent years to control around 65 per cent of the total global rough diamond trade (*The Times* 2003), yet it is still difficult to prove that such diamonds are clean and free from conflict despite measures such as the Kimberley Certification Scheme.

In a broader context, a World Bank Report (Collier et al. 2003) found that economically marginal countries like Sierra Leone that have low incomes and who depend on primary exports like mineral wealth are actually more vulnerable to conflict. There appears to be a clear link between natural resources and conflict, particularly in Africa (Report on Commission for Africa 2005). Indeed, the propensity to civil war lies far more in issues of underdevelopment than it does in ethnic and/or religious strife (World Development Report 2003), though issues of governance can facilitate divisions that lead to conflict. Moreover, those nations involved in civil war have a greater risk of returning to conflict even after 10 years of peace.

The bigger picture – African political economy

Sierra Leone is one of 48 independent sub-Saharan African states that are as wide and diverse as any continent in terms of political stability and economic growth. Excepting the economic growth and political stability seen in the likes of Senegal, Botswana, Mauritius and South Africa, much of Africa has experienced decline in relation to other peripheral economies, both relatively and absolutely since the early 1980s. This development has been noted in journals such as *The Economist* (2000); in the academic literature (Arrighi 2002, Leys 1994), and by IFI like the World Bank (1989, 1994). Explanations for this state of affairs tend to fall into two categories: those who see external factors such as declining terms of trade and Cold War interventions as of primary importance and those who emphasise internal explanations that relate to governance such as authoritarian rule and corruption for example, the World Bank. This work argues that it is often a complex mix of both internal and external factors and that the political instability seen in many African nations can have causal explanations that are external in nature (see McGowan 2003). Many states in Africa have developed the way they have in response to dealing with global capitalism and internal power struggles. The global economy offers ways of dealing with 'politics' through the use of resources and for Reno (1998) offers an explanation to account for the phenomenon of 'Warlordism' in some African states, including Sierra Leone. He argues:

> [In Africa], the social and spatial distribution of resources, the availability of external partners, and the success of earlier efforts to implant a popular idea of state all play critical roles in shaping the options available to rulers who must innovate in efforts to survive [...] It is not inevitable that Africa's increasingly intense commercial ties with the rest of the world will favour the building of sovereign, territorial states. Indeed, rulers of other political units take advantage of opportunities conventionally organized states would be incapable of seizing. (Reno 1998: 39)

Internal explanations that attempt to account for Africa's economic decline often relate to notions of 'poor governance'. This perspective first emerged during the 1980s and was articulated in the Berg Report (1981) that had been commissioned by the World Bank. This came to dominate Washington's policy towards Africa more generally for much of the 1980s and 1990s. Out of this came structural adjustment policies (SAP) that were based on neoliberal economic thinking. SAP was premised on a pro-privatisation agenda, particularly as this related to state industries and the simultaneous removal of state controls of the market. It was argued that this would stimulate economic growth and lead to greater private capital investment. In fact, much of the evidence suggests the opposite. External factors like structural adjustment policies in Africa generally have not brought the economic growth that was promised and have actually seen the lowest rates of growth ever (Ferguson 2006). Moreover, SAP has eroded the control that national governments have over their domestic economies and in particular, their ability to secure social and economic rights. Indeed, the process of economic globalisation has undermined the will of governments to rectify social and economic rights because such processes act in the interests of global capital rather than people. This is the logic of the system (Falk in Dunne & Wheeler 1999). The South's political rights are also undermined in the running of their own national states, and in the bigger political arena of the UN Security Council which is dominated by the five veto-carrying members (only one is from the South). SAP has been shown to make the position of the poor worse, and pre-existing hardships sharper (see Killick 1994 in Thomas in Evans 1998; Mohan et al 2000). Such policies also undermine economic diversification and increase dependence on primary products (see Simon et al 1995 cited in Castells 1998: 85). The economic austerity imposed from outside by SAP violated basic social and economic human rights in Africa. Moreover, evidence suggests that SAP strengthened neo-patrimonialism in Africa and increased corruption (van de Walle 2001 cited in Ferguson

2006). In addition, this 'privatisation of the state'[16] has had a debilitating effect on state capacity to provide basic social amenities for its people. At the same time, such developments have strengthened enclave economic resource exploitation by multinational firms (who hire private armies to protect their interests). The notion of the weak or failed state has particular relevance here. Whilst not new, this appears to have taken on a different dimension in recent years. For Ferguson:

> Endemic violence, "weak states", and resource-extracting enclave production are hardly new features of the African political economy, of course. But there does appear to be a new extremity in the way that many African states have withdrawn from their putative national societies, leaving export production concentrated in guarded enclaves that are increasingly detached from their surrounding societies. (Ferguson 2006: 13 fn 10)

The failure of neo-liberal and pro-market economics (as pursued by the major IFI and UN development agencies) to kick-start development saw a shift in strategy by the end of the 1990s. This new strategy, which formed part of the newly emerging post-Washington consensus, placed greater emphasis on poverty reduction. However, this strategy was still underpinned by free trade and privatisation and came to be reflected in both the *Millennium Development Goals* (2000) and the *Commission for Africa* (2005). The Millennium Development Goals (MDGs) were agreed at the UN Millennium Summit in September 2000 with around 190 countries signing up to these. Their aim was to encourage the international community to commit to development changes, particularly in relation to reducing poverty in the developing world. Eight goals[17] were identified including a commitment to eradicate extreme poverty and hunger (DFID 2006). The MDGs have been seen to be 'overly-ambitious' by some with unrealistic expectations placed on aid. By September 2005, sub-Saharan Africa was already falling short by a 'wide margin' (Clemens & Moss 2005). Moreover, whilst the emphasis has been on reducing poverty, issues of governance and corruption figure prominent with little attention focused on the adverse affects of mining corporations and other private enterprise, nor on the issues raised by the policies of the IFIs themselves. This is hardly surprising given that the whole MDG strategy is underpinned by the belief that private enterprise will not only stimulate economic growth but is also a key element in providing state provision. However, an assessment undertaken in 2004 by the Extractive Industries Review (EIR) involved extensive consultation with civil society groups, government,

[16] To use Hibou's term. See Hibou, B (2004) *Privatising the State*, New York: Columbia University Press.

[17] The Eight Millennium Development Goals were; 1. Eradicate extreme poverty and hunger. 2. Achieve universal primary education. 3. Promote gender equality and empower women. 4. Reduce child mortality. 5. Improve maternal health. 6. Combat HIV and AIDS, malaria and other diseases. 7. Ensure environmental sustainability. 8. Develop a global partnership for development. See DFID 'Millennium Development Goals' www.dfid.gov.uk/mdg/

industry and academia. Various issues previously highlighted in the Millennium Development Goals were raised for the attention of the World Bank Group (WBG). This included governance and transparency; benefits to the poor and social and environmental risks. The EIR report addition-ally highlighted issues surrounding the rights of those affected by invest-ments in mining and concluded that in a number of cases, the World Bank's policy on oil and mining does little to either benefit local commu-nities or protect human rights and the environment (EIR World Bank 2005).

With the ending of war in Sierra Leone in January 2002, further aid came in the form of a huge international intervention effort that included the stationing of UN peacekeeping troops in rebel-held territory, millions of dollars of aid and the setting up of a UN backed war crimes tribunal in March 2004. The peace keeping process in Sierra Leone was estimated to have exceeded $2 billion by mid-2002, with the UN mission overall thought to have been the largest in the world in 2002 with 17,000 ground personnel during its peak. Moreover, international NGOs have invested large amounts of funds into projects for integrating ex-combatants (Hoffman 2004). The IMF made available $12m in low-interest loans to Sierra Leone in 2002 part of IMF programme aimed at reducing poverty and aiding economic growth (BBC News Online 13 March 2002). Whilst such efforts have helped to maintain stability and have been coupled with a commitment to global poverty reduction and sustainable development by the major powers, nevertheless nations like Sierra Leone continue to be afflicted by stagnating growth rates, deep seated and widespread poverty and low levels of human development.

A main criticism levelled against aid to the developing world is the way it is administered and in particular, the levels of dependency it creates. Creating dependency actually does more harm than good. Moreover, the attaching of conditionalities not only interferes with domestic economic and welfare policies, aid is often conditional upon promoting and accepting neo-liberal ideologies that benefits the economies of the global North. Aid has also been responsible for reinforcing the image of Africa as a helpless victim, unable to aid itself. A worrying and dangerous conse-quence of this is the way some have used such arguments to propagate damaging racist views that poverty, disease, low life expectancy and high infant mortality rates in Africa are the result of inherent racial inferiority and lower intelligence.[18] In other words, Africans are responsible for their own plight. Aid has also to some degree masked the real reasons for Africa's plight. This includes the legacy of colonial exploitation; the burden of debt and former structural adjustment policies (SAP); unequal terms of trade (with high tariffs that make African crops uneconomic);

[18] See newspaper coverage in *The Guardian* Friday 24 March 2006 on Dr Frank Ellis (former lecturer of Slavonic Studies, University of Leeds) who claimed Black people and women are genetically inferior. Also, see *The Observer* Sunday 5 November 2006 for similar views expressed by lecturer in evolutionary psychology (LSE) Satoshi Kanazawa.

ruthless exploitation of natural resources by multinational corporations; internal and external corruption, and the continent playing host to a multitude of international criminal dealings from money laundering to arms trading. The issue of aid would again be raised in the *Commission for Africa* (2005) as part of the IFI policy towards tackling poverty here.

In February 2004, UK prime minister Tony Blair launched the *Commission for Africa* (CFA). This report was published in March 2005 and immediately preceded the Gleneagles summit of the G8 in July in that year. Its stated aims were to 'take a fresh look at Africa's past and present and the international community's role in its development path'. The solution to Africa's continuing development problems was couched in terms of neoliberal policies of privatisation of infrastructures through public-private partnerships, forced trade liberalisation, and deregulation (Commission for Africa 2005). These policies were not only designed to encourage foreign investment in Africa but were actively developed with business in mind given that major multinational corporate interests had a hand in the development of the CFA report. (Corporate Watch 2005). The Commission's follow up Report that coincided with the UN Summit in New York (September 2010) noted that between 2003 to 2008, the continent sustained average annual growth rates of 6% with foreign investment and exports quadrupling largely as a result of African governments' efforts to make it easier to do business here. The increased demand for Africa's natural resources was also noted (*Still Our Common Interest* September 2010).

Whilst there has been some acknowledgement by the CFA of the way natural resources can precipitate conflict, the part played by multinational corporations in this have yet to be acknowledged. Instead, the Commission's report criticised the Organisation for Economic Co-operation and Development (OECD) guidelines to multinationals for failing to give clear guidance on resource exploitation and conflict. Moreover, the Commission explicitly stated that 'liberalisation must not be forced on Africa through trade or aid conditions and must be done in a way that reduces reciprocal demands to a minimum' (Commission for Africa 2005: 75). However, the G8 summit that followed in July 2005 proved disappointing in terms of what was on offer to aid poor countries. In the vast majority of cases, overseas aid would indeed be tied into conditionalities such as free market reforms and reciprocal liberalisation of developing economies. Moreover, much of what was promised 'explicitly ties aid to co-operation in the US's "war on terror"' (Hodkinson 2005: 2). Poor nations in Africa and elsewhere then, as ever, would not be free to determine their own economic policies. The government of Sierra Leone had already begun to embrace a promarket policy through its encouragement of private sector investment in the mineral industry in preference to investing state assets here. In its 2003 Core Mining Policy the government of Sierra Leone stated that:

> The Government of Sierra Leone is committed to a 'free market' approach and economic policies, which will ensure the development of

the minerals sector in accordance with international best practice, and within an enabling environment competitive with other countries that have similar exploration and mining potential. The Government will ensure the sector is managed in a transparent, open and accountable manner. (Diamond Development Initiative International 2008)

The Commission for Africa opened up greater opportunities for business. In particular, opportunities for public-private partnerships (PPPs) were created to build infrastructures and provide utilities like water and electricity. Such schemes are sold as being more efficient. The privatisation of public services (that first occurred in the UK itself) has led to the spending of UK aid in Africa on deals with, and for the services of, private enterprise. This includes UK management consultancy companies as well as companies that specialise in infrastructure building. Whilst many UK companies have disproportionately secured contracts and benefited from such business deals,[19] evidence suggests that such schemes are not always more efficient, often cost more and provide huge opportunities for corruption.[20] At the same time, such schemes do not appear to benefit the vast majority of the poor who are subjected to higher prices and continue in their struggle for access to clean water (Corporate Watch 2005). Nevertheless, the CFA is clear about the role of business in Africa and the expectations demanded of multinational companies:

> Clearly, the responsibility for managing resources lies with the state. But the international community also has a role to play in maintaining high standards of governance. If it does so in its own activities – and demands it in the activities of private sector agents, like the multinational companies active in developing countries – then it will be better positioned to encourage similar high standards in the way African countries manage the cash from their natural resources. (Commission for Africa 2005: 146)

One of the recommendations of the Commission for Africa was that:

[19] Companies involved in such schemes include the management consultancy firm Adam Smith International, infrastructure companies like Jacobs Babtie and Halcrow who have provided 'technical assistance' to Africa, UK water company Northumbrian Water and BiWater, a Dorking-based company who have both had public-private partnership contracts across Africa, including Tanzania. Other UK companies include GSL that was part of Group 4, HSBC who form part of Trans African Concessions. The Africa World Economic Summit (1–3 June 2005) was sponsored by global giants like Microsoft, Coca-Cola, McKinsey & Company and Pfizer all looking for business opportunities. See Corporate Watch (2005) 'The Commission for Africa and Corporate Involvement' June. www.corporatewatch.org.uk/?lid=1535 cited in Mines & Communities (2005) 'Edinburgh G8 summit and mining companies' www.minesandcommunities.org/Action/press662.htm Accessed 18 October 2005.

[20] This is according to a report published by Farlam, P. (2005) 'Working Together. 'Assessing Public-Private Partnerships in Africa' February. *The South African Institute on International Affairs* www.oecd.org/dataoecd/44/4/34867724.pdf cited in Corporate Watch (2005) 'The Commission for Africa and Corporate Involvement' June. www.corporatewatch.org.uk/?lid=1535 cited in Mines & Communities (2005) 'Edinburgh G8 summit and mining companies' www.minesandcommunities.org/Action/press662.htm Accessed 18 October 2005.

> Developed country governments, company shareholders and consumers should put pressure on companies to be more transparent in their activities in developing countries, and to adhere to international codes and standards for behaviour. (Report of Commission for Africa 2005: 146–7)

Unfortunately, much of this has yet to be translated into practice. The lack of transparency in the involvement of multinational corporations in Africa continues to be a cause for concern. This particularly relates to the links found to exist between foreign extractive industries and illegal activities, including arms trading, money laundering and terrorism. (*The Guardian* June 2005). Nevertheless, the solution to Africa's development problems continue to be seen in terms of free-market economics, including government enlistment of mining firms to invest and exploit diamond and other mineral reserves (World Bank 2001). However, the EIR (2006) advised the World Bank Group to discourage extractive industry (EI) investment where 'good governance' (including the ability of citizens to hold their government accountable or where conflict is absent) is lacking. This is based on the view that in conditions of political instability and where human rights and political freedoms are weak or absent and there is a lack of capacity to manage environmental and social impacts, EI development does not bring development that is favourable to that country as a whole. Instead, the EIR (2006) point out that revenue from EI continues to be hijacked by the political and economic elites of such nations. It is of little surprise then that the EIR (2006) is critical of the World Bank Group's neglect of governance when considering issues of EI especially since the Group had made previous commitments to issues of governance in 2004 (Lawrence & Reisch 2006). At the same time, evidence suggests that where significant capital investment has taken place in Africa, that it has generally been concentrated in mineral-extracting industries (like those in Angola, Equatorial Guinea, Nigeria and Sudan). Moreover, poor governance, corruption and human rights abuses have not prevented such investment by private companies. Indeed as Ferguson (2006: 196) has argued:

> The countries that (in terms of World Bank and IMF reformers) are the biggest 'failures' have been among the *most* successful at attracting foreign capital investment. African countries where peace, democracy, and some measure of 'rule of law' obtain have had very mixed records in drawing capital investment in recent years. But countries with the most violent and 'corrupt' states, even those with active civil wars, have often attracted very significant inflows.

It is within this broader context of the continent as a whole that we have to position Sierra Leone's recent history and position today. Only then can we begin to understand this country's future prospects particularly in relation to the way natural resources like diamonds can or cannot lead to poverty reduction and greater social justice.

PART I   Sierra Leone & Diamonds

1
Colonialism, Post-colonialism & Resource Predation

The diamond giveth to a man that beareth it strength and virtue and keepeth him from grievance, meetings and temptations and from venom.....It enricheth him that beareth it, enricheth in value and good. (From the Worshipful Company of Goldsmiths, London 1513 cited in De Beers Group Annual Review 2004: 27)

Sierra Leone's colonisation by the British in the late eighteenth century and the discovery of diamonds in the 1930s had a multitude of consequences. This included urban growth, migration and the uneven development of infrastructures. Yet in terms of developing Sierra Leone's economy and society more generally, revenues from diamonds fell far short of this, only benefitting the colonial government and private companies like the Sierra Leone Selection Trust. Sierra Leone remained an area of peripheral capitalist development despite its diamond wealth. The chapter will argue that patterns of economic development laid down during the colonial era, persisted well into the post-colonial period. The way these manifest themselves will be the subject of Chapter 2.

Sierra Leone and the imperial project

Sierra Leone's recent history is closely associated with its slaving activities and its colonisation by the British in 1787 of the Sierra Leone peninsula area. Freetown became the main town in this area and was named so because it became the home of various diasporan freed African slaves. This included those who gained their freedom from slavery through fighting on the side of the British in the American war of independence, and a small number of London's 'Black Poor', a group of ex-slaves forced to live and beg around the streets of London. A number of these were repatriated or deported to Africa in the late eighteenth century.[1] Freetown also became the home of other diasporan Africans, including those liberated from slave ships intercepted by Royal Navy anti-slave patrols that policed the waters around West Africa. (Fyfe 1962, Harrell-Bond et al. 1978, Braidwood 1994). Between 1808 and the 1870s thousands of these *Liberated Africans* were settled with a total of 43,057 being taken from slave ships and re-settled here in 1833 (Harrell-Bond et al. 1978).

The colony of Sierra Leone (that included the indigenous inhabitants) was ruled commercially between 1787–1807 by a British firm – the Sierra Leone Company and was taken over by the British Colonial Office in 1808 (Harrell-Bond ibid., Oliver & Fage 1988). Though Sierra Leone was not formally colonised until 1896, the Sierra Leone Company and the Colony Government had made political and economic inroads in this area. The land on which the early peninsula colony was established had resulted through negotiations with the local population (Harrell-Bond ibid.). A series of treaties forged with political leaders in the interior promoted trade and protected trade routes. In turn, African political leaders sought support from the colony government in order to promote their own political and economic interests (Skinner & Skinner 1971, 1973, 1974 in Harrell-Bond ibid.).

Those areas involved in production or located along trade routes had the closest connections with Freetown and the colonial presence. Other areas, whilst they could be physically close to Freetown might actually be furthest in terms of colonial influence. This influence gradually extended when the hinterland area of the colony peninsula, the Protectorate, was formally colonised in 1896 (Harrell-Bond ibid.).The colonisation of Sierra Leone by the British formed part of the European *Scramble for Africa* where the major European powers formally sanctioned the division of Africa at the Berlin Conference of 1884–85. This imperialistic move gained impetus from the need to acquire new markets for manufactured goods from Europe, for new sources of raw materials and for the need to invest surplus capital. Explanations offered to account for this imperialist expansion have come from conservatives, liberals and Marxists, with each stressing the primacy of political, economic or other factors. The overall effect of Africa's colonisation is seen by conservatives to have resulted in the positive development of the continent. For others, the ruthless exploitation of colonialism led to the continent's underdevelopment.[2]

Gallagher & Robinson (1961) for example stress the political elements of imperialist expansion that began with the British occupation of Egypt and the securing of the Suez Canal, the lifeline of the empire. The need to

[1] The repatriation or deportation of the 'Black Poor' was justified on the grounds of the strain they and other poor people were putting on poor relief. See S. J. Braidwood (1994) *The Black Poor and White Philanthropists,* Liverpool: Liverpool University Press. These 'Settlers' as they became known, also included Nova Scotians and Maroons. See Fyfe (1962) *A History of Sierra Leone,* Oxford: Oxford University Press.

[2] See O' Collins, R. et al (1994) *Historical Problems of Imperial Africa*, Princeton: Marcus Wiener Publishers for a greater discussion of this.

occupy territories to safeguard trade routes led to nationalist rivalries between the major European powers. Hobson (1902) and Lenin (1917) among others offer economic explanations for colonial expansion, albeit from different perspectives. Hobson, an English liberal economist, produced one of the first accounts of imperialism in 1902. He argues that a small section of the capitalist class was benefitting from imperialist expansion at the expense of the rest. He identifies 'the great manufacturers for export trade', 'the shipping trade' but 'by far the most important economic factors in imperialism are the influence relating to investments.' (Harman 2003: 4). For Hobson the solution lay in government intervention to expand the domestic economy and defend industrial capitalism against finance capitalism (ibid, 2003). Lenin's famous *Imperialism: The Highest Stage of Capitalism* (1917) followed in the wake of Hobson. Here, Lenin acknowledges Hobson's identification of the dominance of finance and further incorporates Hilferding's use of *finance capital* as being central to European imperialist expansion. For Lenin, this later led to the First World War. Indeed, Hilferding, Lenin and Bukharin all noted that the rise of finance capital was characterised by the merging of relations between industrial capital and finance capital (Brewer 1980). Lenin also described this period as the *monopoly stage* of capitalism because of the shift away from the 'free market'. Writing at the time of the First World War, Lenin pronounced:

> Marx had proved that free competition gives rise to the concentration of production, which, in turn at a certain stage of development, leads to monopoly. Today, monopoly has become a fact…The rise of monopolies, as the result of the concentration of production, is a general and fundamental law of the present stage of development of capitalism. (Lenin 1933: 20–21 in Harman 2003:1)

Lenin's concept of monopoly capitalism found expression in the division of the world into empires between the major European powers. Colonial conquest was not the only feature of monopoly capitalism but this is perhaps the most important from our point of view. To go back to Robinson & Gallagher (1961), the carving up of Africa and other territories around the world was indeed a political act and in some cases political motives overrode economic ones, like in the case of Egypt.[3] Yet, the new phase of capitalist development has to be understood in economic terms whilst simultaneously acknowledging the inter-connectedness of this with political and social processes. The last quarter of the nineteenth century was a period of great economic growth for the major European powers. Britain, the world's dominant capitalist power at the time increased its capital exports with total investment in foreign stocks rising from £95 million in 1883 to £393 million in 1889. (Feis 1935 in Harman 2003). Many of the raw materials needed by the technologically advanced nations came from colonial areas like Africa. Palm oil for example, became crucial to new

[3] Control here ensured that trade routes via the Suez Canal to India remained open.

industries like soap and margarine manufacturing. Capital export to the colonies was invested in infrastructures such as roads, railway, port and wharves. The bulk of this capital investment however went to the US and places like Argentina. What is clear in this global economic network is that political control through colonisation in some parts of the world like Africa contributed to the protection of economic interests elsewhere. Harman aptly captures the intricacies of ties between economic and political interests:

> Colonies offered the capitalist of the colonial power protected outlets for investment. They also provided military bases to protect routes to investment elsewhere. For Britain possessions such as Malta, Cyprus, Egypt, South Yemen and the Cape were important not just as sources of profit in their own right, but as stopping-off places to India [....]. The empire was like a woven garment which stopped British capitalism catching a cold: a single thread might seem of little importance, but if snapped the rest would start unravelling. At least that was how those who ran the empire, their colleagues in the city of London and their friends in British industry saw things. (Harman 1999: 397)

Colonialism in Africa was closely tied into the socio-economic and political interests of Britain both at home and in the global economy. Whilst diamonds and other resources like gold, iron ore, bauxite and rutile would not be discovered in Sierra Leone until later, (though this was not true in other parts of Africa), there were other advantages to empire. This included not only the exploitation of land and resources but also the utilisation of local labour in the harnessing and transportation of these resources to the economies of Europe (Frost 1999, Fyfe 1962).

Whilst there was widespread resistance to the colonial conquest of Africa, there were also instances where weaker African rulers allied themselves to Europeans as a bulwark against stronger neighbouring countries. The tactics of 'divide and rule' proved useful where the colonisers could seize upon existing political and ethnic rivalries in an effort to undermine local solidarity (Gellar 1995, Boahen 1987). Legitimate trade that came to replace the slave trade was characterised by the exchange of raw materials like palm oil, timber, cocoa, coffee and other crops for the manufactured goods created in the factories of Europe. Colonialism actively discouraged technological innovation and the development of indigenous industrialisation, except in the growth of crops for export to Europe. In British West Africa the cultivation of such crops continued under African farmers and despite advances in metalworking and metallurgy, the technology used in terms of tools and implements had remained unchanged for a thousand years. Colonialism and the slave trade before it had disrupted farming and agriculture and had stifled inquiry and innovation making advances in technology almost impossible (Okigbo 1993).

Colonialism also saw the demise of political and economic independence and has been described by Okigbo (1993:28) as 'enslaving Africans in

their local environment by imposing alien conditions – laws and jurispru-
dence, religion, customs and dress, language and culture – on the subject
peoples'. Boahen (1987) supports this view and adds that colonialism
delayed the political development and maturity of African states:

> The loss of sovereignty , in turn, implied the loss of the right of a state
> to control its own destiny; to plan its own development; to decide
> which outside nations to borrow from or associate with or emulate; to
> conduct its own diplomacy and international relations; and above all,
> to manage or even mismanage its own affairs, derive pride and pleasure
> from its successes, and derive lessons, frustrations, and experience
> from its failures. (Boahen 1987 in Collins 1994: 311)

Colonialism was also responsible for reinforcing conservative traditional
elements in some areas. In Sierra Leone for example, patriarchal tenden-
cies were encouraged as these reflected European perceptions of all
women, European and African. A decline in the status of African women
occurred, who in pre-colonial Sierra Leone for example, had served as
chiefs among the Mende here. The economic status of certain African arti-
sans was also weakened. Blacksmiths, jewellers, weavers, woodworkers
and musicians were all undermined economically, with the importation of
European goods. Whilst colonialism brought with it new opportunities for
some workers[4] and it created new social classes and new relationships,
overall the slowness of economic development meant that opportunities
for social mobility were few (Gellar 1995). The minority of Africans who
benefited from the little education on offer prepared them not for equality
with Europeans but for the inferior positions, they would come to occupy
in the colonial system (Gellar 1995).

Colonialism in Africa served the economic and political interests of
the colonial power and in doing this the British in West Africa relied on
traditional rulers and chiefs to carry out colonial policy, including the
unpopular task of the collection of taxes and help in the governing of
large swathes of territories and populations (Gellar 1995). Such measures
could undermine the authority of the chiefs, seen by many as agents of
the colonial power (ibid.). Moreover, according to Reno (1995) the system
of indirect rule in Sierra Leone through traditional paramount chiefs was
indicative of the incompleteness of colonial power since the co-operation of the chiefs was needed in such tasks as the collection of taxes. This
collaborative relationship, described as tributary by Reno, sowed the
seeds of what he terms the shadow state. The desire for social stability
saw modifications to indirect rule outside of Freetown. In Kono for
example, which would become an important diamond mining area, we
see:

---

[4] Such as employment opportunities for some groups for example Kru sailors. See Frost, D.
(1999) *Work and Community among West African Migrant Workers*, Liverpool: Liverpool
University Press.

a colonial rule that increasingly depended upon personal understand-ings with local strongmen not only to maintain social peace, but also to buttress expanded state institutions. Economic and administrative expansion, coupled with political reforms, gave intermediaries addi-tional resources for extending their personal authority. (Reno 1995: 31)

When diamonds were discovered in Kono in the 1930s, moves to increase state power came about that simultaneously threatened the authority of the chiefs, especially as European mining companies were given a monopoly on mineral exploitation. Yet while decisions over mineral exploitation and the collection and spending of revenues remained firmly in the hands of the colonial government, local accommodations with chiefs soon emerged that added to their powers over alienation of land, control of settlement and immigration. Such factors paved the way for informal diamond markets. Moreover, these developments served to even-tually undermine state control and legitimate government institutions as control over mineral production and export led to this parallel shadow state. This had no responsibility or accountability to the public and opened the way for widespread corruption (Reno 1995).

Colonialism in Africa did lead to uneven economic growth and the imposition of infrastructures that benefitted some Africans. Such devel-opments, however, were to serve the economic interests of the coloniser. With the formal colonisation of the Sierra Leone Protectorate, it was neces-sary to build infrastructures, including railway lines and roads. Yet such developments were uneven. As a result, the transport system served some sections of the protectorate and left others isolated. Some areas became more developed than others leading to differentials in wealth. The devel-opment of infrastructures led to increased trading activities by European merchant firms and those of settlers and Lebanese traders. The gradual spreading of the cash economy, the importation of manufactured goods from Europe and the extension of waged employment led to a broadening of the economic system whereby greater numbers were compelled to participate in this cash economy (Harrell-Bond et al. 1978). The demand for payment of colonial taxes added to this burden.

The expropriation of communal lands throughout Africa led to the enforced uprooting of populations and their transformations into poorly paid urban and rural workers (Gellar 1995). In Sierra Leone, the number of wage earners increased in the 1930s with the discovery of iron and allu-vial diamonds. This contrasts with South Africa where Kimberlite diamonds and gold had been discovered much earlier in the 1870s and 1880s. Here mineral wealth led to rapid industrialisation and the financing of railway enterprise and mining towns by private money. In South Africa and the Rhodesias, European settlement here led to the recruitment of male African 'migrant labourers' recruited temporarily from surrounding rural areas that could stretch hundreds of miles (Oliver & Fage 1988).

In Sierra Leone by contrast, it is estimated that tens of thousands left their villages to work in these new mining industries (Harrell-Bond et al. 1978). Diamondiferous areas like Bo and Kono became centres that attracted increased populations from the 1930s onwards. This was also true of iron mining around Marampa and Port Loko District. Resources like diamonds served to strengthen the links between these areas in the Protectorate and Freetown. Of course, the mining of diamonds would also affect the populations living in and around these areas. The diamond mining boom in Bo, Kenema and other towns from 1953 onwards was decisive in the migration of people to these areas (Harrell-Bond et al. 1978). Yet population movement was not simply from the rural countryside and neighbouring territories to the urban centre of Sierra Leone's capital, Freetown. Movement also occurred from one part of the protectorate to another where perceived economic opportunities were up for grabs.

Colonialism in Africa led to the control of the land, its resources, its imports and exports and retained the power to monopolise economic policy through political and military control. Colonialism also bound economies like Sierra Leone to a global capitalist system that operated in the interests of the colonising powers. Areas that developed economically did so with the interest of the dominant metropolitan power in mind. This included the financial and insurance companies who invested in Africa, shipping firms who traded manufactured goods from Europe and exported Africa's raw materials and mining companies that exploited valuable mineral resources (Gellar 1995). In all of this, African initiatives were thwarted, especially in the modern sectors of the economy using non-indigenous 'middlemen', like the Lebanese in West Africa and Asians in East Africa (Gellar 1995). Many areas were not developed or industrialised and remained areas of peripheral capitalist development, including the diamond areas of Sierra Leone (Zack-Williams 1995).

Colonial rule and the growth of Sierra Leone's diamond industry circa 1930–1961

In February 1930 a letter was sent to the colonial secretary in Freetown from the director of the geological department, Freetown. It stated that whilst prospecting for gold in the Gbobora stream at Fortingaia, in Kono District, Eastern Province a crystal was found that he at once recognised as a diamond. After a further two hours, another diamond was recovered from the stream and each was estimated to be about a fifth to a quarter carat in size (CSO Confidential Series 3 February 1930). This would mark the beginnings of Sierra Leone's diamond industry. The accidental discovery of diamonds in Sierra Leone was not so different from the discovery of those first found much earlier in Brazil and South Africa. In

Brazil, diamonds were discovered in alluvial gold deposits in 1725 in the state of Minas Geraes, 70 miles north of Rio de Janeiro. In South Africa, the son of a Boer farmer found the first diamond on the bank of the Orange River near Hometown in 1867. The first diamonds ever found though were those in India, which were mined not later than 600 BC. These were again alluvial and were found in river gravels and clays (Burke, 1959).

After the first diamonds were recovered in Sierra Leone, it was not long before the Consolidated African Selection Trust Ltd (CAST) who had been working in the Gold Coast undertook further explorations for diamonds. In 1930–31 'Gold Coast people' came to Sierra Leone with a prospecting team from CAST because of their experience in diamond mining (CSO Open Policy Files, Allocation of Crown lands and mining sites). Gold Coast Africans would bring with them their techniques of diamond prospecting and show Sierra Leoneans their methods, which they did. Lines of pits measuring 5 feet by 2 feet were dug across the Gbobore stream at 100–foot intervals. After several days' work, small deposits were found. This prompted CAST to apply for and win exclusive prospecting rights over an area of 4,170 square miles of eastern Sierra Leone. The discoveries of additional diamond deposits outside CAST's control saw the company entering into further negotiations with the colonial government to extend mining rights over the whole of Sierra Leone. In 1935, this was granted for a period of 99 years (Burke 1959: 324–5).

In the meantime, the press in Britain were reporting on the increased demand for diamonds in Europe. The *Daily Telegraph's* (3 September 1932) headline announced a 'Boom in Diamonds' and referred to the 'very brisk business' taking place on the Antwerp diamond markets where all available stocks had become exhausted. It reported that prices on ordinary stones had increased by 20 per cent and on higher quality stones by 10 per cent. *The Daily Express* (5 October 1932) reported on the 'World Rush for Diamonds'. The apparent world-wide increase in demand for diamonds had pushed prices up by 20–25 per cent and had left London, (where 90–95 per cent of the world's diamond trade passed and where the London Diamond Corporation controlled the trade) unable to meet demand.

A new company called the Sierra Leone Selection Trust Ltd (SLST) was created as a subsidiary of CAST and was formed to take over diamond mining operations in Sierra Leone. It was incorporated in London in 1934.[5] In 1935, the SLST was granted a monopoly of diamond production by the British colonial authorities. This gave the company exclusive rights

---

[5] CAST was jointly owned by the Selection Trust Group of Companies who owned 95 per cent and De Beers Consolidated Mines of South Africa who owned 5 per cent. See Zack-Williams, A.B. (1995), *Tributors, Supporters and Merchant Capital*, Aldershot: Avebury: 175; Greenhalgh, P. (1985) *West African diamonds 1919–1983: An Economic History*, Manchester: Manchester University Press: 47–52; Van der Laan, H.L. (1965) *The Sierra Leone Diamonds – An economic Study covering the years 1952–1961*, Oxford: Oxford University Press Chapter 3 for detailed discussion of this; L.J. Burke (1959) 'A Short Account of the Discovery of the Major Diamond Deposits' in *Sierra Leone Studies*, Dec New Series No. 12: 325.

to prospect for, produce and market diamonds throughout the colony with the exception of Marampa and Tonkolili, areas held by another company for the mining of iron ore. The SLST was obliged to pay a rental of £7,000 a year but was exempt from all rents, taxes, royalties, export duties, charges or impositions, except a tax on profits which would not exceed 27 ½ per cent of the Trust's net profit (CSO Open Policy Files File, SLST 1930s; CO/029/63; Burke 1959).

In 1951 a unitary constitution was created giving Sierra Leoneans greater political rights. The cabinet, now made up of African ministers became responsible for internal government. Similar advances occurred at local government level where greater responsibility was now invested in District Councils (Van der Laan 1965). The Protectorate-based Sierra Leone's People's Party (SLPP) won a majority under its leader Milton Margai, a Mende from the southern province. Bangura and Dumbuya (1993) have argued that these political developments signalled the decline of Britain's control over Sierra Leone's minerals, including diamonds. It came as no surprise to the British that with increased political rights, Sierra Leoneans would voice their dissatisfaction over agreements made with the mining companies, including the SLST. The then minister of Mines, Siaka Stevens had in 1946 pressed the protectorate assembly to push for better terms from the mining companies (Van der Laan 1965).

In 1953, a secret memo was sent from the acting governor to the secretary of state for the colonies in which the former warned of the 'deep feeling' that underlies the debate amongst Sierra Leonean leaders concerning mining concessions. It was stated that companies such as the SLST needed to 'get or keep the co-operation of the people' and the goodwill of the leaders. This letter followed in the wake of a debate in the legislative council. Eleven Sierra Leonean members spoke, (including the mover of the resolution, the member for Kono district, the Rev. P. Dunbar), in favour of the following (amended) and subsequently passed resolution: 'Be it resolved that this Government negotiates with the Mining Companies with a view to reviewing the existing agreements and concessions' (CO/029/63 1953). The original resolution had been much more strongly worded and was a warning to the government of the strength of feeling on this issue.[6] The member for Kono justified changing the existing agreements with the mining companies on a number of grounds. These included the fact that the existing agreements were made between the companies and three paramount chiefs. This was no longer adequate representation given the increase in the legislature brought about by recent constitutional changes. More pertinently, he pointed out that the mineral

[6] The original letter had stated: 'Be it resolved that this Council on behalf of the entire country of Sierra Leone hereby registers its strong dissatisfaction with the terms and conditions of the existing mining agreements and concessions, and calls upon government to take immediately all possible constitutional means to change or improve them, so that Sierra Leone may obtain and secure the maximum amount of financial benefit she really deserves.' Letter from Acting Gov of Sierra Leone to Rt Hon Oliver Lyttelton MP, Sec of State for the Colonies File No S.F. 3630/3. Despatch No. 287 Secret. CO/029/63 PRO, Kew.

resources of the country belonged to the public, but such agreements gave the company all mineral rights. In addition, the intention of placing between 68 and 72 police constables at Yengema and the estimated cost of £70,000 for the building of quarters, not including the cost of maintenance, was forcing government to commit large amounts of revenue with no financial benefit to the country. Various members supported these views and Wallace Johnson, member for Wilberforce and York seconded the motion. He complained of the injustice of the 'amount of minerals and raw materials that are being drained from this country', and that this was not commensurate with the money received. Wallace Johnson also criticised the absurdity of the existing agreement that could charge, convict and imprison anyone found in possession of a diamond, even if this was found on his or her own land because this belonged to the SLST. Johnson ended his support for the resolution by arguing that he hoped that these agreements would be reviewed 'so that we as a people will be able to benefit from the mineral wealth of our country'. The member for Bo District went on to explain how those who negotiated the agreement with the SLST did not know the monetary value of diamonds. He went on to explain how people began to realise their worth when increasing numbers began to be imprisoned for being in possession of diamonds. Such actions caused much dissatisfaction amongst the people of Kono. The member for Kono finished the debate with the following statement:

> One important thing is this: this country will hardly be self-supporting without the change, which is so necessary, and we can hardly move towards self-government in this country if we really could not avail ourselves of the maximum benefit from our mineral and agricultural wealth. I would like this statement to be printed in the most grotesque type. (Transcript of Legislative Council Dec 1952 CO/029/63)

The secretary of state for the colonies in secret correspondence with the acting governor, acknowledged the significance of this last point. He explained (my emphasis):

> The belief that handsome profits have been and are being made by the company and that the country needs a larger share of them in order to increase revenue for development inevitably exacerbates feeling among the public and among unofficial members of the legislative council [Sierra Leoneans]. No executive council could retain public confidence – if it could retain its hold on office – unless it strove for and succeeded in obtaining a review of the Sierra Leone selection trust agreement and it would be quite impossible for it to exercise a moderating influence when wage demands were being pressed by miners. If these handsome profits were not being made it would be possible to convince many members of Council that even though the Agreement was out of accord with present day sentiment there was not a good case for revision. *But an examination of the*

Company's accounts fully supports popular belief that large profits are made. (CO/029/63, 1953)

There was also some discussion concerning the question of diamonds which had been found anywhere in Sierra Leone automatically becoming the company's property. It was decided that if diamonds were found outside the SLST concession area, they became the property of the Government. This would ensure the continued monopoly of the SLST and it was hoped this would placate resentment towards the Company (CO/029/63).

In 1955, an agreement between the government and the SLST reduced the rights of the company to an area of 450 square miles in the Kono and Kenema Districts. Rights for diamond digging in the rest of the country now came under government control. After various discussions and compromises, the final boundaries of the areas to be worked by the company were agreed upon (Binns 1982, Bangura & Dumbuya 1993). In addition, the company was permitted to prospect in the rest of the country for deeper deposits of at least 15 feet and could apply for a mining lease if successful. The SLST also had a form of veto, according to Van der Laan (1965) in case foreign companies wanted to mine diamonds in the rest of the country. Whilst some, especially those in the Bo and Kenema Districts, welcomed the agreement, the compensation paid to the SLST of £1,570,000 was criticised. Siaka Stevens, the minister of mines, defended the amount of compensation by arguing that originally the company had demanded a much higher sum of around £10,000,000. Those who lost out through this agreement were the Konos since in addition to the six mining leases already held by the SLST, an additional 200 square miles were given over to the Company. Konos feared that any areas left for local diamond diggers would be barren of diamonds. Relations between the Kono District Council and Central Government continued to be strained into the early 1960s (Van der Lann 1965).

In 1956 the SLPP government established the Alluvial Diamond Mining Scheme (ADMS) which issued licences to native Sierra Leoneans for legalized diamond digging (Binns 1982, Bangura and Dumbuya 1993). Later in 1959 the scheme set up an official buying agency to purchase diamonds found (The Government Diamond Office GDO). This became the sole legal exporter of diamonds under the scheme (Bangura and Dumbuya 1993, Van der Laan 1965). In the meantime, the Diamond Corporation based in London established the Diamond Corporation Sierra Leone (DCSL) to buy stones from licensed dealers and established offices in Bo and Kenema. Whilst licences for diggers could only be issued to native Sierra Leoneans, dealer's licences were not so restrictive and many went to Lebanese dealers (Van der Laan 1965). The Mines Department under the Minister, Siaka Stevens, received the revenue from the licences and put in place procedures to legalize digging in or near a town. After 30 days, already eight Chiefdoms in Bo and six in Kenema had become legalized diamond areas under the scheme and between February and March 1956, 1,500 licences had been issued. It was estimated that with up to 20 diggers or tributors on each licensed plot, there would have been in the region of around 30,000 diggers working under this scheme by the end of March (Van der Laan 1965).

There was an expectation that with legalization the industry would be modernised, and 'mining' rather than 'digging' would describe the work process. This preference was reflected in the name of the Alluvial Diamond Mining Scheme, though both terms would be used interchangeably throughout the 1950s. Some ad hoc modernisation was introduced through the importation of hand and mechanical pumps, washing pans and diamond scales. The recently established Sierra Leone Diamond Mining Company of Gerihun bought machinery worth several thousand pounds. The speaker of Baoma Cheifdom had organised the SLDMC and had planned to sell shares in the company at £100 to provide capital for the Company. New techniques were also introduced in this period, including the use of dams during the dry season to recover diamonds from riverbeds. This was first used on the Sewa River in 1959 and the practice quickly spread (Van der Laan 1965). Apart from these initiatives, the exploitation of diamonds in Sierra Leone outside of the SLST was not highly developed or wholly systematic and relied in the main on ad hoc methods.

To what extent did the SLST operations represent an enclave development? Van der Laan (1965) has argued that the SLST operations displayed all the characteristics of an enclave economy since its activities were largely self-contained, with little integration into the surrounding economy. The company rarely bought local products, relying instead on foreign supplies. Its use of foreign capital, expatriate managers and foreign markets further distinguished the economic activities of this company from the rest of the economy. The highly mechanised methods of production again set this apart from the surrounding economy where farming, manual diamond mining and other activities relied on labour intensive, non-mechanised methods. Whilst there was some notable secondary effects that the SLST had on Kono's economy, seen in the purchasing power of its employees, Van der Laan (1965) argues that overall, its effects on the economy of Kono have been limited. This contrasts with the effects of SLST on the national economy, where revenue from all mining companies' boosted government funds.

Binns (1982) has also commented on the issue of enclave development with reference to Sierra Leone's mineral wealth. He defines this as being characterised by large inputs of expatriate plant, personnel and finance. Yet whilst this was certainly the case for the SLST, Binns argues that not only have diamonds been a significant feature of the local and national economies of Sierra Leone, but also they have had a greater developmental impact than other mining industries. Moreover, expatriate companies unlike other mineral industries here have not exclusively mined diamonds. Rather, they have also involved local labour. For Binns (1982), this factor distinguishes diamond mining from other mining operations that are truly 'enclave' and suggests that diamonds in Sierra Leone are not an 'enclave' industry as defined here (Binns 1982). Zack-Williams' (1995) work has also argued that whilst the economic activities of SLST can be defined as a capitalist mode of production, it does not constitute an enclave development in terms of being independent or removed from the non-capitalist ADMS section of diamond production.

In 1961, Sierra Leone became politically independent from the British under the first prime minister, Milton Margai of the Sierra Leone Peoples Party (SLPP). His brother Albert, also of the SLPP succeeded him on his death in 1964 (Fyfe 1971 in Bangura and Dumbuya 1993). Milton Margai gave an assurance to foreign companies that he did not intend to nationalise such companies, including any mining interests. In an effort to maintain good relations with the new independent government, the Diamond Corporation Sierra Leone (DCSL) funded the creation of a department of geology at the University of Sierra Leone, and the SLST created a school in Lower Bambara and a community centre in Kono. Moreover, high profile Sierra Leoneans, like Joseph Momoh (chairman of the Public Service Commission) who went on to become president, became director of DCSL in 1961. A new director of SLST was also announced in the same year. He was the principal of the University of Sierra Leone, Dr D.S.H.W. Nicole. In 1967, the opposition party, the All Peoples Congress (APC) won the election but power was snatched from them in a series of military coups. Civilian rule was restored when Siaka Stevens, the leader of the APC became the new prime minister in 1968. The APC ruled Sierra Leone under Siaka Stevens for the next 24 years.

'If you see a diamond....'
Strangers, smuggling, illicit mining and security

The diamonds discovered in Sierra Leone from the 1930s onwards were alluvial deposits (Kimberlite diamonds would be unearthed much later), derived from the disintegration of volcanic rock. Such deposits were carried in river gravels and eventually scattered over wide areas of the country with different degrees of concentration. (Greenhalgh 1985). The Sewa River and its tributaries have been responsible for depositing diamonds over a large area in the south and east of the country. The majority of Sierra Leone's diamonds are of the more valuable high quality gem type as opposed to the less valuable industrial diamonds (Greenhalgh 1985, Burke 1959).[7]

Anecdotal evidence suggests that before British colonial rule, many were unaware of the monetary value of these stones that were found in riverbeds and on farmland. Some believed they had magical powers. One

[7] Greenhalgh (1985: 12) says Sierra Leone has half of its diamond production in gemstones, Ivory Coast 40%, Guinea 30% and Liberia 5% based on sources for 1980s.

story relates to the village of Tongoma where a man allegedly gave out diamonds and told people they were devils to be worshipped since they had special powers.[8] Such myths went hand in hand with the misinformation disseminated by the colonial authorities who attempted to deter local communities from taking these stones. Early stories relating to diamonds have become part of local folklore that relate to when the British first began to prospect for diamonds in the 1930s. One such story relates to the way Sierra Leoneans were instructed by the British not to touch or remove any diamonds found for fear of radiation or electric shock. If the diamond was found in the sand, they were instructed to 'draw a ring around it and immediately inform the Whiteman, who would carefully remove it' (see Chapter 4).

It did not take long, however, before Sierra Leoneans came to appreciate the monetary value of diamonds. The alluvial nature of these stones combined with their high quality made the digging of and dealing in illicit diamonds not only attractive but also relatively easy. The smallness of many of these stones made them easy to conceal and transport inside and outside the country. The colonial government and those involved in prospecting and mining soon became concerned about the growth of this illicit trade and the potential for this to get out of hand. Without proper security, some companies were left vulnerable as anyone could come and pick diamonds from the riverbeds or dig in known diamondiferous areas.

In 1935 the SLST estimated that there were indicative reserves in excess of 3 million carats of diamonds with an estimated value of £5 million. Prospecting in the eastern area around Safadu found some of the richest alluvial diamonds. The discovery of a 78.9–carat diamond in the Shongo mining area with a preliminary valuation of £4.734 confirmed the SLST commitment to this area (CSO Confidential Series Feb. 1935). The company began to investigate the issue of security as illicit mining and dealing was becoming a problem. The company agreed to pay £50 each to the paramount chiefs and tribal authorities of the Nimi Koro, Gbensay and Tonkoro Chiefdoms in the Kono District in March 1935 to secure future mining operations here. The agreement (signed by a regent chief, a speaker, and two section chiefs in each of the three areas) obliged these leaders to withhold their consent to the settlement of strangers or diamond savvy non-Konos within the area until legislation could regulate this (CSO Confidential File S/29/35). Such an agreement was seen as a necessity by the SLST who had a poor view of these three Tribal Authorities. The company feared the alleged short-sightedness of these leaders, which made them prone to sacrifice the wider benefit of these areas for immediate gain. A number of traders from outside these areas had been allowed to trade and squat for the payment of one pound per annum that had resulted in over-crowding and was clearly causing a nuisance to the trade in diamonds. The District Commissioner responded by launching a policy

---

[8] This was communicated in Legislature by member for Kono see File CO/029/63 1954.

of 'Kono for Konos'[9], in an attempt to keep out an 'influx of more intelligent Creole, Mende and Temne who were allowed to settle and trade'. He went on to explain that 'Konos now realising, they are taking bread from their mouths and are in favour of keeping such strangers out' (CSO Confidential Series – Diamonds, Special reports on activities in mining – Allocation of crown lands and mining sites. File; Agreement of SLST with certain chiefs). Such policy found sympathy with local people and is something that clearly resonates with Konos today.[10]

The trade in illicit diamonds was not confined to Sierra Leoneans; Syrians were also identified as being prominent in illicit dealings not only of diamonds, but also gold. The town of Boajibu, where 17 Syrians resided in 1935 had enjoyed some business in illicit diamonds. Cargoes of diamonds were taken by Syrians to be disposed of in Cape Palmas. Once the Colonial Office caught wind of this, maximum sentences were called for, especially where Syrians were concerned, justified on the grounds that money accrued was not being spent in the country. The SLST responded by setting up a special body of government police with its own barracks in this area to deal specifically with the theft and illicit dealing of diamonds. Two measures would come into operation to deal with this. First, the detection and prevention of stealing from mines, including prospecting and mining, and second, the 'tracing and suppression of those engaged in illicit traffic in diamonds, inside and outside the mining areas'. The first measure would involve the employment of trustworthy men who would closely supervise employees mining and working; would police company villages and would constantly patrol identified diamond areas not yet being worked. The second measure, seen as by far the most important was reliant on the work of one or two agents or local informers who proved expensive. Existing measures were inadequate to deal with the ease with which diamonds could be concealed and disposed of. The SLST called for greater police powers including the authority to grant search warrants and the authority to inspect letters, packets or parcels in the post, where small quantities of diamonds could be concealed. The company drew inspiration from the South African experience. Here *extraordinary* powers and authority had been granted to the special police forces employed by De Beers Consolidated Mines, for the detection and suppression of illicit dealings. The SLST, a subsidiary of De Beers explained the situation in the following terms:

> In Sierra Leone, the African is only just becoming 'educated' as to the value of diamonds, and encouraged as they are by unscrupulous non-natives and others the traffic will assume large proportions unless adequate powers and scope are allowed those engaged in combating

---

[9] The term *Konomokwie* means 'Mi na get iya' in Krio. This translates to 'this place is mine' and was also used in 2002 when Konos returned to the area after pushing out the occupied RUF. See K. Peters (2007) 'Reintegration Support for Young Ex-Combatants: A Right or a Privilege?' *International Migration* Vol 45, Issue 5 December.

[10] See oral testimonies and interviews in Chapter 3.

the evil. (CSO Confidential Series – Diamonds, special reports on activities in mining – allocation of crown lands and mining sites. File: The Suppression of Illicit Diamond Dealing in Sierra Leone 6 March 1935)

In a detailed confidential seven page report, produced by the colonial secretary's office in Freetown 1935, descriptions of protective measures undertaken in Angolan diamond fields closely resembling Sierra Leone's was given. This was followed by a summary of the measures in force in South Africa (CSO S/19/35 Protection of Mining). However, any changes in the way diamonds were handled in Sierra Leone would have to wait until the 1950s. In the meantime, the commissioner of the southern province (which included the diamond rich area of Kono) reported that he had supplied the diamond police force with truncheons and was ready to supply guns if the colonial secretary agreed (CSO Confidential Series – The Suppression of Illicit Diamond Dealing in Sierra Leone 1935).

Illicit diamond mining and dealing continued to be a problem. Between 1933 and 1935 a mere 49 were caught with unlawful possession of minerals and received sentences of between 1–9 months imprisonment with hard labour (CSO Open policy files – Allocation of Crown Lands and mining sites File: Summonses and convictions under the Minerals legislation 1935). The problem of defining 'unlawful possession' was an issue taken up in the local press. Under the headline: 'Is Diamond More Important to Great Britain than the Happiness and Liberty of His Majesty's African Subjects'? *The Sierra Leone Weekly News* reported that diamonds were not confined to those areas given over to the control of special diamond police (Special Detective Force) and that it was not uncommon for a Sierra Leonean to come across diamonds whilst for example, digging graves, building huts or fishing in the creeks and rivers. It went on to explain that for centuries, Sierra Leoneans had planted farms on top of diamond beds and had lived and slept on diamonds without any knowledge of their value. With the arrival of Europeans, the value of these stones became all too apparent. Many felt that if white people found diamonds and prospered, then Sierra Leoneans should have the same rights. The report explained;

> The Whiteman would exactly do the same thing (take them and sell them) if he were living under similar conditions on land full of diamonds. In view of this condition of affairs, it seems extremely difficult to arrive at the conclusion that every native who possesses diamond has no right to it or that he has stolen it. (Sierra Leone Weekly News 6 July 1935)

What made matters worse was that the chief of the special detective force in the district of Kono had been brought in from the Gold Coast (at a salary of £1,200 per annum) to oversee the operation. It seems that on at least one occasion, of those arrested the majority were acquitted with the implication being that the chief was being overzealous in his duties causing concern to those who lived in this area. The same chief had also been appointed as an assistant district commissioner to deal specifically with the theft of diamonds and this was causing a great deal of concern amongst Kono residents. *The Sierra Leone Weekly News* argued that such an appointment was not British justice and fair play (6 July 1935).

In January 1945 a huge diamond was found, weighing 770 carats. This is thought to be one of the largest alluvial stones ever found, alongside another stone estimated to have been up to 900 carats (The Star of Sierra Leone) that was later found (Burke 1959; Report Mineral Resources of Sierra Leone 1981 SL Collection). By the early 1950s, the Lower Bambara chiefdom in Kenema district became another source of diamonds. These diamonds were concentrated in the basin of the Male River and had come via the Woa River to the Tongo.[11] The migration of foreign miners and dealers mainly from Guinea to the SLST reserves in Kono District spread south during 1954 and 1955 along the Sewa and Bafi Rivers towards Bo and Kenema (Binns 1982). Sierra Leonean's joined these. It is important to note that the increase in black market diamond activity in the early 1950s was in part related to this discovery of more diamondiferous areas, often referred to as the 'diamond rush' (Van der Laan 1965) but which also coin-cided with partial crop failure (Burke 1959). Van der Laan (1965) estimates that in the month of December 1954 alone, around 30,000 illicit diggers were in operation in these areas.

Why was there such a 'rush' for diamonds in the mid 1950s? Apart from the rise in global diamond prices, there was also an increasing recogni-tion of the relatively easy availability of diamonds and of their monetary value. In addition, rural poverty and poor harvests coupled with the authorities inability to control illicit mining, offered an incentive, not only for Sierra Leoneans, but also to migrants from neighbouring countries to try their hand at making a fortune. The role of Lebanese business in illegal smuggling provided an avenue for diggers to dispose of their findings. There was also growing discontent at the injustice of Africans not being allowed to find and keep diamonds, even if they were found on their own land, whilst foreign companies like the SLST were given monopoly rights to mine and sell. Between 1935 and 1952 out of a total profit of £16.5 million made by the SLST, £5.5m was allocated to the Sierra Leone government and £3.5m to the UK government. The UK government there-fore received three fifths of what the Sierra Leone government received. In addition, in some financial years, the UK share of the profits actually exceeded the Sierra Leone share (see below).

These figures were kept secret from Sierra Leoneans for fear of unrest. Four Sierra Leonean Ministers relayed the feelings of ordinary Sierra Leoneans and the difficult position they occupied as representatives of their people:

> To the minds of the majority of Sierra Leoneans the benefits that have accrued to the United Kingdom Government from the diamond profits

[11] See Binns, J.A. (1982) 'The changing impact of diamond mining in Sierra Leone', *University of Sussex Research Papers* in Geography No: 9 map.

Table 1.1 Share of Diamond Profits, 1938–1946

Year profits £	Total share £	Sierra Leone share £	United Kingdom share £	SLST £
1938–39	334,000	92,000	97,000	145,000
1940–41	317,000	88,000	123,000	106,000
1942–44	1273,000	357,000	370,000	546,000
1943–44	1137,000	313,000	351,000	473,000
1945–46	666,000	82,000	272,000	212,000

Source: *Letter to the Governor from four Sierra Leonean Ministers, 31 Oct 1953 CO/029/64*

as compared with what Sierra Leone as the natural owners of this mineral has received would be morally unjustifiable and our task to defend the situation would be most complicated and embarrassing and might even ruin our political career, especially as we are committed to secrecy and cannot give the figures out for public opinion to be ventilated. (Letter to the Governor from four Sierra Leonean Ministers, 31 Oct 1953 CO/029/64)

With independence looming and the increasing control Sierra Leoneans were acquiring, there was perhaps a greater willingness to break these unjust laws. There was certainly a feeling that the mineral wealth of the country should benefit the people rather than foreign companies who had the support of the colonial structure (Greenhalgh 1985). The *Manchester Guardian* (October 1953) had reported the problems associated with the Selection Trust's monopoly rights:

Among aspiring politicians here, prejudice against the SLST is strong. It is a foreign monopoly, holding legal title to virtually all diamonds in the country, even those which may be picked up almost casually by individuals. It cannot claim to be introducing technical skill and capital equipment on such a striking scale as the corporation which works the iron deposits. On social grounds, it has many strong critics in the Kono District, including Mr Dunbar. The mineral monopolies are potentially the most combustible material in Sierra Leone politics; and newspaper references to the current negotiations have not always been directly related to their substance. (*The Manchester Guardian* October 1953)

Smuggling

The 1950s diamond rush made the issue of security even more pertinent and in 1952 Kono District became the only place in the protectorate that was policed by the Freetown-based Sierra Leone police force. It was not until 1954 that these served the whole of Sierra Leone. As for the rest of the protectorate, the court messengers force, directed by the district commissioners, maintained this. Those transporting diamonds outside of the control of the Sierra Leone police force could do so freely but could be stopped and arrested if they had stones in their possession whilst taking them out through Freetown. In 1952, two Lebanese traffickers were arrested in Freetown by the Sierra Leone police force for possession of 250 diamonds. Between January 1952 and September 1953 the police found diamonds worth £110,910 on traffickers and 186 persons were convicted in the same period for illegal possession. In another case, a Gambian travelling from Sierra Leone to Lebanon via Bathurst was arrested for unlawfully possessing 1,319 diamonds, estimated to be worth £20,000. In another case in 1954 a customs officer at Lungi airport, Freetown found diamonds estimated to be worth £6,000 in the luggage of a Lebanese intending to fly to Beirut (Van der Laan 1965).

Whilst there were many successful convictions brought about by the work of the police, inevitably there was also an unknown amount of police corruption. In one reported case, two police officers in Freetown found diamonds in the house of a woman who had returned from Safadu, Kono District the previous day. It was only when a relative of the woman reported the missing diamonds to the police, it became clear that these had not been officially reported nor handed in to the police authorities. The press made much of such issues (Van der Laan 1965).

Migration was becoming of particular concern and in 1954 and 1955 measures to restrict the migration of Lebanese and Africans from neighbouring countries, particularly Mandingo from Guinea were introduced (Binns 1982). Moreover, following a governor's visit to Kono District in 1956 in which he issued a directive that native foreigners, including Marakas, Mandingo, Foulah, Senegalese and others, should leave Sierra Leone within three weeks, a staggering 45,000 non-Sierra Leonean Africans left. (Binns 1982, Van der Lann 1965). It was now also illegal for *strangers* to be present in the Diamond Protection Areas without a licence.

The expulsions of non-Sierra Leoneans related to the activities of these groups in the diamond mining areas and not those involved outside of here. Moreover, the measure applied to those who had come to Sierra Leone within the last six to seven years. The action was justified by the governor because such groups were taking wealth out of the country rather than as the scheme had intended to give Sierra Leoneans a chance of mining their diamonds. Whilst the scheme no doubt opened up diamond areas to Sierra Leoneans, the irony of the continued operations of the SLST in some of the richest diamond areas was lost on the colonial government. Moreover, the provision of only allowing Sierra Leoneans to obtain licences (native foreigners were allowed to work as tributors or diggers) made illicit mining of greater attraction to native foreigners. It was an impossible task and not all left. Some returned in 1957. (Van der Laan 1965).

The geographical location of diamond-rich areas like Kono, close to the

Guinea border and other such areas like Kenema and Bo in the south that are closer to the border of Liberia meant unfettered movement continued to be easy. In the late 1950s, various arrests were made in the Kailahun and Pujehun areas that bordered Liberia. One parcel seized was valued at £50,000. It was reported that firearms used by smugglers was an increasing problem, especially for the police. In 1957, under more restrictive measures, Lebanese and other foreign dealers had to pay a deposit of £3,000 before they received their licence for that year and this would be confiscated if convicted of a diamond related offence. In addition, the government declared non-dealing diamond areas, which restricted the mobility of potential smugglers. In the same year, five Lebanese dealers were expelled from the country because their being here was, according to *The Economist* 'not conducive to the public good' (Van der Laan 1965: 24).

The issue of smuggling had to be tackled and after discussions between the government and representatives from De Beers and the Diamond Corporation Sierra Leone (DCSL), the Government Diamond Office (GDO) was established in Kenema in 1959 (this later became the Government Gold and Diamond Office). This would become the only legitimate exporter of diamonds produced under the scheme. As an incentive, prices paid for diamonds brought to the GDO proved better than those paid in Monrovia and as a result, purchases by GDO exceeded those of the DCSL in previous years. Such measures did much to undermine smuggling, but it meant that the higher prices paid for diamonds, coupled with a low export duty, reduced profits to an estimated one-thirtieth of their value (Van der Laan 1965).

Policing in Kono

The other problems that continued to occupy the police at this time were the ongoing issues of illicit digging and possession that appeared to be increasing. Between July 1954 to February 1956 not only had there been an increase in the number of arrests of strangers and non-native Sierra Leoneans in the diamond areas, there had also been increased arrests of those involved in illegal diamond activities. The highest numbers arrested were in Kono. This occurred at a time when new areas had been opened up for diamond digging, the so-called 'diamond rush' (Van der Laan 1965) and also at a time when the Police Force was extended to the rest of Sierra Leone. Moreover, legislation introduced in 1954 made it easier for the police to arrest and charge anyone carrying tools used for digging.

In 1956, the Alluvial Diamond Mining Scheme (ADMS) was created after the SLST decided in the light of the widespread problem of illicit diamond digging to give up its monopoly outside the Tongo and Yengema leases, in return for compensation. It was hoped that the creation of ADMS would deal with the problem of illicit digging and dealing by allowing Sierra Leoneans to purchase digging licences. Native Sierra Leoneans over the age of 21 could purchase licences for £9 a year or £5 for half a year. Once this had been implemented, it was believed diamond mining could be more easily controlled by the Mines Department (Binns 1982). This policy had some effect in reducing illicit mining and dealing, though total control was almost impossible (Burke 1959). In some areas, gangs of illicit diggers had their own *protection squads* that acted as lookouts and who would not hesitate in defending the diggers against the police. In such cases, the authority of the chiefs was greatly undermined (Van der Laan 1965).

The problem of illicit mining continued whilst the authorities tried to get to grips with the issue of licences for native Sierra Leoneans and deal with the ongoing problem of illicit mining by strangers. A series of confrontations broke out between labourers (Sierra Leoneans and strangers) and the police in the Kono District involving SLST leases. (Daily Mail 13 Feb, 11 July 1957 cited in Van der Laan 1965). In February 1957, police attempted to stop the digging of around 300 Temnes inside a SLST lease near Yomadu. When the police tried to disperse the diggers, they were attacked with various crude weapons and seven policemen were taken and held for several hours. Later the police station at Yomadu was attacked (Van der Laan 1965). In August, a SLST washing plant came under attack at Koidu by a large group of illicit diggers, whom the Kono District Council blamed on 'aliens, native foreigners and Sierra Leoneans from other districts' (Van der Laan 1965: 30–31). By September 1957, the SLST estimated that 12,000 illicit diggers were working inside the Yengema lease alone and believed that several thousand came from Guinea (Van der Laan 1965). In the same month, the Tribal Authorities of the various Chiefdoms would issue permits[12] to strangers until January 1958. It was hoped this would make the job of the police easier and would help control the movement of strangers in the short term. These permits had to be carried by the photographed holder and shown to the police so they could arrest those who had illegally gone into Diamond Protection Areas (ibid.).

The combined efforts of the police and the SLST own security could not quell the enthusiasm of the illicit miners. In August 1957, troops were moved from Daru and Freetown to Yengema where their presence would allow the police to 'mount full-scale action to control the activities of the illicit diggers' (Turay and Abraham 1987: 90). Yet, illicit digging within SLST leases by both strangers and Konos continued into 1958, partly attributed to the fact that previous illicit mining outside the SLST reserves had depleted stocks. This was especially so in 1956 when an estimated 25,000 native foreigners had been digging in Kono. As a result, the diamond-rich leases of the SLST became honey pots attracting diggers who believed any diamonds found were there for the taking.

In October 1958, the situation in Kono began to worry the authorities

[12] Local government had been invested with greater political control as independence was imminent.

especially as independence looked imminent and as reports came in of lawlessness and attacks on the police by armed gangs wielding machetes, swords and stones. In January 1959, the *Daily Mail* issued a statement from the pre-independence Sierra Leone People's Party (SLPP) government that referred to the future of the country:

> In Kono, illicit mining has got worse during the last two months and has now reached a point where if it is not stopped it will imperil the whole economic and constitutional future of the country. The government intends to take whatever measures may be necessary to stamp out this crime against the country. (Turay and Abraham 1987: 91)

The police were armed in response to the increasing tensions (Van der Laan 1965). In December, illicit diggers directed more attacks at the police and after a serious injury, the police opened fire. The government estimated that gangs of between 50 and 400 diggers had been operating in the richest SLST reserves every day and night throughout November and December 1959. Such gangs had armed members who displayed slings, cutlasses, knives and pistols. Though no pistols had been used, other weapons were used to protect the diggers from police patrols, and to attack police posts or posts manned by SLST guards. The authorities worried that the SLST might pull out of its operations in Sierra Leone that was contributing about £800,000 to government revenue in 1958.

Under the amended Diamond Industry Protection Ordinance, it was possible to impose a minimum sentence of 12 months imprisonment for strangers without a residential permit. Moreover, the amended Alluvial Diamond Mining Ordinance could give a minimum sentence of 12 months for illicit digging and in addition, it excluded non-Sierra Leoneans from mining under the scheme (Van der Laan 1965). Various other steps were taken, including in 1959 the limiting of residential permits to strangers in Kono District to a mere 5,000, forcing many to leave this area and head West and North. Of these many were Temnes returning home to areas adversely affected in social and economic terms by the migration of thousands of young males (ibid.). It seems the issues of illicit mining, smuggling and strangers in Kono was brought under the authorities control by the beginning of the 1960s with punitive measures and hard-line controls. The increase in the numbers of police in Kono, heavy penalties and restrictions on mobility did much to protect the interests of the SLST. Perhaps the issuing of permits for strangers made it a bit easier for local Konos to search for a larger share of diamonds, perhaps not. Opposition groups in Sierra Leone were critical of SLPP security. The People's National Party (PNP) established in 1958 and composed of younger members from the SLPP was especially critical of the use of troops in Kono, as was the Kono based, Kono Progressive Movement (KPM) and the United Progressive Party (UPP) founded by a Creole lawyer in 1954. The latter won seats in the 1957 general election in protectorate areas where the SLPP had traditionally been strong (Turay and Abraham 1987).

Migration and the development of the Eastern Province

The diamond areas became honey-pots especially in the 1950s, for those inside and outside Sierra Leone who fancied their chances at finding diamonds. Others who worked in agriculture gave up their work to dig for diamonds, whilst others still worked on a seasonal basis, working in agriculture during the wet season and turning their efforts to diamond digging in the dry season.[13]

It is difficult to estimate exactly how many were working here at any one time since numbers fluctuated. The census for 1963 showed 25,000 males engaged in the mining industry out of a total labour force of slightly fewer than one million, but this did not account for those engaged in illicit activities or those classed as self-employed. Figures produced by Binns (1982) show average monthly numbers of tributors wildly fluctuating for selected years that range from approximately 37,500 in 1956 to 6,610 in 1977. Added to this, Van der Laan (1965) has estimated that during the mid-1950s, over 20,000 strangers were also engaged in any one year, but some of these were seasonal workers staying for five or six months at a time.

Binn's estimates that during the height in the mid-1950s and possibly through to the 1960s, there would have been a staggering 100,000 persons engaged in all kinds of diamond mining in the country (Binns, 1982, Van de Laan 1965). Diamond digging was a male affair and whilst women and children did sometimes accompany male workers, census figures (1963) show that in the diamond mining areas, the male population exceeded the female. Swindell (1973) suggests a causal relationship between this excess of males and the proportional numbers of miners at work. Swindell (ibid.) has also identified some interesting patterns regarding labour migration and the level of skill of those working in different sectors of the mining economy for the mid-1960s. Whilst statistics are difficult to come by for those working in the informal illicit and ADMC sections of diamond mining, the SLST did keep information on this. Swindell examined a group of workers employed for 12 years or less by the SLST pan plants in Yengema and Tongo in the mid-1960s. He found that those working for the SLST, had an urban background and skills and these factors were important in explaining migration.

He presents four main movements of migrants that came from villages, the local town, the regional town and the capital and divides these into firstly, the illiterate, unskilled and inexperienced migrants and secondly, the skilled, literate and experienced. In some cases, the latter have gained education and job experience en route to working in the company mine, have tended to travel over longer distances to find work and enjoy a degree of social mobility as they move up a hierarchy of settlement. Based on this

---

[13] In the rainy season the open pits and holes fill with water, transport is much less reliable and work more difficult. See Binns (1982: 10) 'The changing impact'.

information, Swindell (ibid.) concludes, that those working in the informal ADMS and illicit sectors were more likely to fall into the illiterate, unskilled and inexperienced migrants. Given the small numbers of skilled workers in the wider labour force, the migration of skilled SLST workers was quite exceptional.

Binns (1982) found the majority of those migrants involved in non-company mining in the 1970s, were Temne, Fulah and Mandingo from the northern province, whilst local Kono and Mende people involved in mining did not undertake significant migration because of their close proximity to the mining areas and because of their continued role in farming (Swindell 1973 cited in Binns 1982).

Urban growth

The effects of migration into the diamond mining areas led to the rapid growth of some areas, where facilities such as shops, housing, transport links and traders increased to accommodate and service the mining population and associated services. Many towns grew rapidly because of increased migration caused by the growth of the diamond industry (Binns 1982). New settlements grew up in areas where diamonds were found and as the mining of diamonds has shifted to other areas, naturally settlements have grown up around them. Some of the smaller towns' populations have fluctuated in accordance with the success of diamond mining. In the early 1960s, the thriving towns of Peyima and Sukudu, north of Koidu, had experienced a decline by the mid-1970s (King 1975 cited in Binns 1982). Other areas, like Yomandu and Jaiama Nimikoro showed to have more stable populations by the early 1980s after a period of boom. The two towns of Kenema and Koidu are of notable significance, as they became the two leading urban centres in the diamond mining areas. Both became large enough and diversified to allow for population stability in this period. However, future events, seen in the outbreak of civil war would see this area becoming centre stage as control of the diamond fields became embroiled in this brutal conflict.

Kenema in the south of the diamond mining area was estimated to have had around 30 houses in 1909 and by 1946 had grown to a town of 4000 inhabitants (Gamble 1964 cited in Binns 1982). In 1963, its population had reached 13,246 and by 1974, this had grown further to 31,300. More recent figures estimate Kenema's district population to be around 515,461 for 2009 (World Gazetteer 2009). Whilst Kenema's population was slightly below that of Bo's (the protectorate capital at this time) in 1974 which stood at 39,400, Kenema's growth rate was far greater than Bo's which only increased by 48 per cent compared to Kenema's growth of 136.3 per cent between 1963 and 1974. This made Kenema the fourth largest town in Sierra Leone. Kenema's growing importance can be seen in the way it became the provincial headquarters of the eastern province and an important centre for diamond selling. Moreover, the Government Diamond Office was established here, as was a branch of the Bank of Sierra Leone. The establishment and maintenance of good transport communications between here and Freetown was indicative of Kenema's importance in the diamond industry (Binns 1982).

Koidu's economic activity before diamonds were discovered in the 1930s had been entirely focused on farming. There were no major trade routes through this area, and the nearest railway, completed in 1908, ran 60 miles south of Koidu. In 1928, the settlement was composed of a mere six huts. By 1963, around 14,309 people resided here, which grew to a staggering 75,600 by the time of the 1974 census. The growth rate in this 11 year period was a spectacular 428.3 per cent, making it one of the fastest growing urban areas and the main centre (often regarded as the capital) of diamond mining (Binns 1982). Koidu developed around the SLST Number 2/4 washing plant approximately a mile south-east of Sefadu, the District headquarters. By the 1950s and 1960s Koidu became the main market centre for this area and developed into a larger area with the merging of Yengema and Safadu into Koidu (Kenneth Scott Associates, 1970 cited in Binns 1982).

In 1969, the Koidu-New Sembehun Town Council was established along with the town planning department. Throughout the 1970s, a significant amount of the money accrued from diamond mining went into making improvements to this area. This included the construction of standardised buildings with new building materials like concrete and glass to replace timber and mud; improvements in water supply, sanitation, roads and markets. Throughout the 1960s and 1970s, Koidu developed a diverse economic structure based on trading, some manufacturing and administrative activities (Binns 1982).

By the time of the 1974 census, the proportion of Sierra Leone's population living in the eastern province increased by 3 per cent from 25 to 28 per cent, while the northern and southern provinces declined by around 3.5 per cent (King 1975). Migrational flows into the area were such that at the time of the 1963 census 57 per cent of the population were of the Kono ethnic group. By 1970 this had decreased to around 52 per cent and if broken down further, in Koidu and Yengema towns only 19 per cent of the people were Konos (King 1975). More recent census figures for each of the provinces can be seen in Table 1.2 overleaf.

These figures show a smaller increase in population size in the eastern province as a whole (between 1985 to 2004) in comparison to other provinces. The eastern province is divided into three districts (Table 1.3) that show a significant decrease in the population of Kono District between 1985–2004, no doubt the result of the higher casualty rate of this district during the civil conflict. Table 1.4 further demonstrates the impact of the civil conflict on population figures, with Koidu (the heart of the diamond mining area) showing a significant decrease in population from 1984 to 2004.

Table 1.2 Population Figures for Sierra Leone's Provinces, 1985 and 2004

Province	Population 1985 census	Population 2004 census
Eastern	960,547	1,191,539
Northern	1,259,621	1,745,553
Southern	741, 377	1,092,657
Western Area	554,243	947,122
Total	3,515,812	4,976,871

Source: *Statistics Sierra Leone*, Sierra Leone 1985–2004

Table 1.3 Population Figures for the Eastern Province, 1985 and 2004

	Eastern Province	
Districts	Population 1985 census	Population 2004 census
Kailahun	233,839	358,190
Kenema	337,055	497,948
Kono	389,657	335,401

Source: *Statistics Sierra Leone*, Sierra Leone 1985–2004

Table 1.4 Population Figures for Sierra Leone's Main Cities, 1985 and 2004

Main cities	Population 1985 census	Population 2004 census
Freetown	469,776	772,873
Bo	59,768	149,957
Kenema	52,473	128,402
Makeni	40,038	82,840
Koidu	82,474	80,025

Source: *Statistics Sierra Leone*, Sierra Leone 1985–2004

Infrastructure/transport

The discovery of diamonds in territories that were a long way off from Freetown meant that infrastructures needed to be built to accommodate the increased populations of these areas, and to ensure the distribution of agricultural foodstuffs and imports. This was especially important when diamond digging was legalised in 1955 to 1956. Communications had to be improved and as more money for road maintenance became available in 1956, measures to accommodate increased lorry transport and new rolling stock were brought in to increase the carrying capacity of the railways. Markets were built and increased money circulation had a knock on effect for shopkeepers and other petty bourgeois traders. Clearly, diamonds created enough wealth for a minority, displayed in the construction of new houses and symbolised by the cars being driven, as well as travel inside and outside the country for trade or for pilgrimage (by air) to Mecca (Van der Laan 1965).

In the early years when diamonds were first found around Kono District there was some attempt by the SLST to invest in infrastructures that would facilitate trade in this industry. Accordingly, by 1935 over 40 miles of roads were constructed and maintained by the SLST at a cost of £117 per mile (CSO Confidential Series: File: Report to Governor from the Managing Director SLST Feb 1935). The British had completed the Sierra Leone Government Railway (SLGR) in 1908 that linked Freetown with the eastern area of Pendembu in Kailahun District. A branch line had also been established from Bauya to Makeni in the Northern Province. It has been suggested that the railway may have played an important part in the movement of people to the diamond areas of the south. Bo and Kenema in particular were served well by rail and road. Kono on the other hand, was neither served well by rail nor road. It remained relatively isolated until improvements were made to the trunk road system in the early 1970s. As railways began to be phased out in Sierra Leone in the late 1960s, road development became more important (Binns 1982).

Minor roads in the diamond areas were improved and some work was done to widen existing footpaths. The SLST/NDMC[14] built and maintained surfaced and unsurfaced roads in and around their mining leases and established link roads between diamond fields throughout the 1970s. A vehicular ferry crossing on the Bafi River at Tefeya and Yomandu was also maintained by the company until 1978. When the company's number 7 plant at Tefeya was closed in 1977 work got underway in 1979 to replace this with a bridge (Binns 1982).

By the early 1980s, the mining areas in the eastern province are thought to have had the densest road network in Sierra Leone and a higher than average mobility rate (Binns 1982). The eastern province has grown in importance because of diamond mining; the related and rapid urbanisation of centres like Koidu and Kenema and the importance of this area for agricultural produce. These factors are indicative of the importance of this area to Sierra Leone's national economy and provided greater impetus for improved road links in the 1970s that linked Freetown with the eastern province, including the towns of Makeni (north), Koidu (east), Bo (south) and Kenema (east).

---

[14] In 1970 the APC government and SLST entered an agreement for the setting up of a jointly-owned company, the National Diamond Mining Company, NDMC. The SLST would be compensated by £2.55 million of government bonds, redeemable over eight years. See Bangura, A.K. & Dumbuya, M.S. (1993) 'The Political Economy of Sierra Leone's Mineral Industry Since Independence' *Sierra Leone Review*, Vol. 2 Winter.

Agriculture

There is no doubt that increased diamond mining activities in the 1950s and 1960s affected agricultural production to the extent that its importance in the national economy was eclipsed by diamond mining. However, it also appears to be the case that as diamond mining activities varied, so too were agricultural activities uneven.

Within the SLST and later NDMC leases alone, diamond digging had devastated large swathes of good quality agricultural land. Moreover, evidence suggests that mining has affected drainage patterns, that NDMC washing plants polluted streams and rivers with discharged waste and that some farms were forced onto upland areas (Binns 1982). Compensation payments paid by NDMC in the late 1970s whilst offered short-term benefit for farmers, failed to keep pace with inflation rates and more seriously, could not compensate for long-term destruction and the taking away of good quality farmland. In addition, whilst NDMC made grants available in its two lease areas of Yengema and Tongo field (for various projects like road building and the construction of schools in the mid-1970s) such grants were short-term.

A report undertaken by Njala University College (1972) highlighted the long-term destruction of these areas through soil inversion, where mechanical digging had buried good quality topsoil underneath tons of poor overburden making this unfit for farming. The report also argued that the environmental destruction was disproportionate to the size of the actual areas involved. It proposed that the company make greater efforts to rehabilitate mined land; that this should follow with re-vegetation and that adequate supplies of safe water and better medical facilities should be made available to those affected (Binns 1982).

By 1978, there were some moves towards the rehabilitation of land by the company, but in at least one known case, mining had reoccurred on previously rehabilitated land. The reason, the dictates of the market as diamond prices began to rise. NDMC appeared to demonstrate little concern for the rehabilitation of land dug up in the process of diamond mining. It was not just private companies that created such problems, areas under the ADMS raised similar issues (Binns 1982). The other issue concerning agriculture relates to the movement of farm workers into mining. Whilst different kinds of workers (labourers who worked in the public works and teachers) had turned their attention on occasions, to the diamond industry, more damaging was the movement of agricultural workers to diamond mining (Van der Laan 1965). Binns (1982) points out that some areas were adversely affected by the loss or partial loss of farm labour, particularly as agriculture here is labour intensive.

An additional issue that increased migration brought was the increase in the demand for foodstuffs. Van der Laan (1965) has argued that with increased migration into these areas in the 1950s, demand for rice and other foodstuffs increased by around 18 per cent.[15] In 1954, concerns were raised as to whether there would be sufficient rice supplies to last until the next crop. As supplies of foodstuffs began to diminish in the markets of large towns like Kenema and Bo and the capital Freetown, prices began to rise. The trade unions came out on strike in February 1955 after negotiations for increased pay failed. It was not until 18 people had been killed in serious riots in Freetown during the second day of the strike that both private and public employers agreed to raise wage rates, some as high as 20 per cent. More disturbances broke out in November 1955 in the northern provinces and spread to the southern provinces and is thought to have been indirectly related to the rush for diamonds (Van der Laan 1965).

The attraction of these diamond areas and subsequent migration also had the effect of pushing up rents and the price of food. In Kono District in 1956, a bowl of rice cost four shillings, a bottle of beer eight shillings, and a chicken cost one pound. In the aftermath of the expulsions, Van der Laan (1965) argues that the prices of foodstuffs went down though this would not of course solve the problem of labour leaving agriculture to dig for diamonds.

Increased migration to the diamond mining areas in the 1950s also provoked concerns of overcrowding, poor housing conditions and lack of sanitation. The fear of disease was at the forefront of the governor's thoughts as outbreaks of small-pox had been reported in Freetown, Bo, Pujehun, Kambia and Port Loko in 1956 and is thought to be one of the driving factors (alongside illegal diamond activities) for introducing expulsion orders against foreigners in October 1956. Sefadu was said to have become a strangers' town, whilst the minister of state for the colonies on visiting Kono in 1956 singled out Mandingo from Guinea who had 'swamped' (as he put it) the local population here (Van der Laan 1965: 20–21).

Levi (1976) has argued that there was not necessarily a straightforward correlation between the importation of rice (because of shortages) and the diamond rush in the 1950s, and that this can be partly explained by government policy of price fixing of rice. Whether Levi's argument is accepted or not, much of the evidence suggests that problems relating to agricultural production, including price increases, occurred because of a combination of factors. These included; increased migration that created greater demand for foodstuffs; a decline in agricultural production because of reduced numbers of farm labour, and the loss of some agricultural land because of being turned over to diamond mining.

By the 1970s, several years after the diamond rush, mining was still adversely affecting agricultural production but evidence suggests that strategies emerged within communities to deal with this. In Kono commu-

[15] The extra demand he argues came from strangers Van der Laan (1965) *The Sierra Leone Diamonds*, 9–10

nities adapted to the two demands of agriculture and diamond mining through a division of labour. As a result, the men concentrated their efforts on mining whilst the women became more involved in farming. Binns' (1977 & 1982) work on the eastern province in the 1970s supports this and adds that positive changes in the scale and type of agriculture occurred, seen in the increased production of root crops like fruit and cassava and in the introduction of garden cultivation by Mandingo migrants from Guinea. Moreover, large-scale production of coffee and cocoa around Kono began after the diamond boom of the 1950s. Such production had been in existence in the south in Mende land before this. Binns (1977) also found that some successful miners had invested their capital in cash crops and farming since this was often their main form of livelihood. Binns (1982) concludes that whilst agriculture was adversely affected by diamond mining in the early years, and notably during the boom of the 1950s, since the 1970s strategies emerged to deal with satisfying demand.

Yet prices for agricultural products and consumer goods has traditionally been high, reflecting, it is suggested, the above average level of purchasing power of those here and the high cost of transporting goods to mining areas (Binns 1982). In 1965–66 prices in three districts of the eastern province were between 42 and 55 per cent above the national average (Binns 1982).

The growth of mining towns has also affected marketing systems seen in the emergence of periodic markets whereby traders and buyers travel long distances to attend weekly or fortnightly markets. One such market was the one established at Tokpombu in 1970. Held every Friday outside the NDMC mining camp it was known locally as 'Pay Friday Market' since the service staff at the company received their pay on Fridays. Traders would travel from as far as the Freetown peninsula and the southern coastal area to trade fish, palm-oil and rice with mining communities. The size of the market fluctuated according to the harvest cycle (it being largest at harvest time) and according to the number of migrants or strangers (Riddell 1974 cited in Binns 1982).

Conclusions

The control of minerals in colonial Africa began with the exploitation of South Africa's gold and diamond reserves in the nineteenth century. Since then, much of Africa's diamond wealth has come under the control of foreign companies (often American and Western European), in part explained by these early links with South Africa. Foreign ownership of South Africa's mineral industry allowed such companies to develop the expertise, capital and mining techniques that were easily transferable to other African countries, including West Africa. Technical skills in geology, skilled engineers and other specialist found in the developed world enabled foreign firms to undertake mineral exploration of the continent.

The existence of a ready market in the developed world provided a big enough incentive for investment into this potentially lucrative industry (Greenhalgh 1985).

For the first 25 years or so of Sierra Leone's diamond industry, it was illegal for Africans to dig for diamonds. The SLST enjoyed monopoly rights in diamond production until the mid 1950s when it became legal for Sierra Leoneans to mine. Gradually, a reduction in the Selection Trust monopoly came about through piecemeal measures and eventually it was (partially) nationalised. However, until these measures, the SLST monopolised ownership and control of this country's diamond wealth. From 1951, African Ministers who had since become responsible for internal government policy did little to challenge this monopoly. Government argued that the unified production of diamonds by the SLST would lead to the development of the industry and greater profits for the government in the form of revenue. Kono chiefs and the main political parties initially supported this policy. The Minister of Mines, Siaka Stevens had dismissed ideas of licensing African diggers in 1954 as unworkable and expensive, even though this existed in gold mining (Greenhalgh 1985). However, with the diamond rush from mid-1954 it was becoming increasingly difficult to control illicit mining through suppression. Pressure to legalise diamond mining from those involved in illicit digging and in the aftermath of much debate and lobbying by Sierra Leonean politicians, (some of whom had since changed their minds), resulted in the decision to issue licences to Africans in February 1956. This attempt to quash illicit digging through legalisation and the abandonment of what had become futile heavy-handed policing measures occurred at a time of unprecedented illegal diamond mining activity.

The erosion of the SLST monopoly began not just through the issuing of licences, but also through a series of other measures. These included the confinement of the SLST to leases in a smaller geographical area; the reduction in the length of leases from 77 to 30 years, and being forced to give up its exclusive right to sell all Sierra Leone diamonds (Greenhalgh 1985). In September 1970, the erosion into the SLST monopoly went even further when the leader of the APC Government, Siaka Stevens, under pressure from more radical elements in the party entered into negotiations with the company. This resulted in the establishment of The National Diamond Mining Company (Sierra Leone) Ltd (DIMINCO), jointly owned between the Government and the SLST (Greenhalgh 1985). The broader political context, within which this partial nationalisation of the diamond industry occurred, is the subject of Chapter 2. Throughout this period, SLST continued overall to increase its profits (Van der Laan 1965) even after its monopoly was broken in 1955. Profits slowed between 1954 and 1957 partly due to old equipment and partly through diamond thefts. Yet with expansion into the Tongo field, modernization of equipment and an increase in diamond prices, the company's fortunes began to pick up from 1958. Indeed, from the mid-1950s the company's expanded production reached a peak of 0.94 million carats in 1970 (Greenhalgh 1985). Van der Laan (1965) has argued that during the period from 1955 to 1962 the SLST invested almost £2.5m and estimated that this investment would have almost doubled the productive capacity of the company and would have given it assets worth around £6 million in 1962. As a wholly owned subsidiary of CAST, SLST was making substantial profits for its parent company (Van der Laan 1965).

There is little doubt that diamonds have affected the local and national economies of Sierra Leone. We have noted the disruption to and shortage of agricultural production caused in part by the drift into diamond mining. Food shortages were also partly attributable to an increase in demand for foodstuffs caused by the increase in migrant labour to the diamond areas. The question remains, did diamond production lead to the economic development of local areas like Kono and what impact, if any, has it had on Sierra Leone's national development? Such issues will be discussed in the next chapter.

2

The Political Economy of Diamonds, Governance & Civil War

Research suggests that where development has been hindered, countries have a higher risk of conflict. Civil war and the increased risk of this are closely aligned to development. Moreover, poor governance is also closely associated with conflict and political instability. This chapter will briefly consider a number of issues that arise from debates on civil war more generally and their impact on development. Such discussions will help to contextualise developments in Sierra Leone and, in particular, the relationship that was forged between various Sierra Leonean governments and the diamond industry from 1951 onwards. It was the protectorate-based Sierra Leone Peoples Party (SLPP) led initially by Milton Margai that was able to secure the majority of votes to form the first Sierra Leonean government. Margai became Sierra Leone's first prime minister in 1961 (Hayward 1987). A succession of governments followed, but it was the All Peoples Congress (APC) led by Siaka Stevens and latterly by Joseph Momoh that came to dominate Sierra Leonean politics and economy in this period. The chapter will consider causal factors offered for the outbreak of war as debated in the secondary literature. It will conclude by examining the way diamonds became the currency through which conflict was perpetuated by several players.

African governance and foreign investment

As noted in Chapter 1, diamonds were first found in Sierra Leone in 1930 with one million carats being mined annually by 1937. This rose to two million in 1960. The majority of these were top-quality gem diamonds. Approximately 55 million carats were mined (officially) between 1930 and 1998, giving a total value of around US$15 billion (Smillie 2000). In the pre-1950s period, the colonial government in Sierra Leone allowed for the unfettered growth and development of mining companies which were composed of subsidiaries of European ones. These closely conformed to

laissez-faire economics with an emphasis on market forces, private enterprise and free competition.

During the 1950s and early 1960s colonial governments in Africa more
generally began to increase the proportion of profits taken from such
companies. By the time of Sierra Leone's independence in 1961, the De
Beers Sierra Leone Selection Trust (SLST) was paying at least 60 per cent
of its profit to government justified on the grounds of the growing participation of government in the economy, including the diamond industry
(Greenhalgh 1985). The question is to what extent the profits were accrued
from diamond exports used by government to aid the country's development and were such profits sufficiently large to contribute to sustained
growth? Although companies like the SLST was given exclusive mining
and prospecting rights over the country for 99 years, this was scrapped in
1955 and in 1956 the Alluvial Diamond Mining Scheme (ADMS) allowed
indigenous miners to obtain mining and buying licences. Many of these
licences came to be held by Lebanese traders. However, the SLST
continued to hold control over important diamond areas in the Yengema
and Tongo Field, which spanned an area of around 420 sq miles (Smillie
2000).

Economic policies pursued by independent African nations continued
in the early years at least, in a similar vein to that which existed under
colonialism. Patterns of mineral resource development came to be
dependent on direct foreign investment and subsequent policies came to
favour foreign investors. The production of primary products was done to
satisfy the needs of overseas markets with little in the way of increasing
development and value to the national economy (Cleeve 1997). The degree
of state intervention varied between different independent nations and
could be seen in differences in attitudes towards the role of foreign, state
and indigenous business. Limited state intervention became the preferred
option of many independent African nations since the lack of financial,
technical and managerial resources that many colonial governments had
endured compelled them to rely on private enterprise. This continued in
the early years of independence in Sierra Leone and was probably the
motivating factor for the All Peoples Congress (APC) Government under
Siaka Stevens to resist calls for nationalisation during their early years in
power. It is within this context that diamond production and trade in
Sierra Leone was undertaken.

A consistent feature of diamond production was the issue of illicit
mining and smuggling. The Alluvial Diamond Mining Scheme aimed to
alleviate the endemic problem of illicit digging, but as we saw in Chapter
1, illicit diamond mining in Kono District remained rife. Large scale smuggling operations also continued throughout this period, involving amongst
others, ethnic groups like immigrant Mandingo and Lebanese traders who
were favourably placed to dispose of diamonds with their contacts beyond
Sierra Leone's borders. As security was tightened between Kono and Freetown in the early 1950s, diamonds began to be smuggled to Liberia. Soon

diamond merchants from Israel and Antwerp set up offices in Monrovia alongside De Beers. Yet not only were opportunist immigrant entrepreneurs involved in this illegal parallel economy, so too were large multinational companies and poor Sierra Leoneans. Moreover, under Prime Minister Siaka Stevens (with the aid of the Afro-Lebanese businessman politician Jamil Mohammed) diamonds became more explicitly embroiled in political affairs from 1968 onwards.

Under the Sierra Leone Peoples Party (SLPP) and during the short military rule of the National Reformation Council (NRC 1967–1968) neither was confident that the economic benefits were sufficient at that stage to justify nationalisation. Other factors that supported this move included government reservations concerning their capacity to develop the industry, the assumed negative effects on foreign investment and a political bias against state control (Greenhalgh 1985). In 1968 when the APC replaced the military government (after private soldiers mutinied and restored civilian rule to the APC), Prime Minister Stevens ditched the criticism he had made of the SLST when in opposition, including the threat of expulsion and instead assured the trust that he would continue in the previous mode as far as economic policy was concerned. Yet pressure both inside and outside the APC forced the government to announce in December 1969 that it aimed to take control of mining, including diamond mining from the SLST. Stevens did eventually succumb to more radical calls for nationalising the diamond industry. This came after the realisation that minerals exported in their primary stage with the limited taxes imposed on profits did not significantly aid the domestic economy (Cleeve 1997).

In 1971 the National Diamond Mining Company (NDMC) effectively nationalised the SLST. This was followed by deportations of trust personnel and by the famous diamond theft involving the disappearance of around one and a half million pounds worth of SLST stones. Stevens government justified its taking control by referring to the need to reduce illicit mining and the pressure to increase the pace of *Africanisation* (Greenhalgh 1985, Bangura & Dumbaya 1993). However, as Rimmer (1973 cited in Bangura and Dumbuya 1993) has argued, it actually worsened the control government had over the industry. The government's National Development Plan for 1974/75–1978–79 explained the drop in the export of diamonds from 1,192,000 carats valued at Le35.0 million in 1969 to 870,000 carats in 1972 as due to 'progressive exhaustion of deposits' (Ministry of Development and Economic Planning 1974). Yet the problem of illicit diamond mining and trade continued unabated and must surely have had some influence on the levels of legitimate diamond exports that continued to steadily decline from over 2 million carats in 1970 to 595,000 carats in 1980 to 48,000 in 1988 (Smillie 2000).

Reno (1995) argues that control of the diamond economy affected the amount of political autonomy local chiefs in Kono had acquired[1] and they

[1] In 1967, 75 per cent of Kono's parliamentarians claimed chiefly lineages. See Reno, W. (1995) *Corruption and State Politics in Sierra Leone*, Cambridge: Cambridge University Press.

were anxious to protect these privileges and authority. Kilson (1966) had previously offered an analysis of chieftaincy politics and the patronage powers of politicians at the centre of this patron-client system. He argues that a mutually advantageous association and dependency existed between the traditional chieftaincy and the modern political parties but that a shift towards authoritarianism would develop as elites sought to hold onto power. Illicit mining could not be controlled without local chiefly cooperation, nor could revenue be collected from taxes.

Stevens dealt with those chiefs who opposed the APC Government under him by depriving them of influence and income as development grants were blocked and the authority to approve mining licences now rested with the Ministry of Mines in Freetown (Reno 1995). Yet chiefs continued to benefit from illicit mining. Doing business with illicit diamond dealers allowed these chiefs to pay for political support in their locality. This meant that the APC government came to further alienate Kono opposition elements, ultimately affecting government influence here. Reno (1995: 86) explains that 'This local political independence blocked direct APC influence in Kono and access to local revenues, depriving Stevens of resources to build his own political support'. Yet, Stevens' political authority depended on the generation and control of diamond resources and not state institutional power alone and would involve balancing both formal and informal elements of the diamond industry if he was to survive (Reno 1995). The system of patronage meant that much of state revenue went into lining the coffers of politicians and in the payment of their clients, with many, including Stevens amassing great personal wealth. Stevens is thought to have amassed around $500 million in 1979.[2]

The eventual deal that was struck with the SLST was thought to have been greatly influenced by what had happened in the copper mines under Kaunda of Zambia in terms of the nature of compensation.[3] Negotiations continued with SLST and in September 1970 an agreement was reached with the company that split the cabinet and precipitated the resignation of the ministers of finance and development. A state of emergency was announced (Greenhalgh 1985). In June 1970 the Commercial and Industrial Corporation (COMINCOR) was formed between the government and the multinational company Lonrho with a remit to develop 'all known viable mineral resources in the country'. Another company, the National Diamond Mining Company – Sierra Leone, a subsidiary of a British company (NDMC and part of DIMINCO) was incorporated in Sierra Leone in October 1970. The government acquired a majority share of 51 per cent

[2] 'Sierra Leone's Currency Conflicts', *Africa Confidential*, 25 April 1979 cited in Reno, W. (1998) *Warlord Politics and African States*, Boulder, CO: Lynne Rienner: 117.
[3] The Sierra Leone government agreed to pay for 51 per cent of SLST assets of £2,500,000 through bonds bearing interest at 5 and a half per cent redeemable in 16 half-yearly sterling payments. See Greenhalgh, P. (1985) *West African Diamonds 1919–1983: An Economic History*, Manchester: Manchester University Press: 218.

and the SLST 49 per cent share. DIMINCO produced about half of the total diamond output with the remainder being produced by small-scale producers who were licensees operating under the Alluvial Diamond Mining Scheme (Ministry of Development and Economic Planning 1974). Binns (1982) has argued that the NDMC had parallels with other mining companies operating in the developing world in terms of the level of expatriate finance and managed operation, and in terms of the fairly limited investment in the development of the mining areas. However, whereas other mining operations may be classed as 'enclave' industries,[4] diamond mining in Sierra Leone as a whole does not constitute a true 'enclave' industry (Ministry of Development and Economic Planning 1974). However, Binns (1982) argues that the operations of NDMC more specifically did conform to this model and in particular in terms of its failure to develop the mining areas.

Diamond production under DIMINCO (the Sierra Leone government appointed SLST as managers) steadily declined during the period 1971/2 to 1983 due to a number of factors discussed below. Given that minerals accounted for almost 80 per cent of the total value of exports in 1974 with diamonds constituting the bulk of these (see Table 1.1) this was not good news. The Government set about plans to diversify the economy so that it was less vulnerable to the adverse effects of falls in the value of exports of diamonds. The Government's National Development Plan (1974) aimed to shift the balance in mineral exports so that by the end of the Plan period (1978/79) there would be a greater balance between mineral exports.

Table 2.1 Percentage of Total Value of Mineral Exports, 1973/74 and 1978/79

					1973/74	1978/79
Diamonds	...	...	...	...	79.6	57.2
Iron Ore		...	...	...	15.3	9.1
Bauxite	...	...	...	...	5.1	12.0
Rutile	...	...	...	...	—	21.2
Ilmenite	...	...	...	...	—	0.4
					100.0	100.0

Source: National Development Plan 1974/75–1978/79, Ministry of Development and Economic Planning (Freetown, 1974)

The declining fortunes of the economy more generally under the Stevens administration throughout the 1970s led to political instability and social unrest seen in the outbreak of student protest in 1977, and was quickly followed by school children's demonstrations throughout the county. A state of emergency was announced and elections held in May

---

[4] Enclave industries are often characterised by exploitation of resources without significant development to the surrounding area, a heavy dependence on overseas finance, large-scale, capital-intensive, expatriates in key management positions and organised to meet the demands of the developed countries.

1977 where the APC were returned amidst much violence and alleged vote rigging. Just over a year later, Stevens and the APC declared a one-party state (Bangura & Dumbuya 1993).

DIMINCOs steady economic decline throughout this tumultuous political backdrop can be attributed to a number of factors including the following: diamond recovery becoming more difficult due to the necessity to work lower; deeper and less accessible grades pushing up production costs; the continuing problem of illicit diamond mining; increases in the cost of imported spares and capital items, and reductions in foreign exchange allocations that reduced the buying of stores and equipment. Perhaps the most important factor though was the fall in diamond prices in the early 1980s from Le 225 per carat to approximately Le 125 per carat (Greenhalgh 1985). DIMINCO responded to such developments by taking a number of steps: reducing its personnel (including security), re-working of gravels, searching for new deposits (unsuccessfully) and the closing of some treatment plants. The strains encountered by the company were compounded by the problems of recruiting and retaining appropriate labour and by continued thefts of diamonds and equipment. The future of the company was now dependent on investment in two Kimberlite mines found in Kono in which open-pit mining had begun by the company in 1977 (Binns 1982, Cleeve 1997).

In 1983 the government signed an agreement with the SLST to begin the production of Kimberlite diamonds (Greenhalgh 1985). Full production was expected by 1987 with DIMINCO concentrating on Kimberlite mining leaving alluvial deposits to diggers and smaller firms. Greenhalgh (1985) speculated that because of the high capital investments involved in Kimberlite, direct benefits to government, (including local employment) would be lower than that of alluvial mining (Greenhalgh 1985). Moreover, it was estimated that in addition to the limited area that such deposits could be found (24 square miles of Kimberlite compared to 207.4 square miles of the lease area of NDMC), the majority of these stones were also less than 10 carats and consisted of two variations of clear and coated diamonds. Moreover, by the early 1980s, demand for diamonds began to fall. In 1981 DeBeers sales dropped to half their 1980 level and diamond production in South Africa and Namibia was significantly reduced by the closure of mines near Kimberley and in Lesotho (Bernstein 1982 cited in Williams 1982). In the meantime, the government decided to trade this Kimberlite concession and invited other contenders. The SLST decided to pull out and sold its interest to BP Minerals in 1981. With declining diamond prices BP also pulled out causing a halt to the Kimberlite negotiations. By 1990 the Government entered into discussions with the Sunshine Mining Company of Dallas, USA for a $70 million Kimberlite project at Kono (Cleeve 1997). It is unclear how far these negotiations went before the outbreak of conflict in 1991.

Throughout the 1980s, Sierra Leone's economy under the APC worsened and again fuelled social and political instability. Food shortages and hiking prices for basic commodities led to rioting and demonstrations in 1983 and 1985 by students and by striking teachers and council workers who had not received their salaries or bonuses. Stevens decided to step down and appointed cabinet minister and head of the armed forces Major General Momoh in 1985. Momoh proceeded to implement a new mining policy with a number of measures aimed at maximising economic benefit for the country. The policy also attempted to gain some control over Sierra Leone's two main minerals, gold and diamonds.

Momoh's policies on diamonds ensured that those applying for mining licences had enough capital and knowledge of the industry to execute effective mining. Moreover, the ministry of mines was invested with greater authority to inspect production records now required to be held by licence-holders and was given powers to regulate the number of diamonds sold to dealers for export. Momoh's policy also compelled dealers to export on average $500,000 worth of diamonds (or gold) otherwise their licences would be revoked. Dealers were also required to split their export earnings between themselves (40 per cent) and the Bank of Sierra Leone (60 per cent). In 1990, an annual licence fee of $500.000 was required by all exporters of diamonds. Momoh's government also negotiated agreements with various private foreign mining companies in the latter half of the 1980s, including a deal with Sumatu Raygreen Mining Company (Sierra Leone) to improve diamond mining and update equipment (Michalski 1989 cited in Bangura & Dumbuya 1993, Cleeve 1997). IMF economic reform measures provided the broader parameters within which these measures were executed. The World Bank and the Sierra Leone government attempted to develop a policy on mining investment regulations that would encourage greater input from known mining companies to both mine and export diamonds but this proved difficult[5] (Bangura & Dumbuya 1993).

Momoh's seven years in office witnessed economic collapse, continuing corruption and poor management. Thousands of Sierra Leoneans fled abroad in the 1970s and 1980s as the country slid further into bankruptcy. By the early 1990s, the United Nations ranked Sierra Leone among the poorest countries of the world, despite its mineral resources (Hirsch 2001). Intermittent supplies of electricity and petrol in Freetown meant the city was in darkness most evenings, and it was not uncommon to see long queues of abandoned vehicles left for days at a time outside petrol stations waiting for fuel.[6] Perhaps the most damaging legacy of these years was the effect of non-payment of school teachers who in the absence of salaries began charging their pupils, especially for preparation of exams. Only the well off could afford to do this, the rest were left without education and

---

[5] Explanations given for the lack of enthusiasm include bureaucracy, corruption amongst some government officials and aspects of the mining policy itself. See Bangura & Dumbuya, *Sierra Leone Review* Vol. 2 Winter 1993.

[6] Personal experience of the author who lived in Freetown between October 1989 and May 1990.

economic opportunity. According to Hirsch (2001: 30), 'The alienated and despairing youth who fought with the RUF or were to be seen aimlessly roaming the streets of the capital in the mid-1990s were the product of this situation'. Moreover, events across the border in Liberia would also impact on Sierra Leone. One of the factions that fought to wrest control from Samuel Doe during Liberia's civil war was Charles Taylor's National Patriotic Front of Liberia (NPFL). When Momoh allowed the Economic Community of West African States Ceasefire Monitoring Group (ECOMOG) to use Sierra Leone's main airport as an airbase and sent Sierra Leonean forces as part of the ECOMOG units in Liberia, Taylor began supporting Sierra Leonean rebels. The RUF under Foday Sankoh received arms and ammunition from Taylor (not to mention that both had spent time in Libya receiving guerrilla training, arms and money as Liberia became a Cold War pawn with America backing Doe). The RUF also garnered support from sections of the Sierra Leone Army (SLA) who for reasons discussed below, collaborated with the RUF and became *sobels,* soldiers by day, and rebels by night (Hirsch 2001). These then were the events that led up to and contributed to the outbreak of civil war.

In the arguments discussed above a clear causal relationship was identified between lack of development and the risk of conflict. The economic policies pursued by the national governments in post-colonial Sierra Leone appear to have done little to aid the development of this country. Diamond production was undertaken to satisfy the needs of the global economy and became an important element in Sierra Leone's dependence on primary commodity exports. Government policies came to favour foreign investors whilst the widespread corruption of Stevens' regime meant that the wealth accrued from diamonds and other exports went into paying for both political support and for personal aggrandisement. A combination of the internal factors discussed above with external (global capitalism) factors contributed to the underlying conditions within which this conflict grew and was subsequently sustained for almost a decade.

Civil war in global context

It is perhaps useful to position Sierra Leone's civil war in the wider context of conflict more generally and particularly in relation to recent conflict on the African continent. Globally, the incidence of political instability, civil war and violence is becoming much more common than international wars even though the latter attracts more attention (World Bank 2003). In term of articulations of political instability, coups d'état are more common in sub-Saharan Africa than other areas of the global south and whilst all African regions have experienced coups, West Africa appears to be the main centre of this activity (McGowan 2003). McGowan found that between 1956 and 2001, 80 coups were successful, 108 failed and 139 were reported as coup plots in all 48 independent sub-Saharan African states. The post-independence period has also seen a consistent pattern of prolonged armed conflict in all regions in Africa. This began in the 1960s with the civil wars in the Congo (Zaire 1960–1965), Nigeria (1967–1970) and Sudan (1963–1972, 1983–present). This continued in the 1970s with conflicts breaking out in Ethiopia (1970), Angola (1975), Mozambique (1979) and Rhodesia (Zimbabwe, 1970s-1980s). The 1980s saw eleven wars on the continent, including those which became embroiled in Cold War rivalries like Angola, Mozambique, Somalia and Ethiopia (Busumtwi-Sam 1999). By 2001 all of the world's wars were civil wars except for one.

According to a World Bank report (2003) those marginalised countries whose economic characteristics conform to low income, economic decline and dependence on primary commodities, the risks and incidence of civil war tend to increase. Sub-Saharan Africa as a whole was characterised by economic variables that changed very little between 1970 and 1995. Growth rates in the late 1960s had been high, whereas by the early 1990s they had fallen with per capita income barely rising during this 25 year period, with dependency on primary commodities for exports increasing slightly. A combination of these factors increased the risk of war in Africa from 8 per cent in the years 1970 to 1974 to 12.6 per cent for 1995 to 1999. Other developing regions by contrast had reduced their dependency on primary commodity export from levels that were above those in Africa in 1970 to levels that fell well below those of Africa by 1995. Moreover, other developing regions showed a substantial increase in per capita income overall. Such factors reduced the risk of rebellion. In addition, countries that have been affected by civil war have a tendency to be at a higher risk than before the conflict even if postcolonial peace has been sustained for 10 years or more (Collier & Hoeffler 2001).

The risk of conflict in Sub-Saharan Africa then does not just relate to social factors but additionally and importantly relates to Africa's weak economic performance vis-à-vis other developing nations from the 1970s onwards. Such factors have to be positioned within a broader global context if we are to understand that civil wars are rarely or solely about internal factors. So whilst ethnic and religious conflict has featured large in some conflicts and issues of ethnic dominance increases the risk of conflict, on the whole, ethnic and religious diversity actually acts as a safety valve in terms of the risk of conflict. However, if conflict breaks out, ethnicity can prolong the conflict (Berdal & Malone 2000, Collier & Hoeffler 2001).

The depth of destruction that conflicts have wrought on this continent has in recent years been acknowledged by both African and Western Governments. The Organisation for African Unity (OAU) has issued five declarations and agreements on the threat that internal wars pose to Africa's security. In 1990, the OAU issued a 'Declaration on the Political and Socio-economic Situation in Africa', which recognised that unless conflict was managed, economic development and political instability would continue to undermine efforts to bring this increasingly marginalised continent into the global economic system. The Kampala Document presented in 1991 proposed new conflict-resolution mechanisms which were adopted at the Cairo Summit in 1993. While the emphasis had been on prevention, by 1995 the OAU at its annual summit in Addis Ababa began to consider more interventionist responses whilst at the same time emphasised the relationship between socio-economic development, governance and peace and security. Of course any discussion of political stability and economic development necessitates a discussion of the role of international financial institutions (IFIs). Structural adjustment policies are closely bound up with socio-economic and political factors that affect national security and conflict (Busumtwi-Sam 1999). The question is, are such institutions part of the solution or part of the problem? If we accept that unequal distribution of resources lies at the heart of conflict in Africa, then the solution to this problem has to be sought in global economic forces, and in particular those factors that have a negative and exploitative impact on the continent. There has been some recognition of the destructive effects of uneven economic development that exists between Africa and the developed world as seen in the *Report of the Commission for Africa* (March 2005) and in the G8 Summit at Gleneagles in July 2005. The Commission for Africa states:

> Violent conflict has killed and displaced more people in Africa than in any other continent in recent decades. This has driven poverty and exclusion, undermined growth and development, and deprived many of their right to life, liberty, and security as enshrined in Article 3 of the Universal Declaration of Human Rights. (2005:157)

The role that natural resources play in such conflict and of the need to 'weaken the link between natural resources and violent conflict in Africa' is also being addressed (Report of the Commission for Africa March 2005).

Underdevelopment and the risk of conflict

Research suggests that globally, where development has been hindered, such countries have a higher risk of conflict and conversely, where development has been successful, the risk of violent conflict is lessened (Collier et al. 2003). Cramer (2006) further suggests that we need to go beyond domestic factors when trying to understand conflicts in the developing world as these should be seen in the context of global economic markets and their subsequent impact. For Cramer, such conflicts are part of the transition to capitalism.

Civil war and the increased risk of this are closely aligned to development. Accordingly, despite popular conceptions, economic characteristics are often more important than ethnic and religious conflicts in the cause of civil wars, (though ethnic divisions have been intensified by issues of governance that relate to access to power, allocation and distribution of resources and the way ethnicity is managed by political leaders (Busumtwi-Sam 1999)[7]. Indeed there are a number of economic variables that increase the risk of civil war including; economic decline, a dependency on primary commodity exports and a low per capita income that is unequally distributed. This combination of economic factors leads to impoverishment and in some cases to the creation of groups of disaffected young men who are ripe for recruitment into rebel factions. Natural resource wealth can finance such organisations and further perpetuate conflict. Whilst divisions can manifest themselves along ethnic and religious lines, there is an increased chance of this turning violent in areas with low and declining incomes (Collier et al (2003).

Poor governance is also seen to be closely associated with the emergence of rebel factions and conflict. In some cases, lack of procedures and mechanisms that allow for peaceful change in governance structures make no allowance for legitimate demands for change by disaffected groups. For Busumtwi-Sam:

> The problem of civil conflict in Africa is essentially a problem of governance. Thus effective prevention and management of conflict ultimately entails development of norms concerning governance and mechanisms and procedures that can channel demands for change into predictable and manageable directions. (Busumtwi-Sam 1999: 258)

It appears that civil wars are increasing in terms of their duration and while each situation has to be viewed in terms of specific factors, it is also necessary to see these individual cases in a broader global context. As a result, conflicts are often supported and sustained by factors outside the immediate area of conflict. Financing conflict through the buying of arms and in some cases private security reflects broader global changes that tie into complex political/economic linkages. These developments allow for the prolongation of civil wars today. According to a World Bank report (Collier et al (2003), low-income countries like Sierra Leone that have experienced economic decline and continue to depend on primary commodities like mineral wealth, have a greater risk (15 times higher than OECD countries) of civil war. Part of the solution, the report argues, rests in the need to kick start development and in doing so development needs to be diverse and not solely reliant on primary commodities. Of those nations that have experienced civil war, the risk of further conflict remains high in the first decade of post conflict peace with estimates forecasting as many as half returning to conflict within the decade. If the reasons for conflict lie in the lack of development, we need to ask what

[7] Colonial rule served to intensify ethnic rivalries through the arbitrary creation of colonial boundaries that became rigid and fixed. By 1989, Africa had 103 areas that were subject to dispute between neighbouring states or led to secessionist or irredentist conflict because of divisions between ethnic groups. See Busumtwi-sam (1999) 'Redefining "Security" after the Cold War: The OAU, the UN and Conflict Management in Africa' in Ali, T.M. and Matthews, R.O. (eds) (1999) *Civil Wars in Africa – Roots and Resolutions*, McGill-Queen's University Press: Montreal & Kingston London Ithaca.

has caused this underdevelopment in the first place.

Causal explanations for lack of development fall into those who might broadly be defined as coming under the remit of the Washington consensus[8] and more recently a post-Washington perspective that sees lack of development having its roots in internal factors that relate to poor governance like corruption and authoritarian rule. The Berg Report (1981) commissioned by the World Bank articulated this influential perspective that would come to dominate explanations for Africa's lack of development. In the 1980s, the IMF and World Bank Structural Adjustment Policies (SAP) were soon imposed on affected African states who after initially challenging the World Bank perspective (by pointing out factors such as the deteriorating terms of trade for primary products, the protectionism of wealthier nations, increasing interest rates and debt repayment) heeded to their demands and acknowledged the alleged responsibility of African governments for the crisis. By the late 1990s, the World Bank called for greater state involvement in the implementation of SAP. Although Africa had complied with IMF and World Bank policies, there continued to be a lack of confidence in the continents governments to deal with its problems (Arrighi 2002).

Alternative perspectives that had emerged in the 1960s and 1970s, especially on the left, emphasised external factors for the retardation of Africa's development. These include the more general constraints that capitalism has on development (including the effects of colonialism) as well as specific external variables, such as declining terms of trade and cold war interventions (ibid.). Some also offered causal explanations that incorporated both internal and external factors that were seen to form a complex inter-relationship. Arrighi and Saul (1973) were critical of the role of African elites in the continent's development and in particular the conspicuous consumption of some urban elites, the transfer of profits abroad and the restraints on agricultural production and domestic markets. Such developments they argue, led to a greater dependency on world demand for primary products. At the same time, Arrighi and Saul (1973) acknowledged the role of international capital in restraining and 'perverting' Africa's economic growth. Indeed they argued that the high consumption levels of the elite at least in part derived from the integration of those economies into global capital and was not merely or solely the result of policies pursued by such elites. For Arrighi:

> In sharp contrast to East Asia, sub-Saharan Africa inherited from the pre-colonial and colonial era a political-economic configuration that left little room for the construction of viable national economies or robust national states. Attempts to build these against all the odds did not on the whole get very far, in spite of the considerable legitimacy that they enjoyed at the time of independence. (Arrighi 2002: 5)

[8] This has been briefly defined as global economic policy as defined by the IMF and the World Bank.

Arrighi (ibid.) further argues that up until 1975 Africa's performance as a whole was no worse than the world average, was better than that of South Asia and even North America. However, after 1975 and throughout the 1980s and 1990s Africa's performance fell dramatically whilst that of East and South Asia improved. Arrighi makes the point that since Africa's economy and development is closely entwined with broader global capitalist forces, explanations to account for Africa's deterioration from the mid-1970s onwards have to be sought in these wider global forces. While not absolving Africa's elites of any responsibility, at the same time, human agency is forced to operate within the constraints and indeed perversions of global capitalist development. It is in the light of these broader factors that we can attempt to contextualise the minutiae of one of Sierra Leone's important primary commodities for export – diamonds – and examine how these featured in the country's post-colonial development and eventual descent into civil war.

Sierra Leone's civil war 1991–2002

A wealth of literature[9] has emerged in the past ten years or more that has addressed the background and causal explanations for the conflict in Sierra Leone. Many would agree that the political and economic climate in Sierra Leone before the civil war with widespread inflation, increasing unemployment and what Zack-Williams (1990) calls 'the pauperisation of the mass of the Sierra Leonean people' prepared the ground for political instability and eventual civil war. This conflict saw some of the worst atrocities in recent human history. It is apparent from examining some of the literature that integral ties between politics and economics are tightly woven together. Between the early 1960s when Sierra Leone gained independence and the outbreak of civil war in the early 1990s, a combination of political corruption by elements of the Sierra Leonean elite and economic crisis, (itself the result of political mismanagement and broader global political/economic forces) has destabilised the country. This has resulted in greater and greater inequality. Various commentators have offered explanations of the civil war that have been couched in terms of political corruption and/or economic crisis, though one commentator, Kaplan (1994) in his controversial 'The Coming Anarchy' emphasised endemic cultural and sociological failures in African society for the uncontrolled warfare and what he saw as the inevitable return to primitivism that awaited much of the Third World. Kaplan's contribution to the debate reflected and in turn encouraged Washington's policy on Africa at that time, namely withdrawal from direct involvement in African crises.

[9] See amongst others P. Richards (1996) *Fighting for the Rainforest: War, Youth & Resources in Sierra Leone*, Oxford: James Currey; I. Abdullah (ed) (2004) *Between Democracy and Terror: the Sierra Leone Civil War*, Dakar: Council for the Development of Social Science Research in Africa; D. Keen (2005) *Conflict & Collusion in Sierra Leone*, Oxford: James Currey.

This followed on the heels of the US withdrawal from Somalia after eighteen American Army rangers were killed in the capital Mogadishu (Hirsch 2001).

Bangura (2000) has argued that the Sierra Leone conflict relates to a crisis of youth brought about by government misrule by the All Peoples Congress (APC). Abdullah and Bangura (1997) identifies a culture of marginality, characterised by drugs, violence and disrespect for official institutions. It is the Sierra Leonean youth who are most affected by this argues Abdullah, since as their economic opportunities declined, they fell into a 'lumpen culture'. It was this that provided fertile breeding ground for the rebel Revolutionary United Front (RUF), whose lumpen and criminal lifestyle offered a 'natural constituency'.

The 'youth crisis' discussed by Abdullah and Bangura (1997) which they argue formed the centre of the Sierra Leone conflict can be seen in the high proportion of youth who failed to complete primary or secondary education. Those between the ages of 15–29 constitute 25 per cent of the population, and more than 80 per cent of the population are below 40 years of age. With one of the lowest literacy rates in the world at 24 per cent, many Sierra Leonean youths have to rely on the informal economy to eke out a living. Those who live close to gold and diamond mining areas, earn a living through illicit or informal mining, whilst others may engage in petty trading. It was these marginal youth involved in mining, and other 'alienated youth' in rural areas who had little respect for traditional authority, that the rebel RUF were initially able to recruit from (Muana 1997).

The descent into civil war some would argue was the inevitable result of twenty-four years of misrule and intimidation by the one-party regime of the APC under Siaka Stevens (Kandeh 1999, Zack-Williams 1999), referred to as the 'seventeen-year plague of locusts' (Hirsch 2001: 29). The pursuit of personal gain and political patronage by the political elite, particularly Siaka Stevens, resulted in irreparable damage to the social, economic and political life of Sierra Leone. Those who attempted to challenge this were quickly dealt this as APC rule under Stevens and his allies:

> destroyed and corrupted every institution of the state. Parliament was gutted of significance; judges were intimidated or bribed; the university was starved of funds; many professors compromised their integrity by joining the cabinet; the value of education itself was deprecated in favour of the quick acquisition of wealth; and the professionalism of the army was undermined. Those who opposed the imposition of the one-party state in 1977 were either executed, forced into exile, or reduced to a condition of penury. Bank of Sierra Leone governor Sam L. Bangura was killed under mysterious circumstances in 1979 after challenging the wisdom of lavish expenditures on the OAU summit. (Hirsch 2001: 29)

A shadow state had emerged, (to use Reno's (1995) term), whereby the building of a 'parallel political authority [emerged] in the wake of the near total decay of formal state institutions'. This was firmly rooted in colonial rule argues Reno. Many were excluded from this process and this effectively sowed the seeds for rebellion. The general erosion of welfare provision provided by family and community and the almost total collapse of educational provision led to a decline in moral values and what Kandeh has termed the 'criminal terror' of civil war (1999). The raping of public resources by the political elite directly contributed to the *lumpenisation* of large swathes of Sierra Leonean youth, who in turn formed the core of the RUF.

Richards (1996: xvii) has argued that the violent nature of the conflict was 'moored culturally in the hybrid Atlantic world of international commerce'. This refers to the international nature of the worlds media and the influence of a 'transatlantic creolised culture' that informed Sierra Leone's youth of world events, and in particular raised issues of social exclusion in films like 'Rambo' which many youths could empathise with. Whilst Richards (ibid.) emphasised a 'patrimonial crisis' as one possible explanation for the outbreak of war, Bangura (1997) describes a 'fiscal crisis' impacting most severely on state expenditure and services, and particularly on those who rely on this as a source of income.

Zack-Williams (1999) adds that a combination of political and economic factors were paramount in causing the civil war. The 1970s and 80s saw an increase in Siaka Stevens' personalised rule as economic decline set in. This was the period when the diamond mining areas around Kono District, came under state control and a network of client-patron relationships flourished. (ibid.). In the 1980s, Stevens turned to International Financial Institutions (IFI) to correct the shortfall between government revenue and expenditure and a series of Structural Adjustment Policies (SAP) were introduced, which further strained political and economic conditions. SAP led to 'devaluation and deregulation [which] triggered off widespread inflation, unemployment and pauperisation of the mass of the Sierra Leone people' (Zack-Williams 1999: 145). Zack-Williams further states that areas of peripheral capitalism, like Sierra Leone, have seen the proletarianisation of sectors of the working population. However, the logic of capital accumulation here means that welfare provisions taken for granted at the centre are denied to those on the periphery. Social and economic human rights are all but absent. Indeed, it seems that those with the least social and economic opportunities – women – 77 per cent of whom have no formal education and who perform between 60 and 80 per cent of agricultural work, have suffered most from rebel atrocities (Zack-Williams 1999) in addition to their sufferance in the pre-war period.

When Momoh took over as leader of the APC in 1985, his government sought to liberalise politics and attempted to control the violence and intimidation seen under Stevens. In opening talks with the IMF, Momoh implemented an austerity programme of raising taxes to increase government revenue (Hayward 1997). Structural Adjustment Policies implemented throughout the 1980s and '90s always hit the most vulnerable groups the hardest and reduced the employment opportunities of many. Austerity measures under the impact of SAP inevitably impact hardest on social welfare provision. Sierra Leone's economy was undermined further when in early 1991 supporters of the Liberian rebel leader Charles Taylor crossed over the border into southern Sierra Leone. This signalled the beginning of the war. Now the nation's development deteriorated further as pressure was put more firmly on scarce resources and as Taylor's forces resorted to pillaging and violence in the diamond areas around Kono (Hayward 1997). Richards (1996) had pursued the line that the rebel RUF emerged from within the ranks of a disaffected intelligentsia. Others have argued that the RUF emerged because of a youth crisis dating back to the days of APC misrule. In either case, disaffected Sierra Leoneans joined rebels who came across the border from Liberia.

Diamond resources should have aided Sierra Leone's economic development. Instead, attempts to manage these became steeped in corruption. By the end of the 1980s, only a small percentage of diamond production was exported through official channels causing considerable grievance amongst local populations well before the rebellion in 1991 (Goreux 2001).

Resource predation and war: the currency of diamonds

While the immediate origins of the civil war have to be explained with reference to a series of complex and multidimensional factors (injustice and inequality, social exclusions, endemic corruption, economic and political crisis and poverty), the struggle to control diamond resources quickly became embroiled in the war in Sierra Leone. Diamonds fuelled the conflict that had destabilised the country for almost three decades. They also became an important part of the larger regional conflict involving key international interests (Smillie 2000).

After a Sierra Leonean Army captain, Valentine Strasser marched on Freetown in April 1992 with the intention of overthrowing Momoh's government, it was not long before he and his troops were mining diamonds in Kono in exchange for weapons in Belgium and Romania. Indeed the control of the diamond fields became integral to this conflict and it was not long after Strasser's occupation here that RUF rebels took this area around the middle of 1992 (Reno 1995). The role of private security firms in the protection of mineral resources is important (see Chapter 6) since not only did foreign companies who were engaged in operations here utilise their services, but so too did government and anti-government rebels enlist their services.

The South African private military company – Executive Outcomes (EO) – is perhaps the best known of these and was certainly the most effective in the context of Sierra Leone. This company provided security, mining, civil engineering and financial interests to Sierra Leone between April 1995 and February 1997 and in return was given a stake in the country's mineral wealth. During this time, EO's role was to uphold the military government of Strasser and later support the civilian government that followed elections in February 1996 (Duffield 2001). The use of private military companies like EO during its 18 months or so in the country saw a degree of success as the RUF were pushed from the outskirts of Freetown and were forced out of the diamond areas. The presence of EO also allowed elections to take place in February 1996. Yet the use of private security like EO did not provide a sustainable solution since not long after the company left, the government was taken over by the military who proceeded to invite the rebel RUF to join them (Duffield 2005).

While the manifesto of the RUF called for the 'national salvation and liberation ... the historic responsibility of each patriot ... for a national democratic revolution involving the total mobilisation of all progressive forces', the war in Sierra Leone was mainly waged against the civilian and rural population that claimed the lives of at least 20,000 people and some estimate this to be as high as 70,000 (Zack-Williams 2000). It also led to the displacement of more than half the population as people fled their homes (Douglas 1999). Attacks on civilians occurred in all regions, including the capital Freetown (since early 1998) and a high number occurred in the Koidu-diamond mining area in the east (Human Rights Watch 1998). When the RUF occupied and controlled Kono in addition to Kailahun and much of the Kenema area from January 1996, widespread atrocities were inflicted against civilians (Bangura 2000). This occurred whilst diamonds were simultaneously mined at the war front by various factions, including the Armed Forces Revolutionary Council (AFRC) who had been involved in fighting with civilian militias or civil defence forces like the Kamajors[10] (the largest and most powerful of these) in the Tongo diamond fields. Even in the early days of the war when the National Provisional Ruling Council under Strasser had overthrown the Momoh government in 1992, the army outside of Freetown quickly realised that profits could be made from diamonds at the war front, particularly as their economic position declined and wages stopped. Moreover, the introduction of conscription by the NPRC saw many ill-equipped youths (in terms of training and discipline) being taken off the streets and sent to the war front. Stories of banditry and military collusion with rebels became rife as the phenomenon of the *sobel* (soldier by day, rebel by night) emerged with both RUF

---

[10] The Kamajors are traditional hunters of Mende ethnicity (the largest ethnic group constituting around 30 per cent of the population) and come from the southern and eastern parts of Sierra Leone. They believe in supernatural and ancestral powers. During the conflict civil defence forces like the Kamajors were created when the Sierra Leonean army were implicated in collusion with rebels to exploit the country's diamond reserves. The army was accused of exchanging weapons for diamonds from the RUF, giving them military information, and withdrawing from bases so as to allow rebels to take over diamond rich areas. See Human Rights Watch, 'Getting Away with Murder, Mutilation and Rape', *Sierra Leone* Vol. 11, No. 3 (A) June 1999.

and the Sierra Leonean army (RSLMF) existing by looting and 'foraging' to use Douglas's term (Douglas 1999: 178).

As the war developed, fighting occurred between AFRC troops and the RUF in the second half of the 1990s (UN Security Council 1997). The continued and endless supply of diamonds enabled rebel RUF forces to continue to finance its rebellion by exchanging diamonds for weapons, drugs and the services of foreign mercenaries (including Israeli, Ukrainian and white South Africans to name just a few – see Chapter 6, Goreux 2001). The subsequent terrorising of the civilian population through the use of random violence and the brutal and widespread practice of limb amputation and other injuries, increased fatalities and precipitated population displacement as people fled in search of safety. There were also widespread abductions, including that of children who were used as child soldiers and of women and girls who were used as sex slaves.

The control of the diamond mining areas by various factions led to a massive drain on the country's mineral wealth. Between 1999 and 2001 official diamond exports by Sierra Leone had dropped to half, to US$30 million (HR Watch Report 2001), whilst in 1999 alone, official exports amounted to a mere $1.2 million. According to a report commissioned by the World Bank (2001), export earnings from diamonds in 1999 were estimated at a staggering $138 million in total. This can be broken down into an estimated $70 million that went to the RUF, at least $10 million to the Civil Defence Force (CDF) and a further $50 million taken by those who were outside the control of the RUF and the CDF. Of these $50 million, much was used to finance imports of consumption goods like rice which was then used to buy more diamonds from diggers and their agents. The diamonds that were exchanged for rice were then sold for dollars in a barter-like system (World Bank 2001). Diamond exports from Liberia (which has a negligible number of diamond fields) rose to US$300 million. The former Taylor government of Liberia had been strongly implicated in arms deals with the RUF in return for Sierra Leonean diamonds. The US Ambassador to the UN, Richard Holbrooke, claimed to have evidence to show Charles Taylor and RUF leaders had personally taken large commissions for aiding illegal diamond and arms dealing. In May 2012, Taylor was found guilty of aiding and abetting rebels in Sierra Leone during the 1991–2002 civil war by the Special Court for Sierra Leone and was sentenced to 50 years in jail[11]. He became the the first former head of state to be convicted of war crimes by an international court since the Nuremburg trials of Nazis after World War II (BBC Online 30 May 2012).

In July 2000, the UN Security Council threatened sanctions against both Liberia and Burkina Faso for perpetuating war in Sierra Leone through

---

[11] The counts brought against Charles Taylor included: Acts of terrorism, Murder; Rape; Sexual slavery; Outrages against personal dignity; Violence to life, in particular cruel treatment; Other inhumane acts; Conscripting child soldiers; Enslavement; and Pillage. See Global Witness, (2012) 'The Charles Taylor Verdict: A Global Witness briefing on a dictator, blood diamonds and timber, and two countries in recovery', 24th May.

Plate 2.1 Peaceful protestors outside the Special Court for Sierra Leone during the Judgement in the trial of former President of Liberia, Charles Taylor, Freetown, 26 April 2012 (© Diane Frost)

Plate 2.2 The back premises of the Special Court for Sierra Leone, Freetown, April 2012 (© Diane Frost)

illegal arms and diamonds trafficking (HR Watch Report 2001). In the same month and in an attempt to identify and control *conflict diamonds* the International Diamond Manufacturers' Association and the World Federation of Diamond Bourses agreed at a meeting of the World Diamond Congress in Antwerp, a global certification scheme for rough diamonds (The Kimberley Process). It was also agreed that all rough diamonds be shipped in sealed packages certified by exporting nations and verified by a new international diamond council. Countries knowingly involved in illegal diamond trading should also lose their export accreditation. Yet as has already been said, between 1999 and 2001, Liberia increased its diamond exports to US$300 million (Human Rights Watch – World Report 2001); see also Chapter 4.

In January 2002, the civil war in Sierra Leone was declared over by the UN following the disarmament of rebels in May 2001 and the deployment of UN peacekeeping troops in rebel-held territory. Since then there has been massive international intervention aimed at reconstructing the state and securing peace and stability. In March 2004, a UN-backed war crimes tribunal commenced to try senior militia leaders from both sides of the war. These developments will be discussed more fully in Chapter 7. In the meantime, the following chapter will examine the concerns and worries articulated by some but which are shared by many in post-civil war Sierra Leone.

3

Digging Work, Workers
for Diamonds & Hidden Voices
c.1930s–1990s

Diamond mining along with other mineral mining has accounted for a significant slice of exports and government revenue in Sierra Leone, though it has never been the largest employer of workers. Agriculture has traditionally been the largest and continues to be so. However, mineral production has always been perceived as an avenue for economic development, not least amongst those communities who have remained marginal in discussions on development. Yet as we have seen in the previous chapter, diamonds and other minerals have not led to the development that many had hoped for. Poor management, increasing economic dependency on the export of primary commodities like diamonds and a heavy reliance on foreign investment has had a detrimental effect on development. Not only has this stifled economic change but it has also had a distorting effect on more general socio-economic and political developments. Independent governments in Sierra Leone inherited (unchallenged) an authoritarian colonial economic and political structure that was subsequently used in the interest of the new African elite. Little was done to utilise this mineral wealth for the betterment of wider civil society. Instead, much of this wealth was squandered and misused by governments to buy amongst other things political patronage and to add to the accumulation of personal wealth. Wider structural factors that were external to post-colonial Sierra Leone also had a role to play, particularly those involved in the trading and buying of diamonds, and the mining companies involved in their exploitation. It is within this broader context that the following two chapters examine work and social organisation respectively, from 'below' by utilising the personal testimonies of a small group of Kono people[1]. Both Chapters 3 and 4 will examine the views and perspectives of those communities who have remained marginal economically, socially and politically from the process of development.

Discussions on development (undertaken by governments, interna-

---

[1] Some of the names used here are real whilst others are fictional to protect the person's identity. A list of those interviewed can be found in the bibliography.

tional financial institutions and mineral companies), have rarely included those communities affected by diamond production (either through living in a diamond producing area, through working in the industry or in some other capacity) and have been conspicuous by their absence or have been the least regarded. The lives and livelihoods of such groups and the way diamond production impacts are rarely taken account of in negotiations between government and mineral companies (International Institute for Environment and Development 2002). In documenting some of these unheard voices we are at once attaching significance to their perspectives, their truth and are acknowledging what is important to them. The theoretical framework that informs the approach used here is far removed from positivistic notions of neutrality and objectivity. Instead, it adopts an approach that sees human agency as an important factor in articulating a critical perspective of, and challenge to, wider socio-economic and political forces.

Alluvial mining – workers and multinational enterprise

There have been two main methods used in the mining of alluvial diamonds in Sierra Leone. The first is mechanised mining, as used in the main by foreign companies, where earth-moving machinery and the establishment of washing plants make the working of diamondiferous areas more efficient and profitable. The second method of mining is that first used by local diamond miners under the Alluvial Diamond Mining Scheme (ADMS) and by illicit diggers. This relies on hand digging and the washing of gravels by hand panning, using mesh sieves. The use of motor pumps to clear water from filled pits is also used. Such methods today have barely changed since the 1950s, and indeed before this when SLST monopolised production and mining was deemed illegal for Sierra Leoneans. There is also a third type of mining; semi-mechanised, that falls between the two and will not be discussed in any great detail here. Interviews with those who had worked or had associations with both types of mining activity will be used where possible as a point of cross-reference with other sources. Additionally, they will act as a means of enhancing the secondary and primary archival material, as well as filling the gaps and omissions here. Finally, such testimonies provide alternative perspectives from *below*.

Cleeve (1997) has argued that employment conditions for those working for multinational mining enterprises were better than those who worked for local employers. The Labour Congress adds that mining companies generally implement labour agreements more effectively than other employers implement and attribute this to the existence of better organised labour unions and the larger size and profitability of mining companies operations. Those who worked for large mining companies did organise in trade unions in the 1940s and 1950s. In September 1940 for example, the Yengema Diamond Workers Union (YDWU) was formed and in 1945 it combined with DELCO's Mining Employees Union to form the United Mine Workers Union (UMWU) headed by Siaka Stevens as General Secretary. During the Second World War, changes in social and economic conditions with inflation, shortages of manufactured and consumer goods and the failure of wages to keep up with prices saw increased political and industrial unrest. Whilst Sierra Leone did not experience the same level of industrial unrest as say the Gold Coast during the war years, nevertheless there were instances of strikes in 1944 and 1945 and in the latter case workers succeeded in raising daily wage rates and reduced hours to a daily rate of eight (Greenhalgh 1985). Several factors have been offered by Conway (1968, cited in Greenhalgh 1985) for the apparent stability in industrial relations in the mining industry in Sierra Leone. These include the establishment of collective bargaining procedures in the form of a wages board in 1946 where unions and employers were represented. More importantly, was the confidence that the union had in this structure, strengthened as it was by the boards' responsiveness to labour's demands. Other factors that contributed to relatively good relations include the promoting of leadership security and patronage, the stable nature of unions attributed to the prohibiting of rival organisations and the practice of extending negotiated agreements to workers not on the union bodies. By the 1950s, the mining industry as a whole experienced increased strike action. In April 1951, 2,600 SLST workers came out in support of substantial pay increases which were conceded. This led to increased illicit diamond mining activities. The 1955 General Strike saw riots in the capital Freetown and unofficial strikes at Yengema, which occurred again in 1959 (Greenhalgh 1985).

Under the 'Regulation of Wages and Industrial Relations Act 1971', wages and salaries, fringe benefits, leave, accidents, redundancy and union recognition were determined through collective bargaining procedures. Moreover, it has been suggested that a consensus existed between multinational enterprise executives, trade union leaders and government that rates of pay in mining were higher than those of other firms, foreign or local, and government departments. In addition, mining companies have also offered other benefits, such as subsidies for rice and fuel, rent and subsistence allowance in a bid to attract workers, though adequate supplies of labour were always available and active recruitment was not necessary (CSO Sierra Leone – Geological Survey and Mines Annual Report for 1938). The payment in kind system no doubt contributed to workers' earnings through the provision of cheaper food, housing and medical care, but employers such as the Selection Trust had a stake in maintaining a healthy and viable workforce, if they were to continue to make substantial profits from diamonds. Maximizing profit was the motivating factor behind the company not philanthropy. Moreover, such companies were to an extent regulated by government legislation

concerning welfare provision. Whether diamond workers felt they benefitted from this system or not was not an issue since they had no choice
in the way they were paid. What is known is that employer-worker relations were not always good and that on occasions, strikes were organised
by unions such as the United Mine Workers Union (UMWU) whose
members worked for the Selection Trust (Annual Report of the Mines Dept
1959).[2]

In the early 1930s, the Selection Trust operated a policy of employing
'new boys' on trial at 6d. per day, for one or two weeks. After this, they
would let him go or keep him on and raise this to 7d. Wage rates were
multilayered in 1938 with a range that started at the bottom end of 6d to
11d per day; 1s. to 1s. 11d per day; 2s. to 2s. 11d per day and for skilled
Africans 3s. to 11s. 4d per day (Sierra Leone Blue Books 1938).
Throughout the 1930s and much of the 1940s, the absence of trade unions
in this industry and the seemingly unlimited supply of labour meant wage
rates were not increased until later (Greenhalgh 1985). These wage rates
were either higher or the same as those employed in similar positions by
the colonial government. With the additional payment in kind provision,
it seems likely that such workers enjoyed a relatively higher standard of
living than government workers did. This did not mean though that industrial relations were always harmonious and while Sierra Leone did not
witness the level of industrial unrest that other West African countries
experienced in the 1930s and 40s, it had its fair share (Conway 1968). The
problems of inflation, the failure of wages to keep up with prices and the
subsequent shortage of manufactured and consumer goods came together
in a potent mixture of general instability in the immediate aftermath of
war. Such instability manifested itself in a series of strikes.

In the diamond industry in 1945, strike action occurred independently
of the UMWU by labourers and semi-skilled workers, who were successful
in raising wage rates and reduced the working day to eight hours. With
the establishment of a Wage Board in the mining industry in 1946, the
introduction of greater formality in the bargaining procedures occurred,
including minimum standards. Moreover, the creation in 1952 of Works
Committees allowed for greater local consultation outside the more
centralised structure of the Wage Board. Both developments may have
gone some way in placating strike action. With price rises in 1951, SLST
workers joined in the general unrest and in April of that year, 2600
workers took strike action for eleven days in support of pay increases
above the minimum level. The Selection Trust eventually conceded with
substantial wage increases. There was also a General Strike in 1955 in

---

[2] The United Mineworkers Union was formed in 1945 with Siaka Stevens as the General Secre-
tary, after the amalgamation of the Mining Employees Union and the Yengema Diamond
Workers Union. See 'Report on the Labour Dept 1945, Sierra Leone Box 1937–1965, Agreement,
Proceedings' and 'Annual Reports', Freetown Government Archive. Trade Unions were not
recognised in Sierra Leone until the passing of the Trade Union Ordinance in 1939. See M.
Crowder 1968: 352.

which workers at Yengema took industrial action and an additional strike involving Selection Trust workers in 1959 (Mines Dept Annual Report 1959). Greenhalgh (1985) suggests that the 1951 strike involving 2,600 workers fuelled illicit diamond activities and acted as a safety valve for workers' frustrations. He believes this contributed to the increased wage rates. Throughout the 1950s and 1960s Greenhalgh (1985) suggests that SLST labour-management relations were good with only minimal strike action and substantial wage increases. This is in part attributable to the need to pay competitive wage rates vis-à-vis other employers as a means of ensuring a stable work force and high productivity levels.

Up until the 1950s, Sierra Leoneans working for the Selection Trust were excluded from the more senior positions of the industry, confined as they were to the lower echelons. Skilled or well-paid positions like managers, engineers and geologists remained firmly in the hands of Europeans until well after the Second World War. With the pressure for political independence on the horizon, steps were taken after the war to train up Sierra Leoneans for such positions.[3] Such moves were indicative of the pressure for change that had been forced by the effects of the war on colonial societies. As Crowder comments:

> The very generous support given by Africans to the war effort had to be recompensed by the social, economic and political reforms which had been demanded by the elite over the past twenty years. (Crowder 1968: 502)

Yet this process of *Africanisation* in the diamond industry (also referred to as Sierra Leonisation after 1971) was slow to take off and did not really achieve significant movement until the early 1970s. In 1958 the Selection Trust had 91 senior staff of whom 97 per cent were expatriates. By 1970–71, this had risen to 298 senior staff of which 66 per cent were expatriates including seven expatriate West Africans. It was not until 1974 that Sierra Leoneans began to make up around half (51 per cent) of the 329 senior staff of what had now become DIMINCO, though it was later still in 1983 before Sierra Leoneans formed the majority (82 per cent) of senior staff (Greenhalgh 1985).

The establishment of multinational companies in developing nations often necessitates the development of infrastructural facilities by the companies themselves. The mining of diamonds in Sierra Leone has taken place in remote rural areas where access and communication has needed to be improved. This has necessitated the construction of not only roads, rail and other transport links as we saw in chapter one, but also housing and amenities like hospitals and schools for those communities concerned. By 1950 the SLST had established its headquarters at Yengema, Kono District and had established several mining or labour camps across the district, where labourers lived with their families (Mines Dept Annual Report 1950). The Kwakwayi labour camp, established in

[3] See Chapter 1 for details of this.

the late 1940s consisted of 120 rooms with kitchen, latrines and bath houses. For the European staff, two double houses with servants' quarters were also constructed. In addition, an existing hospital was extended and a mortuary and isolation ward was built. In Koidu Town, a canteen and meetinghouse for Africans was built in the late 1940s by the SLST. In the 1950s, the Company maintained an active construction programme. In one year alone the Company was able to complete construction on the maternity block at Yengema hospital; improved the areas water supply; completed stores and workshops for the Tongo field; extended the Artisan Training School in Lower Bambara Chiefdom and completed the electrification of the Koidu hospital. Moreover, the Company extended its scholarships scheme for local and overseas study (Annual Report of the Mines Dept 1957)

Annual reports compiled by the Mines Department for 1947 and 1950 show that around 2,700 labourers were employed in mining and prospecting under the SLST monopoly. Around 25 Europeans supervised these. Compared to other mining activities, only iron ore resembles these figures for 1950.

Table 3.1 Average African Labour Engaged in Mining and Prospecting by Quarter, 1950

Mineral	First quarter	Second quarter	Third quarter	Fourth quarter	Year
Gold	304	286321	355	317	
Diamond	2,779	2,834	2,743	2,715	2,765
Iron Ore	2,603	2,613	2,659	2,724	2,650
Chrome Ore	992	921	970	1,086	992
Total					
1950	6,678	6,644	6,593	6,880	6,724
1949	6,442	6,604	6,353	6,511	6,478

Source: Annual Report of the Mines Department for the Year 1950, Freetown.

Table 3.2 Average Labour Engaged in the Mining Industry, 1950

Mineral	British	French	Syrian	Other persons
Gold	1	4	6	317
Platinum	–	–	–	–
Diamond	30	–	–	2,765
Iron Ore	43	–	–	2,650
Chrome Ore	9	–	–	992
Total	83	4	6	6,724

Source: Annual Report of the Mines Department for the Year 1950, Freetown.

Once the diamonds were recovered, companies or individuals were free to buy and export these stones if they had purchased an export licence. Records show that two banks, the Bank of West Africa Limited and Barclays Bank (D.C. & O.) Limited had some interests in diamonds in the 1950s as revealed by their purchasing of exporters' licences in 1957 at a cost £250 each. In both cases, the banks sold their diamonds 'by arrangement' to the Diamond Corporation (Annual Report of the Mines Department 1957, Freetown).

Fieldwork undertaken in Kono by the author (April 2003) involved visiting various sites that had previously belonged to the NDMC (this was incorporated in Sierra Leone in 1970 and was a subsidiary of the British company DIMINCO). According to one of my informants, NDMC employed over 2800 workers during its peak in the 1980s. One site had been a former sorting plant (Number 12 Plant – see Plate 3.1) where diamondiferous gravels were cleaned and processed before the diamonds were extracted. Now all that remained was rusty (dangerous) and dilapidated machinery that was gradually being subsumed under bush. Another site I was taken to held the remains of what can only be described as a piece of England deep inside Sierra Leone's interior. It was clear to see as one approached the large iron gates with the company's initials (Plate 3.2) clearly visible over the top that this was a self-contained 'gated community' complete with club house, golf course, tennis courts, outdoor swimming pool and various sized residential quarters reflecting the hierarchical employment structure of the company. Since its abandonment during the rebel invasion of the area it had been looted and partially destroyed and like Number 12 Plant, was gradually being subsumed by the surrounding bush. Outside the giant gates the African workers quarters were located (Plate 3.3). Today they continue to be used as dwellings by local Kono people. As I walked around the area I spoke to a former employee Mr Fayie (Interviewed 18 April 2003) of the British-owned NDMC about his previous employment with the company.

Mr Fayie left school in 1982 and started working for the NDMC on 28 September 1983 as a security guard. He moved through the ranks of sergeant and security officer, working around the Tongo area. His main job was to 'make sure that the diamonds are not stolen away'. He worked there until the company was liquated in 1994 during the rebel conflict but was kept on as a member of the caretaking committee to look after properties left by the company. Mr Fayie spoke about the policing of diamonds, work conditions, the legacy of British colonialism and whether he thought the discovery of diamonds in Sierra Leone had been a 'blessing or a curse'. He also commented upon the recent activities of Branch Energy, another mining company interested in exploiting newly discovered Kimberlite diamonds.

I was taken to Number 12 Plant and the residential area where former employees lived. Here I was shown what remained of the separating house, where diamonds would be separated out from other stones and gravels. Close by, NDMC workers' dwellings remained. It was explained to me that such facilities were built according to a hierarchical 'class' struc-

Plate 3.1 NDMC Number 12 Sorting Plant, Kono District, 2003
(© Diane Frost)

Plate 3.2 NDMC former 'Gated Community' behind which European living and leisure quarters were housed, Kono District, 2003
(© Diane Frost)

Plate 3.3 NDMC African workers quarters now occupied by local people, Koidu, 2003
(© Diane Frost)

ture composed of 'A' class for senior workers, 'B' for intermediate and 'C' for junior workers. These were divided between administrators, miners, the security and anyone else employed by the company. Mr Fayie explained, 'For the lower ranks you had outside toilets and baths', as well as a 'canteen'. The company also provided other facilities for workers and their families including schools and a hospital, described by my informant as 'the best hospitals in this country'. Such facilities were clearly demarcated between Sierra Leoneans and Europeans. Tennis courts, swimming pool, golf course and Club House were there for the exclusive use of Europeans whilst 'Africans were not allowed to come here'.

We proceeded through the bush to what remained of the swimming pool, tennis courts and golf course with the latter remarkably identifiable despite the overgrowth. It was astounding to see this partially preserved little piece of England that looked alien against the backdrop of rural Sierra Leone. I reflected on how this must have replicated some of the British expatriate communities in parts of South and East colonial Africa. The NDMC had clearly invested heavily in the area.

Policing and Security

The NDMC like all private companies employed their own security to protect company property, guard extracted gravels and patrol areas of land leased for the exploitation of diamonds. In his capacity as a security guard, Mr Fayie was responsible for catching those involved in illicit activity. Those caught would be tried in Magistrate courts and could receive prison sentences from between two to six months depending on the crime. I was informed of a notorious security guard known locally as 'The Commander', who instilled fear into local people through his reputation as someone who possessed the power of juju. 'People were frightened of [him]... people used to shiver when they heard the name Commander'. He 'creates fear, panic amongst people.' Also, 'He was very powerful; he was a man to fear. I believe that man had mystic powers, if he was here today, [if] you call his name, the next [minute] ... you see commander. He had these powers'. Such beliefs proved convenient for the company with its subsequent effect of deterring some, though not all, illicit mining.

I was also informed of a story relating to the colonial period that has become part of local folklore. During this time, the British allegedly informed Kono people that diamonds contained an electric current that could kill. If anyone found diamonds they were instructed that 'Africans must not touch it', instead they should 'draw a circle round it in the sand and call the British man. He has a clipper in his hand, he picks up the diamond, takes it back to Europe' (Mr Fayie, interviewed 18 April 2003). This story symbolises above all the belief of many Konos that 'outsiders', beginning with the British and continued by 'strangers' (non-Konos), foreigners like the Lebanese, as well as an array of mining corporations have duped local people out of their mineral wealth. Indeed, a sense of bitterness and anger tinged many of the conversations that were had with Kono people, and with good reason. 'He [the British] left Africa suffering, he brainwashed us, brainwashed the black man...' and 'you [the British] came and fooled us [.....] we've been mining over 70 years in this country, we can't show nothing for these diamonds' (Mr Sahr Bendu, interviewed 18 April 2003). Such views are echoed by the ex-security officer, Mr Fayie:

> We have nothing to boast about, nothing to show for the diamonds that are mined here, no roads, no running water, no electricity, no infrastructure here, all the things you are seeing, even with Koidu Town, are private owned buildings. (Interviewed 18 April 2003)

Kimberlite mining and community concerns

Another informant, Mr Amida (Interviewed 19 April 2003) had been an Intelligence Officer at the security division of NDMC. He talked about what he saw as the injustices and problems of diamond mining in Kono and of the time he was imprisoned for speaking out against the National Provisional Ruling Council (NPRC) military government (1992–1996). Mr Amida argues that it was individual politicians along with the company that benefitted from the deal that was struck between the military government and the NDMC. Anyone who voiced criticism of this was imprisoned, as he was:

> The National Provisional Ruling Council government (that was a military government)....they said this company [NDMC] should come and operate [but] people are afraid, they don't have [any] rights because it was a military government...
>
> The politicians, at the end of the day, it is only them and their family or their close relatives, or those that have helped them to be right up there that are enjoying [the proceeds]. We remain to suffer, even when we cry [protest] they take you as an inciter, as a traitor and you are detained. Let me disclose one secret to you, I've been detained during the war period in this country, by the NPRC government. I was detained in their concentration camp at Murray Town Barracks for two months because of my views. (Mr Amidu is a fictitious name to protect his identity)

Mr Amida also spoke of the unequal relationship between the government and mining companies who have in the last ten years or so begun exploiting Kimberlite deposits. He has been highly critical of both since he believes the profits from diamond mining had not benefited the local community. He explains: 'why should we come from one of the richest districts [in terms of mineral wealth] in the world and live in absolute poverty? This has been the question that we have been asking ourselves. The government has not been very fair to us...'

Concerns have also been raised about the use of explosives in exploiting deeper Kimberlite deposits. One issue revolves around the company, Branch Energy, who have been operating in Sierra Leone pre- and post-civil war. Local people have raised safety concerns over their use of explosives here in light of a number of fatalities and have been lobbying for greater accountability of the company to the local community. Mr Fayie explains that:

> All the Kono people [are concerned], because there was an incident, when a stone exploded [and] killed a woman. Before the war, that happened, so because of that experience, we said we need to do something, these guys are coming over again, we need to sit down and talk to them. (Interviewed 18 April 2003)

ALLUVIAL DIAMOND AND GOLD MINING ASSOCIATION
KONO DISTRICT EASTERN PROVINCE
SIERRA LEONE WEST AFRICA

MOTTO: PEACE, REHABILITATION AND DEVELOPMENT

174 Circular Road
Freetown
Tel: 224088
Fax: 229931

43 SukuTamba Street
New Mbaoma II
Koidu Town
Kono District
Date: 29- 03- 09

REF........................

CAMPAIGN! CAMPAIGN! CAMPAIGN!
AGAINST UNJUST MINING PROJECT 1
AUTHENTIC

The Alluvial Diamond and Gold Mining Association is working on a Campaign against all UNJUST and DESTRUCTIVE MINING activities that is currently happening in Kono District by some Sierra Leoneans as some unpatriotic foreign nationals which has nearly devastated the District and the Kono people over their Native Land and Sierra Leone as a whole. This has even scoped some **Political Authorities** and important NGO's to repatriate the Kono Refugees in areas that is not, and will not be welcome by the **Kono Natives**. As contemption to their living standards, most people from Kono are now living or dwelling in unideal and inhuman places within the country. The Kono people are in Agony, crying and dying everyday, there is need for an immediate solution to their problem.

United Nations latest report has shown and justifies that **rampant** and **unscrupulous** Mining activities are still carrying on in Kono District by some people living in and out side Sierra Leone. By and large, the above mentioned organisation is in cordial tide with their Local Authorities, the vibrant Movement of concern Kono Youths (MOCKY), Kono Development Union (KONDU), Kono Student Union (KONSU), Inter Religious Council, Civic Societies, Kono Union Abroad, NGO's, Patriotic Sierra Leoneans and Immigrants to lay to rest this issue.

In accordance with the environmental research report by our officers, the Campaign is against the Unjust Mining in the following respective Areas:-

1. UNOFFICIAL MINING ACTIVITIES IN MINING AREAS
2. TOWNSHIP MINING
3. LOCAL AND GOVERNMENT INFRASTURCURE
   e.g. Administrative Buildings like Hospital, Schools, Roads, Commercial and Market places, social and Religious Centers, like Mosques and Churches.

4. FOREST RESERVES
5. PRIVATE PROPERTIES eg. Houses, Agricultural PlantationS etc.

The under mentioned Names are Mentors for the Implementation of this Document and Executive Members of the above Organisation.

Co-ordinator   Mr. Komba Kainjama Suku-Tamba...

Secretary-General   Mr. Franklyn Smith...

Public Relations Officer Mr. Prince John...

Social and Technical Secretary   Mr. Gbandewa Tamba Sonsiama...

Financial Secretary   Mr. Saafea Songu Mbrewa...

Auditor   Mr. Komba Fillie Faboe...

Fig. 3.1 Campaign letter to Freetown politicians from the Alluvial Diamond and Gold Mining Association against unjust mining in Koidu Town, Kono District, 29 March 2001

In conversations with people, there was an overwhelmingly strong conviction that the communities that live in this area should see some benefit from diamond exploitation by mining companies. 'We are not against them coming to Kono, but when they come, let them come with something good for us ... making provisions in the interest of the Kono people, [like] water supplies, electricity... It appears that these Kimberlite managers are coming now and we're looking at what happened when [they came before]... which hasn't given us anything in return...' (Mr Fayi, interviewed 18 April 2003).

Clearly, there are deep concerns over the mining of any diamonds by multinational companies, not least because the community is concerned with what they may or may not gain from this. Past experience teaches them that the wealth from diamonds has not benefitted their community or the country at large. Moreover, there are real concerns about the dangers of mining close to residential areas because of the instability this causes to the surrounding land, particularly subsidence (Plate 3.4). Such concerns are forcing organisations like the Movement of Concerned Kono Youth (MOCKY) into battles for representation in meetings taking place between the government and mining corporations like Branch Energy. These activists are pushing to have their voices heard so they can safeguard the well-being of their community and negotiate future benefits. In talking with people, the anger and sense of betrayal that many felt towards the

Plate 3.4 Mining in Koidu Town close to roads, residential dwellings and other buildings, 2003
(© Diane Frost)

government because of the lack of transparency and inclusion in negotiations was tangible. Many were suspicious of government and felt they had been 'tricked' and 'pushed out' of negotiations between the government and companies like Branch Energy who are pursuing plans to develop Kimberlite deposits. While the war exacerbated poverty and inequality and set back the country's development even further, conditions before the war were still very difficult for the majority. This dichotomy continues to feed the anger, pain and perplexity that many in Sierra Leone carry with them today.

Mining operations carried out by large multinational companies necessarily demand an amicable and cooperative relationship with government, yet those communities likely to be affected by their operations are often the last to be consulted. Clearly, the future mining of Kimberlite reserves has caused much consternation within Kono communities because of the potential dangers involved in deep mining. Such communities are not adverse to this kind of investment per se, especially if negotiations are transparent and inclusive, their concerns are informed by past experience and in particular the effects of profit repatriation that hinders sustainable development, economic growth and social improvement.

In October 2007, a spokesperson for the Network Movement for Justice and Development (NMJD), a community activist organisation made a number of claims with reference to diamond mining in Sierra Leone. Allegations of human rights violations, environmental degradation and threats to health and security were made against Koidu Holdings SA[4], a Kimberlite diamond mining firm and one of the biggest direct investors in Sierra Leone. The NMJD also accused Koidu Holdings of routinely using state police forces to arrest community leaders who oppose their mining practices. The company was said to employ around 400 workers in the Kono district in eastern Sierra Leone for around $200 a month, a sum deemed inadequate for a family of five. Moreover, two workers were killed in accidents in 2006 involving machinery, raising concerns about safety (Gonzalez 2007).

Mechanised mining stands in sharp contrast to what is often referred to as indigenous mining or hand mining undertaken by those who have a licence to mine or who are 'supported' by a licence holder. The labour process involved in this type of work is based on crude pre-industrial; pre-capitalist techniques and remuneration (see Chapter 1). Illicit activity is also easier in this sector because of the absence of systematic security that only mining companies or government can afford.

---

[4] Koidu Holdings is 65 percent owned by global private resource group BSG Resources Ltd and 35 percent by Magma Diamond Resources, a subsidiary of Geneva-based Beny Steinmetz Group. See 'Sierra Leone to review mining contracts' Reuters 1 November 2007.

Indigenous mining and the labour process

In the 1960s a government scheme encouraged the setting up of so-called 'native firms'. This scheme specified that 51 per cent of the share capital had to be held by natives of Sierra Leone and allowed for those not defined as 'native' such as Lebanese traders to participate. In 1958 only 5 native firms had been established. By 1960 this had increased to 22 and by 1962 to 44 (Swindell 1973). Under ADMS, Sierra Leoneans could apply for a licence and work a specified number of feet for a period of 6 or 12 months. Since many of these did not have sufficient capital to employ labourers on a wage basis, the conventional employer-employee relationship was absent from this tributor system. Instead, tributors or labourers were provided with daily food and actual earnings became dependent on diamonds recovered.[5]

Greenhalgh (1985) has argued that this 'tributing' system has a long history in mineral production as it was first used in the Cornish tin mining industry. The system in Sierra Leone, he suggests, is based on traditional labour employment practices and was used in gold and tin mining throughout West Africa in the nineteenth and twentieth centuries. Zack-Williams (1995) has argued that this form of diamond mining (carried out under the ADMS) was reminiscent of a pre-capitalist mode of production, which resulted from SLST domination of this industry. He argues that the mining of diamonds under the scheme did not constitute wage-labour for a number of reasons, including the continued economic attachment and traditional rights to use the land that many tributors retained (seen in seasonal mining). This meant that many tributors were not reliant on diamond mining for survival because they were part of a larger economic unit through the peasant family and communal land-owning system:

> Thus unlike the modern wage worker, the tributor does not suffer from an ability to gain a livelihood other than by concluding a contract of employment with those who have the land or capital to set him to work. This means that the tributor is not dependent on his 'employers' as his counter-part employed by the capitalist is on his employer. (Zack-Williams 1995: 167–168)

Moreover, a client-patron relationship existed between the licensee and the tributor rather than a capitalistic buyer and seller of wage labour. Zack-Williams (1995) suggest that this system is more akin to the metayage system used in share-cropping in the southern United States. Here former slaves lacked capital to buy land and land owners lacked funds to pay wages. Former slaves provided their labour as tenant farmers and landowners provided the land, each would receive a share of the proceeds.

[5] See Zack-Williams 1995: 143–145 on recruitment of labour.

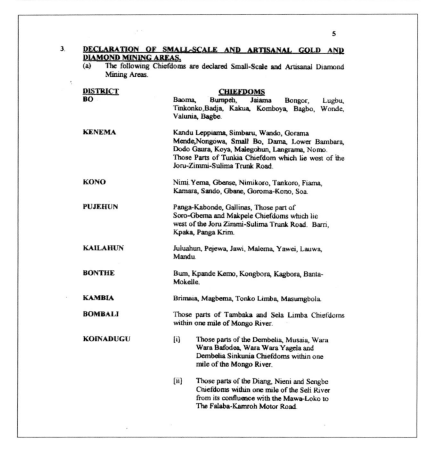

5

3. **DECLARATION OF SMALL-SCALE AND ARTISANAL GOLD AND DIAMOND MINING AREAS.**

(a) The following Chiefdoms are declared Small-Scale and Artisanal Diamond Mining Areas.

DISTRICT	**CHIEFDOMS**
BO	Baoma, Bumpeh, Jaiama Bongor, Lugbu, Tinkonko,Badja, Kakua, Komboya, Bagbo, Wonde, Valunia, Bagbe.
KENEMA	Kandu Leppiama, Simbaru, Wando, Gorama Mende,Nongowa, Small Bo, Dama, Lower Bambara, Dodo Gaura, Koya, Malegohun, Langrama, Nomo. Those Parts of Tunkia Chiefdom which lie west of the Joru-Zimmi-Sulima Trunk Road.
KONO	Nimi Yema, Gbense, Nimikoro, Tankoro, Fiama, Kamara, Sando, Gbane, Goroma-Kono, Soa.
PUJEHUN	Panga-Kabonde, Gallinas, Those part of Soro-Gbema and Makpele Chiefdoms which lie west of the Joru Zimmi-Sulima Trunk Road. Barri, Kpaka, Panga Krim.
KAILAHUN	Juluahun, Pejewa, Jawi, Malema, Yawei, Lauwa, Mandu.
BONTHE	Bum, Kpande Kemo, Kongbora, Kagbora, Banta-Mokelle.
KAMBIA	Brimaia, Magbema, Tonko Limba, Masumgbola.
BOMBALI	Those parts of Tambaka and Sela Limba Chiefdoms within one mile of Mongo River.
KOINADUGU	[i] Those parts of the Dembelia, Musaia, Wara Wara Bafodea, Wara Wara Yagela and Dembelia Sinkunia Chiefdoms within one mile of the Mongo River.
	[ii] Those parts of the Diang, Nieni and Sengbe Chiefdoms within one mile of the Seli River from its confluence with the Mawa-Loko to The Falaba-Kamroh Motor Road.

Fig. 3.2 Small-scale artisanal gold and diamond mining areas by chiefdom

The dominance of the SLST meant that hand miners were restricted in the areas they could work, confined as they were to 400 x 400 ft (and in the case of tenant farmers in the US indebtedness meant they too lacked the freedom to move). They were additionally confined to areas outside SLST leases, which were less diamondiferous and therefore more risky. In such circumstances, it was extremely high risk to employ tributors on wages. However, in the more developed semi-mechanised sector of ADMS where larger areas had been bought under one licence (for example, the Leone Trial Mining enterprise) and where known deposits were good, it was possible to pay wages to skilled workers such as dragline and bulldozer operators (Zack-Williams 1995). For the majority though, because the tributor system did not provide the basic minimum for survival, it

6

iii] Those parts of Neini, Sengbe, Mongo and Neya Chiefdoms within one mile of the Bagbe River from where it enters Kono District to a point due south of Kamara in the Neya Chiefdom.

[iv] Those parts of Neya Chiefdom within one mile of the Njai River from where it enters the Kono District to a point along the river two miles North Korubola in the Neya Chiefdom.

TONKOLILI Tane; Bonkolenken, Kunike.

PORT LOKO Mangeh Bureh and those parts of Kolenten, Konna and the Little Scarcies Rivers.

(b) The following Chiefdoms are declared Small-Scale and Artisanal Gold Mining Areas:-

DISTRICT	CHIEFDOMS
TONKOLILI	Kafe-Simiria, Kholifa, Sambaia, Konike-Barina, Kalansogoia, Tane, Konike, Bonkolenken.
BOMBALI	Sanda Loko, Sela Limba, Magbaiamba, Tambaka.
KOINADUGU	Mongo, Diang.
BO	Valunia.
KENEMA	Gorama - Mende, Simbaru.
KAILAHUN	Kissi Tongi, Penguia, Yawei.
KONO	Soa, Gbense, Nimikoro, Nimiyema, Sando.

(c) Only people of Sierra Leonean origin and nationality are permitted to reside in the above declared small-scale and artisanal mining areas and participate in mining and/or marketing of precious minerals.

(d) All other nationals shall relocate to Freetown and the other designated areas in the Provinces if they wish to participate in the marketing of precious minerals under the Small-Scale and Artisanal Mining Provisions of the Mines and Minerals Act.

perpetuated reliance on the land, since although some were successful, many did not make enough to live on. Interestingly, the Mines Department in 1959 were of the opinion that tributors 'have the majority's say in what is to be done, leaving the licence holder powerless to an extent.....'. This relates to the inability of the licence holder to pay wages to their labourers (Annual Report of the Mines Department 1959 Freetown).

Labourers today continue to work for individual licence holders. In 2003 the author met with a number of licence holders who 'employed' or supported tributors or labourers to work their areas. Men worked in gangs of four or five and were provided with one meal a day, equipment, and sometimes medicine if they became sick. In one case, the licence holder was a town chief and he provided funds for the schooling and welfare of the children of his managers. Under this clientelism, the licensee or patron takes responsibility for the welfare of the 'client' or tributor, providing food and medicine, paying school fees (in some cases) and financing legal advice when necessary (Interview Mr Mohammed, MOCKY, 17 April 2003).

The manner in which digging is undertaken today appears on the surface to be an ad hoc affair, with pits and overburden haphazardly displayed (see Plate 3.5). Indeed, this less efficient system was used throughout the 1950s, though there had been successful attempts by the inspectors of mines and area superintendents to persuade miners to change to more productive methods through working parallel trenches (Annual Report of the Mines Department 1959 Freetown). However, while digging in trenches is more efficient, it is less easy for diggers to conceal stones and so pitting is preferred because concealment is easier.

On a visit to a site in Koidu Town in 2003,[6] the author found young men and one or two women and male children, some as young as eight and nine years old, digging and panning for diamonds in pits that were knee deep in mud and water in soaring temperatures. Such work, I was informed, is undertaken in return for one meal a day and some remuneration if any diamonds are recovered. Women generally do not work in the digging of diamonds because I was informed, the work is too heavy but that exceptionally, some may work in diamond panning as they did here. Many women however prefer to work in gold mining. One of my informants, Mr Mohammed[7] talked me through the process of working the gravels as we stood observing a site just off one of the main roads and close to shops and housing. I asked about how these areas were policed:

> Security in this type of mining is provided by the people themselves because they are very mindful about the gravel. Sometimes they will rotate and provide security with some people sleeping here tonight and tomorrow another group [will sleep on the site] until the sites ended [depleted]. (Mr Mohammed, interviewed 17 April 2003)

He also spoke of 'sponsors', that is, those who support the diggers and the problems of mining close to residential areas. He explained how the area had been 'plotted out' and distributed by the Ministry of Mineral Resources into chiefdoms and how each licence holder 'employed' anything from three workers upwards, depending on their ability to 'support' these workers and on the size of their plot. In the past, one licence holder would be responsible for the plot, supporting the workers and finding a buyer for any winnings. Today, these stages have become fragmented, with different people involved. This is indicative of greater levels of expediency being employed as access to resources has become even tighter. It also points to the resourcefulness of those involved, particularly their ability to adapt to ever more difficult ways to eke out a living.

---

[6] Fieldwork April 2003 Koidu Town, Kono District.
[7] Mr Mohammed also held an executive position in MOCKY.

Plate 3.5 Overview of dug out pits where overburden can be haphazardly thrown on top of virgin land, Kono District, 2003
(© Diane Frost)

Plate 3.6 Chief Bondu (Town Chief of Koiqema) in the white suit inspecting his site, Kono District, 2003
(© Diane Frost)

In this situation, you have somebody who likes to mine in this plot right, so there's one person who sponsors from that angle. You have another person who comes with his workers and he takes care of his workers and they all work together …. You have a person who will spend his money and make sure they get the right equipment, shovels, water pumps, shakers, so you have various stages in the process, that's of now. Before this time, mining was done by one person at a time…. But now it is breaking up into various groupings at various locations. (Mr Mohammed, interviewed 17 April 2003)

Whilst certain elements of this system have been modified, other practices have remained the same, and in particular, the issue of 'winnings':

At the end of the day when the job is done the tributors will go round the table with the investor or the person who provides the finance for the job to negotiate what the actual content of the gravel is. If nothing comes out of the gravel then they get nothing, only the food that is provided for them. (Mr Mohammed, interviewed 17 April 2003)

One problem that exercises many of those I spoke with is the opaqueness of the criteria used to classify the value of diamonds recovered in hand mining and the subsequent remuneration paid:

There are problems between the miners and the financiers because there is no fixed price for diamonds here within this community. Especially the fact that the World Bank or the Diamond High Council does not do anything to fix or regulate the price for the category of diamonds. Our people within this community will not want the local miners to have access to such information because they want to make higher profits. Against the backdrop that the miners themselves will toil so hard to get the diamonds, you can see for yourself there's none among them that will be able to acquire a daily living because they are being suppressed by those who have come to buy all the diamonds themselves. So that's one of the reasons why the Kono Peace Diamond Alliance wants to raise their sanity so the Kono miner is able to achieve something at the end of it. (Mr Mohammed, interviewed 17 April 2003)

On another visit to a diamond area the town chief of Koiqema, Chief Bondu had a licence to dig in the area and accompanied the author. Chief Bondu said he employed over 300 diggers who worked on commission and provided various services for the community:

Commission …. I give him a percentage, we provide food for them …. medical facilities [for them] and their families out there. I try for hospital; I try for school [try to build]. I built a mosque for the people, I'm not Christian, I am Muslim, but I built a church for Christians …. I paid for some people to go to university, to go to the US. Everybody phone me, I will have something for them. (Chief Bondu, interviewed 20 April 2003)

The paternalist client-patron relationship apparent from this brief communication with a town chief exists throughout the socio-political hierarchy of Sierra Leonean society. The term 'supporter' has been used to describe the tied relationship that existed between the patron (in the past it was well-off Lebanese or Sierra Leoneans, today this is not always so) and those 'supported' (licensed miners who depended on the patron to sell his winnings) through a series of tacit commitments (Zack-Williams 1995). This client-patron relationship could also be seen in the chief's dealings with the community he represented. During my stay I observed[8] a steady gathering of men (occasionally women) including a number of elders and 'holy' (Muslim) men who would sit in and around the large porch waiting for the chief's arrival. He would see or speak with each of these in turn. On one occasion, a manager arrived with quite a large but discoloured stone and an argument broke out in which the chief accused this man of selling (good quality) diamonds behind his back. It was later communicated to me that the chief had paid this man well and had looked after his family by paying for his children to go to school in the US, had provided medical care and so on but yet he had allegedly cheated on the chief. The man was subsequently dismissed.

In the early 1970s, the number of tributors per licence was eleven and covered 400 feet by 400 feet (Swindell 1973). It was common then and today for as many as 20 to be employed by one licensee, working in groups of four or five. On one visit to a working area in Koidu Town (April 2003), one licensee had at least 20 men working for him for whom he provided food and equipment. In another case, a woman with a small business had bought a licence and was employing 10 tributors in return for supplying one meal a day and basic equipment. The payment in kind system and the avoidance of paying wages has particular implications, not least, the lack of control a licensee has over the tributors, reflected in the relatively low recovery rate of diamonds. Moreover, payment in kind enables licensees with little capital to employ labourers at minimum cost and risk. Licence holders (including miners) might also ask for financial assistance from the dealers who purchase their winnings. This ensures such dealers have priority in purchasing diamonds recovered and allows anyone with a licence (including miners) to mine without capital but with some assurance of a profit at the end. The actual remuneration that each of those involved receives is not clear and varies from area to area and between individual agreements. This supporter system emerged in Kono in 1963/64 partly in response to hiking costs in working increasingly exhausted shallow deposits and the need to mine deeper ones using mining equipment (see Zack-Williams 1995 for a detailed study of this).

The way digging is organised along a pitting system leads to production in small and less efficient units and results in low returns. In addition, areas worked in this way cannot be reclaimed and worked by mechanical

[8] This was also an opportunity for the community to make sense of my stay there. Thus rumour had it that the chief had taken a third wife

methods because of the disturbance to alluvial gravels and the potential risk of uneconomic digging. Systematic mining by hand has not been successful because the organisational structure of hand mining has meant that maximum earnings have not been achieved by maximisation of production (see Greenhalgh 1985). The Alluvial Diamond Mining Ordinance 1956 enabled native Sierra Leoneans (and others) to set up mining companies provided that half of its members were natives of Sierra Leone (Lebanese born in Sierra Leone were not considered natives). The aim was to encourage the pooling of resources by bringing all nearby leases under one, allowed for greater mechanisation and therefore made mining more efficient and systematic. There was a sharp increase in firms registered in the early 1960s[9] with 22 registered in 1960 compared with only eleven in 1959 (Report of Mines Department 1960; Zack-Williams 1995). The Mines Department commented on the degree of enterprise seen in this business. It also observed that the demand for licences in swamp areas was greater than the ground available. Consequently, applicants were:

> encouraged to form simple native firms, so that all would have the opportunity to benefit from their land. Such firms overcome to a greater extent the small man's bane of insufficient capital and provide better supervision against theft of diamonds by tributors. (Mines Department Annual Report 1960)

However, this initiative was short-lived only lasting from 1956–77. After the initial flurry of establishing native firms in the early 1960s, the figures declined until the mid-1970s when they began to rise. However, by 1977, there was none. Throughout the whole period, there were 134 native firms in operation. Of those, only 19 (14 per cent) were wholly owned by Sierra Leoneans. The rest were mixed or owned by Sierra Leoneans and non-Sierra Leoneans, with the Lebanese being the single most dominant group with interests in 86 of these 134 companies (64 per cent). Other groups involved included other Africans from outside Sierra Leone, British, American, French and Belgians (Zack Williams 1995). It is difficult to find a full explanation in the literature for the failure of these native firms. Suffice it to say that suspicions and underhand dealings appear to have played some part in their failure, alongside the fact that the SLST dominance in this industry and their ability to hang on to the best diamondiferous areas greatly disadvantaged native firms. Zack Williams (1995: 154) has argued that the monopoly position of the SLST/NDMC 'led to the atomization of indigenous enterprises within the industry'.

Another scheme that is worthy of mention is the Cooperative Contract Mining Scheme (CCMS, not to be confused with the SLST contract

---

[9] This was attributed to the end of the 'honeymoon' period when alluvial deposits were easier to find and individuals were forced to co-operate in mining. Also, numbers increased as a result of larger capital requirements of the more ambitious mining schemes. See Report of Mines Dept 1960; Zack-Williams, A.B. (1995), *Tributors, Supporters and Merchant Capital: Mining and Underdevelopment in Sierra Leone*, Aldershot: Avebury.

mining scheme). This scheme involved partitioning off land formerly mined by NDMC in the 1970s so that private individuals could re-mine there. While this was intended to benefit ordinary Sierra Leoneans who reside in the diamond areas, evidence suggests that this served the interests of the elite:

> In short, the Co-operative Contract Mining Scheme (CCMS) has been an important source of capital accumulation for those supporting the ruling All People's Congress (APC) party; and far from promoting the interests of the people in the diamondiferous chiefdoms, it has enriched both traditional elites and the political class. (Zack-Williams 1995: 165)

The number of plots allocated to high echelon APC personnel or organizations, six out of 20 (30 per cent) supports Zack-William's argument that political patronage was at work here. In addition, seven (35 per cent) of the plots were allocated to chiefs. The largest group with 12 plots allocated (60 per cent) was non-Konos and only three (15 per cent) were allocated to development agencies in Kono (Zack-Williams 1995).

Artisanal mining continued to provide some cash flow into the economy during the war years at a time when large-scale industrial mining declined, though artisanal mining also fed the civil war. Between 1995 and 2005 diamond mining consisted of almost entirely artisanal mining that generated income for private operators but little in terms of government revenue. Moreover, the continued operation of informal diamond trading pre the 2000 Kimberly Process Certification Scheme again resulted in significant loss of government revenue. The Certification Scheme has not prevented the continued smuggling of diamonds across the border to Guinea and Liberia seen in the fact that the average value of diamond exports in November 2007 was lower than expected compared with historical averages and after taking note of recent world price trends (*Standards Times* Press News 28 November 2007).

Artisanal miners continue to be disadvantaged when selling diamonds to a dealer because of the lack of expertise and equipment to verify value. The lack of transparency and the apparent mystery surrounding valuation serves to limit the control that the artisanal miner has over valuation and as such his ability to secure a fair and realistic price.

Child labour

As noted above, it is not uncommon for children as young as eight and nine years of age to be found working in diamond digging in Kono. This is in contravention to Article 32 of the (UN) Convention of the Rights of the Child, and Article 15 of the African Charter of the Rights and Welfare of the Child (Diamond Industry Annual Review, Sierra Leone 2004: 7). One source claims that as many as 80 per cent of children within the age range of 9–18 found in the Kono, Tongo, Kenema, Pujehun and Bo districts have been used in diamond and gold mining exploitation (Alluvial Diamond and Gold Mining Association [ADGMA] letter 26 September 2002). In a wider global context the International Labour Organisation (ILO) estimates that around one million children work in small scale mining and quarrying around the world where they face high risks of injuries, health and death through working long hours in appalling and dangerous conditions (ILO 12 June 2003). Indeed evidence suggests that child labour is increasing globally and relates to the growing impoverishment of large sections of the population, particularly in the developing world (Castells 1998). Sub-Saharan Africa does not contain the highest number of child workers but child labour here is more prolific in terms of their proportion of the total labour force (ILO 2003).

Poverty-stricken families often feel that they have little choice but to send their children to work in order that the family or even the individual child has a chance of eating that day. Others have no family and as orphans and street children may be forced to work by adults as a means of survival. During the civil war, children had been used as soldiers and labourers in the diamond fields around Kono and beyond. The use of child labour to mine diamonds continued after the war.

A 2002 *World Vision* study surveyed 500 child miners in Kono District. They found these children often became involved part-time at an early age and this increased to the extent that their education was affected. The report states that 'those who were doing well in school but had to abandon their educational pursuit to follow their peers who transiently became rich and admirable.' The study also found that 83 per cent of child miners (mainly male) surveyed said they were actually involved in mining activities while a much smaller 8.6 per cent said they were involved in the preparation of food on site and would spend the whole day there. When asked why they became involved in this, 75 per cent of those surveyed said they did so 'to get money', 15.2 per cent said they had no alternative, 6.2 per cent had been influenced by friends and 4 per cent said they had been sent by their parents (Diamond Industry Annual Review, Sierra Leone 2004).

By early 2003, around 1,200 child miners had been registered by the ministry of gender and children affairs in collaboration with the NGOs *World Vision* and *Aim Sierra Leone,* with the intention of taking them out of the mines and placing them in school. Several thousand children between the ages of seven and 16 are believed to be working there digging and sifting soil and gravels from 8:00am to 6:00pm in search of diamonds.

Those who have become involved in grass roots organisations like MOCKY[10] recognise the continuing problem of child and youth labour in

---

[10] There have been reports that such organisations, whilst doing much good work in their communities, have also been involved in diamond smuggling across the border into Guinea and have been involved in the intimidation of local communities. See Global Witness (2003b) *The Usual Suspects.*

diamond mining and in particular, the potential to cause serious problems of disaffection later on. One of my informants was an executive member of MOCKY when I interviewed him in 2003. Here, he explains what he sees as the problems underlying the use of child labour in diamond mining, particularly during the civil war period (1991–2002):

> During the last 10 years the children did not go to school because they are living in displaced camps and refugee camps, so the education standard dropped drastically in this district ... the accommodation in some of our schools are very poor, in fact we have no furniture in the schools, just bare bricks.
>
> In fact the majority of the miners have been recruited from the youth. So for the past 20–30 years virtually, they have been mining and no new developments. ... They are virtually getting no benefit from mining and at the end of the day; we will see some leaving school, joining the mining activity, making it as a permanent job. And we have seen that this has contributed to some extent in destroying this nation ... because that makes him not proceed with his education, cannot further his education. So at the end of the day, we came to realise that the majority of the dropouts in Sa Leone are coming from this part of the country. (Mr Abdullah, interviewed 18 April 2003)

Mr Abdullah explains that many of these young miners were recruited or taken forcibly by the RUF and that even after the war, children and young men continue to be recruited for mining at the expense of their education:

> There are many smaller boys, kids you know, using them from the age of, let me say eight to 15, even now it is still continuing. If you go to the mining areas, you see a small amount who are supposed to be in permanent school engaged in mining. You see their parents are living in squats maybe they cannot get them out of because they are using the boys as a source of income for them you see. ... [a worker] can spend maybe 10–20 years there [mining] without actually seeing anything [finding diamonds]. The next thing he can do is become very prone to, you know, causing destruction in the community. So that is one problem we are facing actually ... Let the kids get out of the mining and go to school because they are the future. Without them the future will be bleak. (Mr Abdullah, interviewed 18 April 2003)

Such views were also reiterated by others interviewed, including the vice-president of MOCKY, interviewed 18 April 2003. He believed that diamond mining was seen as 'the only avenue to get money, to get quick money' Gladys, a school teacher in Kono and also a member of MOCKY was passionate about the need to educate children and young people, particularly boys who are vulnerable to the pressures to mine. 'Let's encourage our children to go there [school] and learn something for themselves, so in the future they will be good fathers of this land, because our great grandfathers, their own sons, we are going to step our foot into their shoes, so let us encourage our children to go to school, not to go and mine' (Gladys, interviewed 18 April 2003).

The ILO has argued that the existence of child labour is a political rather than economic issue requiring political commitment and action from national governments if it is to be challenged. Poor families are often unable to take children away from paid work (or payment in kind) with the subsequent loss of income in order to send them to school. Governments have to compensate families for lost earnings so that children can be encouraged to go back into education. One way of doing this is through 'income transfers programs' so that families of children taken out of paid work are compensated for lost earnings (currently operating in Mexico, India and Brazil). Moreover according to the ILO, governments also need to invest in educational resources and infrastructures like new schools, books and teachers. The ILO argues that investing in children's education brings huge economic benefits in terms of productivity and increased wages once the child becomes an adult worker. The increased productivity would benefit the economy and business, higher wages would bring benefits to these individuals and their families and governments would gain from higher tax revenues. The initial cost of investing in children's education is thought to cover a period of about 15 to 20 years but the benefits continue for 40 years beyond that. It is believed that the poorer the country is, the greater the economic benefits and based on their research, the ILO suggest that 'as a percentage of annual gross national product (GNP), Sub-Saharan Africa could experience a gain of more than 50%' (compared with Asia, North Africa and the Middle East in the range of 22% to 28%)' (ILO 2003).

Conclusion

Diamond mining in Sierra Leone has developed and grown into an industry based on a division between mechanised mining undertaken by private multinational companies and what is referred to as indigenous hand mining based on pre-industrial methods and pre-capitalistic social relations. There is another category, semi-mechanised mining (not discussed here).[11] The chapter has attempted to combine existing secondary literature with archival material and oral testimonies. It is hoped that the oral testimonies have served to enrich and bring to life the secondary and archival material by investing the reader with the experiences of those working in, or having close associations with, diamond mining in one way or another.

The decision to use the particular testimonies presented here was based on two main considerations. Firstly, from a practical and organisational point of view, such accounts tend to concentrate on those issues the

[11] I was informed that Lebanese businesses often use these machines but that since the ending of the war, this was not being undertaken on any significant scale.

chapter is concerned with, namely the process of work and how work impacts on wider social life experiences. While such narratives may not be 'typical' as defined by more scientific methodology, at the same time broader structural factors that impact on these individuals are not unique to them. Second, these accounts have been chosen because of their comprehensiveness and ability to elaborate at length on particular subjects. Some accounts gave very brief and limited one word answers that did not add anything significant to the research. For these reasons, they have not been included here. Notwithstanding the above, the accounts used here nevertheless contain gaps and omissions either because the author did not ask about particular areas or because the respondents chose not to go there. We need to be mindful as social researchers that what is left out can be as significant as what is included and that whilst the content of the narrative is important, so indeed is the form. The asking and the telling are as significant as the not asking and not telling. Such 'evidence' has to be seen within the broader parameters of social and historical structural relations that impact on social interaction. During the visits to diamond sites, I was keen to talk with those occupied with the process of digging. However, interrupting the work process itself was problematic and effectively hindered my ability to talk or interview them. Moreover, my presence and the presence of others also appeared to hinder my attempts. Those I did try to speak with (through an interpreter) held back either through shyness, lack of confidence or because they did not want to say anything that could compromise their position in some way. One digger claimed he was 16 but looked much younger and again was reluctant to talk.

What is apparent from the accounts used here is that many individuals felt they and their families benefitted from working for private companies like NDMC. The reasons include the payment of a wage or salary; the regularity of work and the provision of housing to name just a few. There was a feeling that today whole communities in particular areas of a town or village could benefit from company investment in diamonds. The belief was based on the assumption that this would bring development in infrastructures usually provided by the state such as electricity, roads, piped water, housing, schools and hospitals. In post-civil war Sierra Leone that continues to be afflicted with major infrastructural problems, it is no surprise to hear local Kono people arguing in favour of investment by large mining companies. The one proviso that many activists are rightly demanding is that those at the bottom of the *diamond chain*, have a voice in any negotiations taking place between such companies and government. Otherwise, as discussed in Chapter 2, such investment could be limited to particular areas and consequently constitute 'enclave development',[12] with

---

[12] See Binns (1982: 7) 'The changing impact of diamond mining in Sierra Leone', in Chapter 2 who argues that diamond mining as a whole did not constitute an enclave development but that NDMC activities did in terms of repatriation of profits and lack of development to the surrounding areas.

little benefit to the rest of Sierra Leone. It is because of the continuing problems surrounding the diamond industry today, like issues of child labour, lack of economic opportunities as well as the destruction that the civil war brought to these areas, that grass roots organisations and others have attempted to raise the profile of these concerns. Such issues will be discussed in Chapter 4.

4
The Grass Roots & Social Organisation

Community-based resource conflicts often arise over issues involving the exploitation of these resources by transnational corporations. This can cause subsequent problems of environmental damage; the undermining of rights (including human rights, the right to consultation and information, the right to compensation and the right to share in the benefits) and the inability of national governments to regulate transnational corporations and protect their citizens and the environment. Governments and companies invariably formulate mineral policies in the developing world with little consultation with those communities affected.

Such communities are regarded as objects of development and not participants in this process. When such communities begin to organise themselves it is possible for them to articulate the adverse affects that some mineral production can have. For example in Sierra Leone the development of Kimberlite mining has been undertaken in some cases close to residential areas. Giant pits have been left using large earth moving machinery and old decaying plant and machinery have been abandoned. Both these represent death traps for curious children. Moreover, much of this mining has led to environmental destruction of agricultural land. In highlighting these factors through community-based organisations, such communities become important social actors that need the acknowledgement of governments if not foreign investors.

Communities like those in Kono have questioned the role of government and the motives of foreign investors in diamond production because of the adverse consequences discussed above, and because of the carnage and destruction the civilian population was subjected to during the civil war. Organisations like the Movement of Concerned Kono Youth (MOCKY) are conscious of the fact that the Revolutionary United Front (RUF) found support among sections of a disgruntled and disempowered youth. Many of the youth who came together to form MOCKY had been involved in the ex-Civilian Defence Force (CDF) who fought the rebel RUF. It is for this reason that MOCKY are targetting youth and pushing for both wider opportunities and greater empowerment of the youth since they believe to ignore this component of society is storing up problems for the future. Moreover, organisations like MOCKY rightly feel that their community have not gained from mineral production (mechanised or non-mechanised) and want the opportunity to articulate their concerns and their needs to foreign investors like Branch Energy/Koidu Holdings Ltd that have entered negotiations and agreements with government on present and future diamond development.

MOCKY was set up in 1999 in an attempt to mobilise the community of Kono to improve conditions there both during and after the war[1]. According to one of their documents (see Appendix D) 'It was formed by disgruntled Kono youths who were then resident in Freetown as a result of the occupation of Kono district by the combined RUF and AFRC junta forces in February 1998'. Its raison d'être was in the words of one of its executive members who wished to remain anonymous, to 'serve as the mouthpiece for the Kono people in Freetown and outside Freetown during that time' (Interviewed 18 April 2003). It would also agitate against the 'neglect and marginalisation' experienced by Kono people through a campaign that would publicise their plight to the national government and the international community. To that effect, two initial demonstrations were organised in March and April 2000 in Freetown (the latter was referred to as 'Black Monday' as demonstrators wore black) in which Kono residents staged a demonstration against the RUF occupation of the Kono district.

MOCKY has also been involved in other activities. In a newspaper article (*The New Storm* 23 July 2002) it was reported that tension had erupted between ex-CDF fighters (mainly from MOCKY) and the Sierra Leone Police over crime and security in Koidu town. It seems that cases normally reported and dealt with by the police were being 'hijacked' in the words of the paper, by MOCKY who were 'threatening civilians not to report cases to the SLP but to their office' at Opera, Koidu town. The newspaper went on to claim: 'The MOCKY youths allegedly have boasted that they would not close down the office as they are entitled to take part in the security of their area.'

During interviews with two executive members of MOCKY (18 April 2003) who wished to remain anonymous, the devastation caused by the war and by diamond mining over many years was something of great concern to the organisation. They were particularly keen to motivate young people in the area to get involved in practical activities that would make residential areas safe as well as to make these young people feel valued and belong.

Some people were seeing the youth as destructive people, to be people of less importance in the community. But out of those discussions we

---

[1] See Peters, K. and Richard, P. (2011) 'Rebellion and Agrarian Tensions in Sierra Leone' *Journal of Agrarian Change* Vol 11, Issue 3 July, for a discussion of similar organisations in Tongo fields.

were holding, most of the youth came to realise that they have their role to play and some of those youths today have made their roles very very good. And we are seeing some improvement within the youth constituency and indeed the youth are cooperating. (Anonymous MOCKY member 1 interviewed 18 April 2003)

MOCKY also embraced what would become the 'Just Mining Campaign'. This was aimed at better safeguards for communities against dangerous mining practices (for example digging close to residential areas causing subsidence as well as the use of explosives to exploit Kimberlite deposits). The campaign was also concerned with lobbying for the wealth produced from diamond mining to have some beneficial socio-economic effects on the community. The continuing problem of smuggling, particularly from Kono and over the border into Guinea has also prompted a number of initiatives, including the identification of 'six entry points where smugglers can pass with diamonds'. This information was passed on to the police and ministry of mines by MOCKY members.

[diamonds] are very small you know. Very high quality, you can put it in your pocket and you move, you know, across the border. We've done that. So even with the [UN] peacekeepers here, they can testify that we gave them a pamphlet about the entry points, also the government and the police and even the Mines Ministry in Freetown [...] so that he can put more plans in place about how they can check the smuggling of diamonds.' (Anonymous MOCKY member 2 interviewed 18 April 2003).

Another informant, is also an active member of MOCKY and a human rights activist. He reflects on the poor physical state of the country despite its mineral wealth: 'Sierra Leone should have been a paradise by now, good roads, we should have got adequate education, our people should have been well paid, the infrastructure should have been improved, but nothing of that nature has happened, look at the roads in Freetown.' He was also critical of the international community, particularly those involved in the diamond industry:

the question that we are asking, if they are talking about blood diamonds, if they want to eliminate blood diamonds, they should start first from their very own countries, because there are people here that are not going by the rules and regulations set by the international community, we call them mafias. They own all over the country, they pop in here to buy diamonds, and some of these diamonds are going to their own very country, there's money laundering, this we know, and all that kind of thing is happening, we've seen that. (Mr Abnoa[2] interviewed 19 April 2003)

Various governments and Sierra Leonean politicians have also been criticised for not doing more and for looking after their own interests. In partic-

---

[2] This is a fictitious name to protect his identity.

ular, Western educated politicians have been accused of taking kick-backs from investors and of making promises, particularly during elections, to negotiate fair deals with mining companies. It is clear for many that national and local government have a responsibility to negotiate a fair deal with mining companies like Branch Energy:

> It's the responsibility of the Government, because it is the Government who is going to have the share [of the profits], the Government [and] the local authorities because they are giving surface rent and the economy. (Mr Abnoa, as above)

Branch Energy returned to Kono after the civil war to explore the possibility of exploiting Kimberlite reserves. This led to a number of concerns, in particular how the mining of Kimberlite would be undertaken from a health and safety point of view; what safeguards would be put in place to avoid environmental destruction and whether local labour would be employed:

> Even when Branch Energy is coming here, we know that most of their staff, even when they have qualified people, are going to be imported....but then our brothers should be employed. Our brothers here on the ground should be employed rather than others [...] you'll find a hell of a problem with this. I must confess, because our brothers will continue pressing on, pressing on, we will not give in. (Mr Abnoa as above)

Questions have also been asked concerning how the exploitation of Kimberlite reserves will benefit Kono? Mr Abnoa reflects the concerns of numerous people I spoke with when he asks: 'What do we stand to benefit? [...] it is the responsibility of the Government to seek the welfare of the people, because Government issues a contract [to the company]'. He continues:

> 'What I am saying here, is that definitely we know that at the end of the day, this district has been marginalised for far too long, *for far too long*, like in the case of Ogoni. [...] Here will not be like another Ogoni [...] the Delta oil region, because when the people are oppressed to a certain level, they will definitely have to explode. (Mr Abnoa as above)

In the mean time people complain of Kono being in total darkness because of the lack of electricity, of schools with no furniture or resources; of dangerous pot-holed roads and of social injustice and suffering.

Since these interviews were conducted Koidu Holdings Limited (formerly Branch Energy) began blasting Kimberlite pipes in the area. According to the pressure group 'Network Movement for Justice and development'[3] (NMJD – Sierra Leone), part of the broader 'Campaign for Just Mining', this blasting began before the completion of the Environ-

---

[3] Also referred to as Network Movement for Justice and Development, based at King Harman road, Freetown.

mental Impact Assessment. Key stakeholders had been invited to be part of this consultation process whose aim was to have the input and partic-ipation of communities and others to ensure a transparent and accountable process. Consequently, broad based organisations like the Kono Peace Diamond Alliance were left out of the process. NMJD argues that by excluding such stakeholders, not only does this contradict the Mines and Minerals Act of 1994, the Environmental Protection Act of 2000 and the set standards of the World Bank but it undermines the fundamental rights of the communities affected. The blasting which began before January 2004 was carried out every week and affected the daily activities of those residing in the area since residents have to leave their homes for safety. The blasting has caused damage to buildings. Whilst a Resettlement Action Plan has been devised to provide housing for those affected, the sub-standard nature of these constructs and their lack of basic facilities has led people to refuse to relocate.

Koidu Holdings Limited was a member of the Kono Peace Diamond Alliance (PDA) before it was disbanded.[4] The Campaign for Just Mining, established in January 2000, has called into question the commitment of Koidu Holdings Limited to the peace, security and development of Kono that the Diamond Alliance pledged a commitment to. Moreover, it has called on the Government of Sierra Leone to protect and promote the inter-ests of these communities with existing legislation to stop and prevent such practices. This has provoked criticism from the Government, including the then president, Kabbah, who said that the Campaign for Just Mining is doing:

> a gross disservice to the people of Kono District and the entire country [by giving] grossly inaccurate and negative information about Koidu Holdings to international financial institutions [...].necessary to give the company the type of financial guarantee that would enable them to stay in business [also]. It is no business of an NGO to feed international organizations with distorted and alarmist accounts with a view to deprive this country of opportunity of realizing the full benefits of its resources. (*Awoko Newspaper* 25 June 2004)

The national coordinator of the NMJD, Abu A. Brima has said of these developments:

> How can this sector contribute to poverty alleviation for the majority of Sierra Leoneans when it concentrates wealth in the hands of a few, especially foreigners, displaces people from their lands and degrades the resources upon which many poor people depend? (Newsletter NMJD Mines and Communities Website March 2004)

---

[4] According to Maconachie, the Peace Diamond Alliance (PDA) had been disbanded by 2008. See Maconachie, R. (2008), 'Diamonds, governance and "local" development in post-conflict Sierra Leone: Lessons for artisanal and small-scale mining in sub-Saharan Africa?' *Resources Policy*.

Increased investment in Kimberlite mining has the potential to generate wealth and contribute to the country's development. So far, however, the impact of this activity on local communities has been negative, particularly in the way this relates to local livelihoods. Communities in Sokogbeh, Saquee and Swarray Towns have reported to the NMJD during a consultation process in February 2004 of the threat that Kimberlite mining is having on three main areas. These are local resources, human rights and the degradation of the environment and natural resources. The issue of resources includes restricted access to traditional bushes and forest that is important for farming and income generation; the prevention of free access to rivers used for fishing and water; that small-scale artisanal mining has been displaced with no alternative income; that sacred sites and burial grounds have been desecrated and that internal conflicts are emerging within communities that is threatening social integrity and cohesion.

The Network (NMJD) has also reported on the human rights violations that have occurred when blasting takes place.[5] These include the closure of schools and businesses during blasting that is determined by the company without local negotiation or respect for the rights or needs of communities; lack of respect of community land rights, with no protection of traditional livelihoods and cultures; people forced to abandon their homes until blasting ceases and constantly in fear of the threat of violent eviction; reports of violence used by the police and arrests and detention of local community leaders for questioning the activities of the company (some people have reportedly been imprisoned without trial for up to six months). There have also been reports of environmental damage resulting in the loss of important resources including clean water; the reduction of farmland and residential areas, increase in traffic, particularly the non-stop use of heavy vehicles that produces noise pollution (Newsletter NMJD Mines and Communities Website March 2004).

A number of people were interviewed by the NMJD (Newsletter NMJD Mines and Communities Website March 2004) during their consultation process with local people and were asked how the activities of Branch Energy/Koidu Holdings were affecting their lives. Some of their views are reproduced here:

> We really want to ask government to tell us whether they've sent Branch Energy to Kono to disrupt our learning, destroy our schools and houses and incapacitate our parents. We also want to ask Branch Energy to tell us about what development plans they have for us in Kono because we have still not seen anything they have built or constructed since they came. It's just destruction all the way. (Gladys Gbonda, Class 6 UMC Girls School, interviewed April 2003)

---

[5] Also see Peters, K. and Richards, P. (2011) 'Rebellion and Agrarian Tensions in Sierra Leone' *Journal of Agrarian Change* Vol 11, Issue 3 July, for a discussion of human rights violations by companies.

A member of the Sokogbe 'Affected Property Owners Association' says:

> 'We are in the middle of a dilemma; we have not been relocated, we cannot put up new structures and we cannot plant anything in our backyards. How do these people expect us to live and take care of our families? There is a piece of bush in Sokogbe community that has some tree crops and fertile land. People used to fetch fuel wood and make vegetable gardens there, but now we cannot access it. The place where they want to relocate us is small with no land for gardening or recreation. How can they build houses/relocate people without consulting them or involving them at least in any of the activities? This is absolutely not right. (Sahr Fea Sarquee interviewed 17 April 2003)

Mrs Memuna Boya has said: 'Sometimes I am caught up in the middle of preparing food for my children, then we are asked to leave, which makes my children to go for hours without food' (Interviewed 19 April 2003).

There have been a number of reports in the Freetown press concerning the negative impact Koidu Holdings is having on surrounding communities. The *Concord Times* (March 26, 2004) for example described residents views of the company's activities as 'irresponsible' because of the danger to local people in the blasting zone evident from the damage to 12 homes so far. The *Standard Times* (March 16, 2004) reported on three elderly women who had to be revived in the Koidu Government Hospital following blasting after they failed to leave their homes despite warnings to do so on national radio. The report argues that the age of the women made it difficult for them to move quickly. The paper also reported that the Town Chief of Sarquee, Pa Kai David Mboma (also chairman of the Affected Property Owners Association) and three others were arrested and detained for several hours on allegations of inciting youths against the operations of Koidu Holdings.

Newly constructed houses for those affected by blasting operations have also come under criticism. The *New Citizen* (April 6, 2004) reported on the views of the Agriculture and Food Security Minister and Chairman of the SLPP, Kono District, Dr Sama Mondeh. He told the newspaper:

> I am here on a fact-finding mission as we have received information in Freetown that the company has constructed sub-standard housing facilities for the people. The three bedroom houses are poorly constructed with only a single exit door. The building itself is too low and lacks adequate ventilation.

He added:

> As SLPP Chairman for Kono District, I will not sit down complacently while Koidu Holdings is building substandard structures for our people. Koidu Holdings is generating a substantial sum of money, which demands the company to construct better housing and offer other amenities for the people.

The Safety Officer for Koidu Holdings, Rex Bonafa has said in response to this that, 'the newly constructed buildings are more durable than the former buildings inhabited by the people which should be accepted'. (Network Movement for Justice and Development, Sierra Leone, Press Statement 23 January 2004)

Women and social organisation

Many of the voices heard so far have come from male activists who have taken a prominent role in organisations like MOCKY and the Network Movement for Justice and Development. MOCKY have acknowledged the importance of women to that organisation and have stated in its aims and objectives that women must be given equality of opportunity to hold executive positions and contribute to decision making. Whilst the nature and extent of gender inequality in the developing world more generally is not always apparent in indicators such as the Human Development Index, women continue to bear the brunt of socio-economic and political imbalances.

Gender inequality is more prominent where people are poorest. Women tend to do most of the work in poor societies, providing income for families while at the same time their subordinate status means they have primary responsibility for childcare. Women are disproportionately the poorest of the poor and continue to struggle for political representation.

The UNDP (2000) identified eight areas[6] where gender equality needs to be addressed. One of these is in the realm of political power and in the need for an increased role in decision-making in organisations like unions, community groups, and governments. In recent years we have seen women across the developing world beginning to get their voices heard through for example, the emergence of a transitional women's movement. Whilst it is unclear in the context of Sierra Leone whether women do indeed presently hold executive positions in organisations like MOCKY, there is a women's group within the organisation that is able to articulate women's perspectives and raise issues and concerns that specifically affect them as women. In trying to document the voices of a small group of women in Kono and learn more about their concerns and involvement in organisations like MOCKY a small group was interviewed.

Mrs Gladys Gbonda (interviewed 18 April 2003) is a member of MOCKY and a teacher and Chairperson in FAWE (Forum for African Women Educationalists) that supports girls and women to acquire education. The Forum (FAWE) was created in 1992 and was registered in Kenya as a pan-African NGO in 1993 as 'a response to the slow pace of imple-

---

[6] These are 1. autonomy of the body, 2. autonomy within family and household, 3. political power, 4. social resources, 5. material resources, 6. employment and income, 7. time (relative access to sleep & leisure, and 8. gender identity. See Gender Equality Index, United Nations Population Fund (UNFPA) New York 2000.

mentation of Education for All goals in sub-Saharan Africa'. It has a particular emphasis on girls' educational needs especially in terms of access to school opportunities to complete their studies and perform well at all levels. Its membership includes women policy makers and male minister who are associate members.

The programme was launched in Sierra Leone in April 2002 and by April 2003 the organisation had around 212 children in the non-formal primary school or attending the skill centre, in addition to 50 other students including mothers and pregnant women involved in training. For Mrs Gladys Gbonda, one of the biggest obstacles to overcome in Sierra Leone surrounds the deeply entrenched traditional views that girls should not be educated and the subsequent expectations on girls and women to perform traditional female roles. But she says: 'We are encouraging women to come into MOCKY, because at first the people of Kono don't believe that women are able to do anything, they believe that we are supposed to be in the kitchen or at home'. Indeed Gladys describes some of the effects that diamond mining in Kono has had on girls and young women in terms of sex work or early marriages. She explains: 'they go into early marriage because of money, because [men with money from diamonds] will impress them with money, so the parents sell her child and give them to them at early ages.' She continues:

> Between 15 and 18 years, they are going into early marriages and early pregnancies, that is affecting us, you will find those girls are going out on the streets to do this prostitution for money, because they have been used to money. Some of them who going through that marriage, they don't like the men, but because they are afraid of their parents or whatever, they will go into that marriage, let me say, [there is] no love [...] the girls will be married [or] they will be out on the streets.

The work of FAWE has campaigned for the education of girls and women and has set up a number of community educational projects. The organisation is also mindful of girls and women who have been forced into sex work and are doing what they can to provide alternative opportunities:

> We want to take the girls off the streets, so that they can be safe and look out for themselves.
>
> We want them to be educated, so do something beneficial to themselves, because before, the girls education in Kono was very poor, they don't like going to school, and some of our parents don't like them in there, because they said women should not go to school.
>
> We are going to talk to our sisters, our aunts, our mothers, to send their girl child to school, because when you educate a woman, you have educated a nation. So I want to encourage parents in Kono to send their girls to school, because we are there to educate them. We have a skill centre, about 50 students, they are training them in skills like dying, adult literacy class, masonry, and we want to add sewing, carpentry,

but we have not yet started the carpentry, it is in the pipeline. (Mrs Gladys Gbonda Gladys, interviewed 18 April 2003)

Another women's group that has emerged is the 50/50 Group which was formally launched in November 2001 by the then president of Sierra Leone Tejan Kabbah in which he endorsed their struggle for the recognition, equality and inclusion of women.[7] Nemata Eshun-Baiden founded the 50/50 Group in an attempt to bring together Sierra Leonean women who want an equal share of political power. One of the group's main objectives is to push for at least one-third female representation in Sierra Leone's enlarged 124–seat legislature. In the 2002 Parliament, there were 10 women among 75 males, including two senior cabinet ministers and two deputies. One of these, the Economic Development Minister Kadie Sesay, said: 'what women want is meaningful and equitable partnership with our menfolk in the furtherance of development of the country.' (*World Press Review* June 2002). Despite this, women made few inroads in Sierra Leone's presidential race in 2002. In the nomination exercise for the presidential race, only one female candidate went forward, former human rights activist Zainab Bangura, who heads the Movement for Progress Party (MOPP) (MOPP'S political structure is 50 per cent women).

The 50/50 Group draws inspiration from other nations (including New Zealand with 30.8 per cent and Sweden with 42.7 per cent female representation) where women have achieved greater representation. This includes Mozambique that currently leads Africa with 30 per cent female representation in parliament (*World Press Review* June 2002).

Gladys is also involved in the 50/50 Group in Freetown, and is motivated by the dominated position women find themselves in here. She explains: 'Africans they like to victimise women, to dominate women, they don't want the women to be in any position. At Kono, that is the real place for that kind of attitude. They like women to be in the kitchen'. Another activist and advocate of women's rights is Mrs Jackson (interviewed 18 April 2003). She is involved in the Kono Women's Task Force that intervenes in areas of Sierra Leonean life where they feel women's voices are unrepresented. For Mrs Jackson, women's position in Sierra Leone is intolerable at many different levels:

All we want is women's rights, women are being dominated [...] they've not got the mouths to speak their minds, as I talk to you, I feel like shedding tears. Do you know our women are marginalised, [we are told] women are marginalised because the men are the vanguards, that is rubbish! [...] They say when a woman marries, the children she has with the husband are named to the husband. We have told them that we have to maintain our integrity, [...] and the women actually have to be appreciated. But do you know our greatest problem, mass illiteracy is our greatest problem [among women] so we are begging the nation to

[7] See Address by President Kabbah: 'Recognition, Equality and Inclusion' 30 November 2001, Sierra Leone Web www.sierra-leone.org/kabbah1130001.html

educate women more. Do you know something, do you know what they do, because of the mass illiteracy, when the husband dies, they call upon the brother of the deceased to come and take her which is very wrong. There is nothing in favour of women, you lose, can you imagine? That is why we become the Task Force.' (Interviewed 18 April 2003)

There were a number of other women in Kono who against all the odds, had set themselves up as supporters of miners through providing tools, food and a portion of any winnings recovered. I met with one woman, 'Victoria' (not her real name) who introduced herself as a business woman who as well as supporting miners also owned a street store in town as a way of supplementing her mining business. For Victoria, small-scale artisanal mining was risky because she only had a small amount of capital to invest in tools and labour with no guarantees of any winnings. This was a real gamble for her since her relatively meagre investment meant she could only afford to excavate a small area with a handful of labourers. By definition, the returns for Victoria are riskier compared to those who can afford to support a larger number of labourers and pay for digging licences for larger plots of land. Victoria is aware of the risks and chooses not to put all her eggs in one basket: 'I do it in small scales because I don't want to go too deep [invest too much], so my business cannot fall down, because I have to support men doing the work' (interviewed 17 April 2003).

The economic squeeze in Sierra Leone has led to even greater expediency in artisanal diamond mining. Here, a system of 'bailing' has emerged whereby those without a licence but enough capital to 'support' a handful of labourers can have a foothold in diamond excavation. Victoria explains how she has been able, in the absence of a digging licence herself, to support a small number of diggers on someone else's plot in return for sharing the gravels excavated:

> Now, because things are hard, everybody doesn't have money now to support the larger mining, but now we do it into bail, we call it bail, to bail me, you have the place [licensed plot], I don't have a place then I come and say "give me this place, let me support my men", when we extract the gravel, we share it, if you have five buckets, then I have five buckets, so that's why we call it to bail, the five buckets is my expenditure, because they have to pull it out, then I buy it from the boys, I will get something. Then the man that owns the place, because he's paying his money or our money for the licence, the same deal, he owns that land, whatever comes out of it, it's his. I feed them [the men] every day, and after, when ever extract the gravel, I buy the diamond from them, whatever it costs.....We have to talk price. They have to sell it to me, when we meet a particular price, then I can buy it, then it's my own business. (Interviewed 17 April 2003)

However, whilst this system enables small entrepreneurs like Victoria to maintain a presence in small scale diamond mining, it remains a precarious business. The risk of losing diamonds recovered remains high as there is little incentive for labourers to hand over all winnings. Victoria and others like her are merely one or two steps removed from the even greater precariousness endured by diggers. She explains her role as a supporter:

> I have to buy the tools. I have to buy them rice, giving them food, even today they harassed me for their food, because I did not give them for two days, so they have asked me, I have to give, at times there are so many headaches, to pull that money, but you have to do it because they are working for you. I've just started, and maybe tomorrow I will start washing my gravel. My boys will wash it. I'm going to send somebody to watch so that they cannot escape with my diamond. (Interviewed 17 April 2003)

Another woman Ms Fasuluku (interviewed 19 April 2003) supported 26 men with her sister. She also had a business in Freetown, a bar that supplemented her diamond business in Kono. She would return to Freetown to run the bar during the rainy season when mining was made more difficult and in this way was able to spread the risk of her investment in diamond mining. Ms Fasuluku further explains how the greater resources one has to invest, the bigger the potential returns:

> I do mining myself, but because of the mining and the way that we are doing it, we are taking a risk, because you don't know where it's productive and where it's not productive, most of the productive places, if you are a poor woman or a poor man, you can't work, you can't make it because you don't have the money, you have to hire caterpillars, you have to have investors, you want to get 100 boys because with big mining, you get big diamonds, but if you don't do big mining, you don't have big diamonds. (Interviewed 19 April 2003)

Women involved in mining as supporters were often made to feel unwelcome as traditionally women have not been involved in the mining industry and are discouraged from being on site. Ms Fasuluku explains: 'When we go to mining places sometimes we hear them say "women are not allowed here".' For her, it is important that those supporting these workers have access to the site so they can see how the work is progressing: 'We want to see productions, we ourselves are the best people to be there when they are even washing our gravels, we found out that they don't even allow us to go there with our boys to see what we have worked for.'

I also spoke with Esther (interviewed 19 April 2003), the sister of Ms Fasuluku. Both women worked together in supporting miners. Esther has had some success in diamond mining and explains: 'It has been good with me, I've bought cars, I've bought land, houses and medication for my children [...] I think the diamonds are alright here, diamonds have been a major career for us.' Esther does not believe that children should work in this industry but she herself has teenagers working for her: 'I don't like the children being miner right now, there's big men [older] that have left school all the years [ago], so they can do the mining. The children [should] go to school, I don't like seeing children doing mining here. The youngest one [working for me] is about 14 years. He should be in school.' This raises the issue of child labour and other issues surrounding development that a number of organisations are involved in. Grass roots organisations like MOCKY have joined alliances with broader organisations such as the Kono Peace Diamond Alliance and the Alluvial Diamond and Gold Mining Association that have representation from international organisations such as USAID, DFID, UNAMSIL (see Chapter 7). Those involved in such organisations have made important contributions to campaigns like 'unjust mining' and 'child miners'.

In March 2003, the *Campaign for Just Mining* launched the first Diamond Industry Annual Review, a three-year project composed of civil society organisations (including NGOs participating in the Kimberley Process Certification Scheme) concerned with mining, human rights and the environment. The review is 'an attempt to describe the country's most important asset within the context of its history and potential .... and outlines what needs to be done to convert diamonds from a liability to a tool for development'. The campaign also sees its role as one of educating and sensitizing mining communities and wider Sierra Leonean society to the activities of mining companies like Koidu Holdings Ltd. In particular, the campaign sees its objective as promoting transparency and accountability in the diamond industry so that some of the material benefits are passed down to those communities involved (Newsletter of the National Movement for Justice and Development, Sierra Leone, March 2004).

Diamonds: A blessing or a curse?
Kono perspectives on diamonds

During a visit to Sierra Leone in 2003, a Freetown newspaper ran with the headline 'Diamonds: a blessing or a curse for Sierra Leone'. People I spoke with in Kono expressed a mixture of views. 'Victoria' (interviewed 17 April 2003) explained 'I can say [diamonds] it is a blessing, because some places are wishing to get it, but it happened that God give it to us, it's a big blessing for us. We are lucky but we are not benefiting as we should, because we lack so many things [...] in Sa Leone.' For others like Mr Amida (interviewed 19 April 2003) he acknowledges the potential of diamonds for Sierra Leone but is critical of Western mining companies and in particular the environmental damage and dangers caused: 'I will not say it is a curse, it is a blessing, but then some people are a hindrance to the development of this country [...] when they [British or American mining companies] come here, they should have covered the areas that they have mined, they don't do that, they leave it open.' He explains that when the pits are left open they become breeding grounds for mosquitoes and a death trap for children who have drowned in them.

Others see Sierra Leone's diamonds as a curse that has caused untold damage and destruction to this country. Gladys (interviewed 18 April 2003) supported four boys after she returned to the area post-civil war and explained: 'to me [diamonds are] not really a blessing, it is a curse, because it's a hinder, many lives in this district, it has made people to go astray one way or another.' The question of diamonds hindering development and opening the way for exploitation by outside interests is something picked up by Mr Fayie (interviewed 18 April 2003). He explains: 'I think that diamonds have been a curse for the people of Kono, we've got nothing to show for all these diamonds that we mined here over 70 years ago.' He continues: 'no roads, no running water, no electricity, no infrastructure here, all the things you are seeing, even in Koidu Town, are private owned buildings.' For him:

> It would be better that there were no diamonds here, maybe develop-
> ment would have taken place here, but you see, 85 percent to 90
> percent of all that's coming in here in the class of being business
> people, to me I will tell you that they are exploiters.

An executive member of MOCKY believed that the industry had not been managed in the interests of the country as a whole and that only external business interests had benefited from Sierra Leone's diamond wealth. For many, artisanal diamond mining was the only work available in this area:

> Well, diamonds in Sa Leone [sic], they are a curse rather than a
> blessing, because they were never managed properly for them to benefit
> the average Sierra Leonean. The diamonds are benefiting people from
> [outside], the average Sierra Leonean have not been able to access the
> diamonds, the value of the diamonds in any shape or form. The infra-
> structure is down, educationally people, most of our colleagues here
> have not benefited from a decent education, not had the opportunity to
> have. So you find a good deal of them in the mines, they have no other
> place of livelihood, they feel the only way they can live their lives is
> only when they come to the diamond mines. (Anonymous Mocky Exec-
> utive, interviewed 18 April)

Yet even then, the prospects are poor, with few ever succeeding in breaking out of this work let alone becoming wealthy:

> Very hard for you to hear them miners who started as a labourer and
> today he is a rich man. The money is mainly among the higher class. If
> you are a miner today, you come in the next year, you find him as a
> miner, you come here three years after, you find him as a miner. They
> will never grow [prosper].

For some, the problems facing Sierra Leone is a combination of what one informant terms 'colonial imperialism' and a legacy of misrule by past governments that eventually led to civil war:

We have to pay the price for what some of our brothers did, although it is because of the misrule of the past Government, what they have not done so wisely, they've taken up arms, and these are the very people who have been mistreated by the Government [...] Sometimes I see it [problems in Sierra Leone] as colonial imperialism. I know there is some amount of colonialism here, and definitely I must confess, it is coming back in Africa. (Mr Amida interviewed 19 April 2003)

Conclusion

The accounts presented here, like those in the previous chapter, cannot claim to be 'representative' or 'typical' in the objective, scientific sense, but they do speak to the subject of social organisation with which the chapter is concerned. Moreover, wider structural factors surrounding the diamond industry today, like the destruction caused by the war (still evident), the issue of child labour, stifled economic opportunities and lack of political representation (especially in negotiations between government and multinational organisations) has a wider impact on communities that goes beyond the individual accounts presented here. So whilst these testimonies cannot claim to be 'representative', their experiences and the issues they are concerned with have wider currency. By contextualising these individual accounts within the broader parameters of socio-economic and political structures (see Chapter 2) we are made aware of the wider impact of such conditions on communities more generally. It is this wider impact that has galvanised some to articulate these concerns and attempt to redress them through the organisations that they have been instrumental in setting up.

.

PART II The Global Context

5

Diamond Wheeling & Dealing From the Pit to the Global Market

The business of dealing and exporting rough diamonds out of Sierra Leone is far from straightforward and presents a myriad of opportunities for illegal practices. Diamonds are bought and exported (legally or illegally) out of Sierra Leone through two main avenues. First, they are taken out through the country's main airport at Lunghi (via Freetown) where they are transported to the main diamond cutting centres in Europe and elsewhere. The majority have historically gone to Antwerp. Second, Sierra Leone's diamonds are smuggled across the border to Liberia or Guinea. Those involved in the export of diamonds have included mining companies (including government owned or partially owned), individual licensed and non-licensed holders. Since the late 1990s, the official procedure for the export of diamonds from Sierra Leone began with an application for a one yearly Export Licence. This had to go through the minister of mineral resources for approval who in turn is advised by the director of mines. The latter also approved of the buying agents used by the exporters. Parcels of diamonds were then made up and sealed in the Government Gold and Diamond Office (GGDO) in Freetown and did not require checking or opening on leaving Freetown or entering Antwerp. However, in practice it appears that many exporters did not go through the GGDO and openly flouted this procedure. This can be seen in the reduction of official exports in 1999 which reached an all time low at $1.2 million (Global Witness 2000). In 2000, the Kimberley Certification Scheme was introduced. Initially this was to ensure that exported African diamonds did not come from conflict areas (*blood diamonds*). All exported diamonds now required a certificate to prove they were 'clean'. However, over a decade on, this scheme has not prevented *conflict diamonds* nor has it prevented the illegal export of diamonds.

The legality of diamonds exported by mining companies and individual licenced holders can sometimes be problematic since 'smuggling' can take place through indirect and/or unwitting means. This includes the unintentional under-evaluation of diamonds so that their full value is lost. In addition, the practice of categorising gemstones as industrials leads to undervaluation. Moreover, even where diamonds are legally exported, some of these will have come via illicit diggers who will sell their stones to dealers at a fraction of their value because they fear being caught with illicit diamonds. The incentives for smuggling, especially at the bottom of the *diamond chain*, relates to the low value received for diamonds from the diggers upwards. This encourages the practice of bypassing those above in the pursuit of a better price through smuggling. Smuggling also takes place at the top end of the hierarchy where again there are many incentives for this continued practice. The illicit trade in diamonds does not end once they arrive in the cutting and polishing centres. The export of polished diamonds is subject to tax and the incentive to avoid this again leads to various illegal practices, the extent of which is difficult to quantify.

Typically, gem diamonds pass through five main stages beginning with the mining and purchasing of rough stones. The Central Selling Organisation (CSO) purchases around 70 per cent of the worlds mining output. During the second stage, stones are sorted by size and quality in various diamond centres before being sold to manufacturers. Eighty per cent of these rough stones pass through Antwerp before being cut and polished during the third stage in centres located in New York, Antwerp, Tel Aviv, Johannesburg and Bombay. The fourth stage involves manufacturing diamonds into jewellery, followed by the fifth and final stage of marketing (Africa Region, World Bank 2001).

Dealers and exporters

National and transnational mining companies
As well as individual dealers and exporters, various mining companies have also been involved in the export of diamonds from Sierra Leone. Historically these have included Consolidated African Selection Trust (CAST), the Sierra Leone Selection Trust (SLST) and later the National Diamond Mining Company Sierra Leone Ltd (Diminco). The business of dealing and exporting diamonds has historically been fraught by the ongoing problem of controlling the flow of smuggled diamonds leading to substantial loss of government revenue. In an attempt to stem the flow of illicit dealing and exporting, the government introduced major changes in 1959. Under the Diamond Corporations Agreement, all diamonds now found under the Alluvial Diamond Mining Ordinance (1956) would be 'exported and marketed solely and only through and by the Government Gold and Diamond Office' (GGDO established in August). 'Natives' (Sierra Leoneans) and 'non-natives' would be charged £100 and £250 respectively (this had been raised from a mere £25 in both cases) for a dealer's licence. (Sierra Leone Annual Reports 1891–1987).

When Sierra Leone became independent in 1962, government policy stated that diamonds should be sorted and sold in Freetown instead of London. From 1962 until the 1980s, the GGDO checked, weighed, cleaned, sorted and valued stones under NDMC sorting staff. By the 1970s DICOR (Diamond Marketing Corporation -a subsidiary of De Beers Diamond Trading Company) and four other buyers[1] bought diamonds from the NDMC and enjoyed a 10 per cent discount on GGDO prices (Even-Zohar 2003). By the 1980s, the Afro-Lebanese businessman, Jamil Said Mohammed undertook the privatisation of the National Diamond Mining Company. DICOR's operations, including all diamond exports, were taken over by Precious Minerals Marketing Co. (PMMC).

There have been various companies operating off and on in Sierra Leone since then, including Branch Energy (SA) Ltd, a subsidiary of DiamondWorks. DiamondWorks had been involved in intricate inter-related mining and 'security' interests, including the mercenary organisations Executive Outcomes (EO) and Sandline, and is alleged to have received diamond mining concessions in part payment for its collaboration with these (Mines and Communities website November 2003). The company was granted the 25–year Koidu Kimberlite Project Mining Lease Agreement (Decree No. 12) of 1995 and returned to the country in June 2002 after the war had been officially declared over in January of that year. Branch Energy entered into an agreement with Magma Diamond Resources to exploit the rich Kimberlite deposits at Koidu. This new venture became known as Koidu Holdings Ltd and began operations in October 2002. This company's operations have recently aroused much controversy (see Chapter 4) especially from local community groups, not least because of its former connections with mercenary activity (Mines and Communities website November 2003). In addition, the company has more recently been accused of violating human rights by forcing residential communities out of the area in order that blasting can take place (Mines and Communities website November 2003).

The dominance of De Beers

De Beers has a long presence in the production and selling of African alluvial and Kimberlite diamonds though in recent years the world famous company has moved away from the marketing of rough diamonds on behalf of other producers and instead has concentrated on mining and selling its own rough diamonds. The only exceptions are Russia and Canada. De Beers continues to market around 40 per cent of Russia's output and 35 per cent of Canada's Ekati production (Even-Zohar 2003). Still, around 85 per cent of the world's diamond production remains under the control of a small group of multinational Kimberlite mining concerns. Along with De Beers we can include Debswana, Alrosa, BHP-Billiton, Rio Tinto and Namdeb (ibid.). The success of De Beers relates not only to the

[1] These were Leon Tempelsman & Son; Jamil Said Mohammed; Jack Lunzers S.L0 Ltd and Kaplin. See Even-Zohar, C (2003) 'Sierra Leone Diamond Sector Financial Policy Constraints', Diamond Intelligence Briefs Online Tacy Ltd.

production of diamonds over the last 100 years or more, but also in the company's ability to monopolise global sales and marketing of diamonds since the 1950s and keep prices stable.

Typical of some monopolies is their ability to assume various forms in different contexts. For example, De Beers in London assumed the identity of the Diamond Trading Company, whilst in Antwerp it assumed the role of the CSO – an arm of the DTC. In Israel, De Beers was known simply as 'the syndicate' and in Africa it adopted different names, including the Diamond Development Corporation and Mining Services, Inc. De Beers came to own or control all the diamond mines in southern Africa and controlled the trade in diamonds in England, Portugal, Israel, Belgium, Holland and Switzerland. (Epstein 1982).

When diamonds were first discovered in Sierra Leone in the 1930s, De Beers stated in a report (1934) 'These fields are a real menace to De Beers.' The company proceeded to protect itself by seeking control here (cited in Roberts 2003: 89–90). Accordingly, during periods when production exceeded demand, the De Beers cartel maintained price stability by limiting the number of diamonds in the market through stock piling or by buying back diamonds that had entered the wholesale market. In this way, price stability was maintained. Harry Oppenheimer of De Beers (1982) explained:

> A degree of control is necessary for the well being of the industry, not because production is excessive or demand is falling, but simply because wide fluctuations in price, which have, rightly or wrongly, been accepted as normal in the case of most raw materials, would be destructive of public confidence in the case of a pure luxury such as gem diamonds, of which large stocks are held in the form of jewellery by the general public. (Cited in Epstein 1982: 6)

At the beginning of the twentieth century, the Russian Revolution of 1917 precipitated panic in the diamond industry by the decision of the Bolsheviks to sell off the Tsar's stash of diamonds that had accumulated over several centuries. The threat was enough to depress world diamond prices for over a year until the Bolsheviks were offered and accepted £250 million for the entire collection (unseen) by a relation of Barney Barnato – the controller of the diamond syndicate in London. After the delivery of the diamonds in fourteen cigar boxes, assurances were given to diamond merchants that these diamonds would not enter the market for several years (ibid.).

By the 1950s, the CSO of the De Beers Company dominated the world supply of rough diamonds. The CSO is the collective name of De Beers' marketing monopoly that controlled the selling of 80 per cent of the world's rough diamonds in the late 1970s (Green 1984) rising to around 90 per cent by the early 1990s (Kanfer 1993) The London-based CSO acts as a wholesale marketing company sorting up to 14,000 different categories of diamonds and sells to diamond cutters, the majority of the world's diamonds (Even-Zohar 2003). The CSO includes three main organisations.

These are the Diamond Purchasing and Trading Company which sorts and values the stones from De Beers own mines in South Africa and Namibia; De Beers Industrial Diamonds that markets industrial stones and the DTC seen as the great wholesaler of gem diamonds. De Beers through Anglo-American Investment Trust (who in turn owned 26.4 per cent of De Beers Consolidated Mines) controlled the latter in the early 1980s (Green 1984). The DTC, also based in London, is the venue where around three hundred of the world's most notable diamond dealers and manufacturers attend a *sight* by invitation every five weeks to inspect the box of rough diamonds that has been made up for them.[2] The boxes are prepared based on knowledge of the buyers needs (though there are no guarantees) and on what is available. Boxes can contain a huge variety of stones in terms of quality, colour, shape and size (carat weight) with some worth only a few dollars a carat whilst others could fetch up to $15,000 a carat. As there are no available price benchmarks, the eventual value will depend on market conditions and in particular maintaining the stability of rough prices through controlling the production of diamonds (Even-Zohar 2003). Boxes are accepted or rejected without any negotiation of the price or content and may take up to one or two days of inspecting.

Each buyer or *sightholder* inspects the box or boxes in a private north facing viewing room where natural light aids the process. Only those diamonds weighing over 14.8 carats are sold to particular individuals outside of the regular boxes. Buyers are often reluctant to refuse their box for fear of losing their 'invitation' even if this means operating at a loss. Some transactions occur outside of this in the open market where rough diamonds are bought directly from Africa and South America. Diamonds purchased from the DTC are then taken to the main cutting and polishing centres (Green 1984, Global Witness 2000). The strategies pursued by these marketing firms in terms of available size, quantity and production of diamonds are determined by information provided by the mines themselves. A close and coordinated relationship existed between the two and the monopoly position that De Beers occupied gave the company great control in regulating and stabilising the rough diamond market.

Once the diamonds leave the DTC in London, they go to Tel Aviv, Bombay, New York or Antwerp amongst others as the main trading centres for rough and polished diamonds. Diamond dealers, manufacturers and wholesalers are found here. Illicit diamonds smuggled directly from Africa or through the Lebanon and elsewhere might end up in one of these centres (Green 1981). Around 90 per cent of all diamond workers before the Second World War were found in the Netherlands and Belgium and many were Jewish. After the war, some of those who survived the Nazi Holocaust took their skills to Israel and the US and contributed to the growth of cutting and polishing industries here, particularly in Israel (Van der Laan 1965).

[2] According to Green, T. (1984): 128, in the early 1980s the 300 were made up of 80 from Belgium, 64 from the US, 61 from India and 46 from Israel. This practice still occurs today.

Today, a small group of licensed exporters control the export of diamonds from Sierra Leone (see below). De Beers along with other large mining companies like Rio Tinto and BHP Billiton have withdrawn from the alluvial diamond markets in Africa because of concerns over conflict diamonds (Even-Zohar 2003). However, De Beers continues to have an important presence in diamond mining outside of Africa's alluvial diamonds and still dominates in the business of international diamond marketing. The DTC continues to act as the sales and marketing arm of De Beers' Central Selling Organisation (the umbrella name of various companies that market diamonds) and maintains its position as the world's leading supplier of rough gem diamonds. Based in London, the DTC sources its rough diamonds not only from De Beers own group of mines in Africa, but also through agreements with other mining companies. The DTC currently sorts and values about two thirds of the world's annual supply of rough diamonds by value and currently employs several hundred sorting experts around the world in London, Kimberley, South Africa, Windhoek, Namibia and Lucerne, Switzerland. Once purchased, the diamonds are sorted and valued in preparation for sale. Although many of the sorting processes are highly mechanised today, the sorting and classification of rough diamonds into 16,000 individual categories of size, shape, quality and colour, requires a high level of skill and expertise. Once sorted, diamonds are blended into selling mixtures in preparation for sale to the DTC's clients, or Sightholders comprising of the most experienced diamond polishers and dealers in the world. (De Beers 2004) Green (1984) makes a useful analogy of the role of the DTC with a tube of toothpaste through which the majority of gem and industrial diamonds are squeezed before being dispersed to the cutting and polishing centres around the world. Inevitably, some leak out but these represent only a small number of producers who choose to bypass De Beers control. Green additionally likens the CSO to:

> a sponge that absorbs diamonds in bad times and disgorges them in good [and works hard to] tailor the demand for diamonds by the public to suit the supply from the mines... and to make sure that if the inventory is laden with a particular size of diamonds, the customer is wooed to buy them. (Green 1984: 120)

In 2004, the DTC sold rough diamonds to the values of US$5.7 billion, 3 per cent higher than in 2003 and employed around 22,000 people across 19 countries. De Beers invested more than US$ 111 million in diamond exploration during 2004 resulting in the discovery of 49 Kimberlites in seven countries (De Beers Group Annual Review 2004). A scheme used by De Beers in South Africa where buyers pay a reserve price in advance with the remaining paid after sale, has been discussed with reference to alluvial miners in Sierra Leone (Even-Zohar 2003). De Beers is still directly involved in Sierra Leone's diamond interests as a key player in the Kimberley certification scheme and USAID Peace

Diamond Alliance (along with Branch Energy and Rapaport) before this was disbanded.

Diamonds are Forever: Selling the Symbol

De Beers prominence in the supply and distribution of rough diamonds also extends to the retail end of the trade after the diamonds have been cut and polished and made into jewellery. The famous De Beers slogan 'A Diamond is Forever' continues to be used as a clever marketing strategy many years after it first became closely associated with the engagement ring. Diamonds and engagement have become irreversibly synonymous to the extent that engagement rings cannot be anything other than diamond based. The use of advertising to sell diamonds, and in particular, the use of diamonds to symbolise eternal love began in 1948 during an advertising campaign that was launched by De Beers to shift surplus stocks of diamonds that had built up in the US during the depression. Engagement rings had accounted for over half of diamond purchases in the large American market, but had subsequently been dented (Green 1984). The De Beers advertising machine set about making the diamond synonymous with eternal love, drawing on the stones inner qualities of strength, endurance, beauty and longevity as symbolic of a couples love and relationship. Giving an engagement ring came to have powerful emotional capital.

Since then, 'A Diamond is Forever' continued to have an important influence on the selling of diamond jewellery and even became the name of the famous Ian Fleming book, *Diamonds are Forever* later made into a film.[3] Today, De Beers continues to trade on the inner qualities of these stones with special editions given names like the 'Radiance Collection' for example, whilst other diamond jewellery is described in similar adjectives like 'mystical', 'romantic', 'seductive' and 'brilliance' that conjures up a particular image and world (De Beers 2010). Diamonds continue to be marketed as a 'girl's best friend' with much advertising aimed at women's jewellery seen in all kinds of rings, earrings, necklaces, pendants, bracelets (see De Beers www.debeersgroup.com). Moreover, advertising campaigns can be tailored to shift surplus diamonds, especially if the surplus is of a particular shape or size. In the 1970s for example, a marketing strategy was pursued that focused on the eternity ring. This was at the time of the first oil crisis when a surplus of small stones had built up (Green 1984).

Yet diamonds have proved to be more than a mere symbol of eternal love and commitment, they have also become associated with financial expediency. Diamonds retain their value better than other precious stones or minerals like gold, are a safer and more stable bet than currency (including US dollars) and property, which is prone to fluctuate, and therefore are a good form of investment. They are also easier to move physically during times of political instability and conflict. Additionally,

---

[3] Conflict diamonds from Sierra Leone feature in another James Bond film, 'Die Another Day' 2002 (Warner Bros).

diamonds have continued to increase in price since the 1930s through the control and regulation that De Beers' Diamond Trading Company has held (Green 1984, Van der Lann 1965). Indeed the control that De Beers has enjoyed historically has been a major contributor in maintaining a steady balance between the supply and demand for diamonds. By marketing the lion's share of the world's rough diamonds (via the Diamond Trading Company) on behalf of all producers, De Beers was and is still able to control both supply and demand, avoid over-production of stock and maintain price stability.

According to De Beers (2004) themselves, the DTC continues to lead the way in the demand for diamond jewellery through a highly successful marketing campaign that includes the maintenance of consumer confidence and the selling of dreams. De Beers claims that 'the DTC is in the business of marketing dreams and promoting diamonds, nature's most precious treasure, as the ultimate purchase, reserved to celebrate the great moments of fulfilment' (De Beers 2004: 6). De Beers have also implemented an ethical code, the 'Diamond Best Practice Principles' (BPP) to its DTC customers to ensure, in their words 'the highest professional, social, environmental, legal and ethical standards to protect consumer and trade interests and to sustain the reputation and integrity of diamonds and the diamond industry' (De Beers 2004: 7). The principles are meant to ensure that those who comply do not use child labour; trade in conflict diamonds or endanger the health or welfare of individuals. The principles are also meant to ensure that ethical business practices are followed and that where treatments, synthetics and 'simulants' are used, that these are disclosed (De Beers 2004: 54). The group maintains that various means are used to ensure diamonds are ethically sourced and are authentic as opposed to synthetic as a way of ensuring consumer confidence in the industry. The Kimberley certification scheme (discussed more fully below) is one strategy in which De Beers has attempted to disassociate itself from conflict diamonds, defined by the group as 'diamonds which originate from areas in Africa controlled by forces fighting the legitimate and internationally recognized government of the relevant county' (Global Witness 2000:1)

Licensed individuals
The dealing and exporting of diamonds in Sierra Leone is also undertaken through individual licensed dealers and exporters. In Sierra Leone today, the majority of diamonds are transported this way with most of the exporters being non-Sierra Leoneans (Even-Zohar 2003). The business of dealing and exporting Sierra Leonean diamonds particularly from the artisanal mining sector has tended to be shrouded in suspicion with a deep-seated distrust of those involved. This is in part because of the ease with which diamonds can be smuggled in this sector where security in the field is non-existent. It is also partly to do with the alluvial nature of much of Sierra Leone's diamonds, which makes it easier to access them

close to the surface. Moreover, unlike Kimberlite mining, there is less uniformity in alluvial production grade and profitability, it requires smaller investments, yet it yields superior diamonds and grades. In addition, there appears to be less transparency here concerning data that relates to profits when compared to Kimberlite mining elsewhere. This situation can lead to greater involvement of the various stakeholders in the management and control of mining. Dealers or exporters are more likely to have greater 'hands on' experience in the process of mining (Even-Zohar 2003).

Formal structures exist for the dealing, selling and exporting of diamonds outside of the large mining companies in which numerous players form an elaborate and intricate hierarchical chain with each player taking a cut. Those who own an alluvial mining licence (and who in turn may have up to 100 diggers working for them) sell their winnings to licensed dealers or exporters at prices that are negotiated on a case-by-case basis.[4] The value (after production costs are taken into account) may typically be split between the workers (diggers or tributors), the mining licensed holder and the dealer. The dealer in turn will pass the diamonds to a licensed exporter who will arrange for the diamonds to be formally exported. It is at this exporting stage of the process that the *real* value of the diamonds comes into play:

> A trader/agent/dealer/miner may collect his 'added value' (i.e. commission, winnings), but the conversion of the lion's share of diamonds' value into money often occurs outside of the Sierra Leone economy in the cutting centres. For example, a domestic player may earn profits worth 30%-50% of the value of the stone, but he will usually only receive the money overseas after the stone has been sold at arm's length to the first truly unrelated party. The profit supposedly made in Sierra Leone thus may lend nothing to the economy. (Even-Zohar 2003: 8)

New foreign players that have attempted to enter the export end of the trade have claimed that there are greater economic benefits to be had if diamonds are bought in Antwerp rather than in Sierra Leone. It has been claimed that the reason for this is that established traders in Sierra Leone collude to increase the price foreigners have to pay through a process of bidding up. This has the effect of driving away outside competition since prices are too high. The elimination of competition means established traders could subsequently push down the price they pay for diamonds and force miners to sell at lower prices. Those who gain most from these arrangements are the established traders. Any suggestion that diggers and miners be paid more because of the increased likelihood of unemployment and greater hardship, have been dismissed. Yet it is questionable whether such arguments can be justified in the light of the relatively large profits made by traders and others at the top end of the internal diamond

---

[4] Licences are issued by the Ministry of Mineral Resources and can be bought by anyone who can pay.

SCHEDULE A – FORM 11

MINES AND MINERALS ACT

ARTISANAL/SMALL-SCALE MINING LICENCES

APPLICATION FOR PRECIOUS MINERALS DEALER'S LICENCE

Application No. ....

1.   Full Name of Applicant..

2.   Nationality of Applicant..

3.   Applicant of Sierra Leonean origin and nationality
     (i)   Full name of father...
     (ii)   Place of Birth: Village/Town..........................Chiefdom...............
            District...

4.   Occupation of Applicant in Sierra Leone...

5.   Designated Business Address in Sierra Leone

     ....

6.   Application submitted for following Precious Mineral(s)

     ....

7.   Passport Information

     (a)   Passport Number and Nationality...

     (b)   Date and Place of Issue..

     (c)   Expiry Date...

8.   Supporting Evidence of Available Capital (Bank Statement/Guarantee) and
     Professional Experience (attach)

9.   For Applicants illiterate in English, name and address of designated clerk........

     ....

10. Total purchases and value, total sales and value, over past four years, where
     applicable (attach)

I hereby declare that the statements made by me in this document and attachments
are, to the best of my knowledge, correct.

Date........................   ....

                                         Signature of Applicant/Clerk

Fig. 5.1 Dealer's Licence Form, 2003

SCHEDULE A – FORM 15
MINES AND MINERALS ACT
ARTISANAL/SMALL-SCALE MINING LICENCES
APPLICATION FOR PRECIOUS MINERALS EXPORTER'S LICENCE

Application No.....................

1.   Full Name of Applicant...

2.   Nationality of Applicant..............Position in Company.........................

3.   Name of Company...

4.   Occupation of Applicant in (a) Sierra Leone.....................................
                                 (b) Overseas

5.   Business Address in Sierra Leone

    ....

6.   Business Address Overseas

    ....

7.   Application submitted for following Precious Mineral (s)

    ....

8.   Passport Information (where applicable)

    (a)   Passport Number and Nationality...
    (b)   Date and Place of Issue...
    (c)   Expiry Date..

9.   Supporting Evidence of Available Capital (Bank Statement/Guarantee) and Professional Experience (attach)

10.   Corporate bodies – Photocopies of Certificate of incorporation, Business registration and M & A are to be attached.

11.   Total purchases and values, total sales and values, over past four years, where applicable (attach)

12.   References: (From foreign new applicants) Letters of recommendation from Diplomatic Mission / Home Government.

I hereby declare that the statements made by me in this document and attachments are, to the best of my knowledge, correct.

Date...............   ....
                                          Signature of Applicant

Fig. 5.2 Exporter's Licence Form, 2003

market that buy cheap and sell at considerably higher costs.[5] Even-Zohar (2003) refers to this group as a 'dealing and exporting cartel' since they work together to finance and profit from the bulk of Sierra Leone's diamond production today and hold considerable power over the earnings and conditions of Sierra Leone's thousands of diggers (Even-Zohar 2003).[6]

According to the Sierra Leone Diamond Industry Annual Review (2004), there were 135 diamond dealers' licences issued by September 2003, many to non-Sierra Leoneans. These dealers are also *supporters* who provide the necessary capital for artisanal mining and who often support small time mining licence holders. The dealers in turn may also have supporters, especially if they are smaller Sierra Leonean players who rely on Lebanese or Maraka traders. In addition, some dealers may act as agents for foreign exporters and can employ up to five (Sierra Leonean) buying agents. By mid 2003, Kenema, an important diamond trading town, had a total of 66 diamond trading offices the majority run by Lebanese dealers with only six run by local Sierra Leonean dealers (Sierra Leone Diamond Industry Annual Review 2004).

By September 2003, 39 individuals held diamond export licences and whilst 33 of these were Sierra Leoneans, the fact that they came under one licence gives an inaccurate picture. According to the Government Gold and Diamond Office (GGDO) which values and taxes diamonds for export, 'foreign nationals out-performed the indigenous citizens and by a very wide margin, even though more indigenous citizens participated in the export process than last year.' Exports for the first half of 2003 totalled $37 million and of this 78.4 per cent ($29 million) was accounted for by those defined as 'non-citizens' and includes Lebanese who hold Sierra Leonean passports. Those defined as 'indigenous' citizens exported only 21.6 percent ($8 million) of the total. From 2004, all exporters pay $30,000 for a licence (Sierra Leone Diamond Industry Annual Review 2004).

Today, this 'dealing and exporting cartel' dominates the alluvial diamond export sector since the large mining companies who left during the civil war are gradually returning to invest not in the country's alluvial diamonds but in the untapped Kimberlite reserves. Whilst it is difficult to know how much alluvial production is exported illegally, international political pressures to reduce the flow of conflict diamonds and the subsequent introduction of a certification scheme has served to increase the cost of smuggled diamonds. Consequently, this has contributed to more diamonds being exported from Sierra Leone through official channels between the years 2001–2002 and subsequently, though this does not mean the total elimination of smuggled diamonds, which continues, even through official channels (Even-Zohar 2003).

[5] The mark up here whilst considerable relative to what the diggers and licensed miners receive is modest compared to what the finished product will fetch once cut and polished.
[6] Even-Zohar (2003) estimates this to be in the region of 300–400,000 diggers.

Tens of millions of dollars worth of diamonds continue to leave Sierra Leone without any certification. In 2003, approximately $75 million worth of diamonds were exported through official government channels compared to $40.7 million in 2001. Yet as much as half of the gems mined continue to be smuggled out of the country. Monetary incentives to report illicit diamond mining have been initiated seen in the so-called '40 per cent law'. Under this, informants receive 40 per cent of the value of the illicit stones seized by the authorities. However, there are other issues that impact on the ability of government agencies to enforce controls. In Sierra Leone, lack of police training and basic infrastructural facilities including transportation and communication technologies, make it extremely difficult for mines wardens and monitoring officers to monitor and enforce diamond regulations. Moreover, poor remuneration for those involved in enforcing the certification scheme increases the likelihood of bribes and leads to accusations of malpractice by mines wardens, monitoring officers and custom officials (Sierra Leone Diamond Industry Annual Review 2004).

By the end of 2004, there were around ten export licence holders held by companies and individuals, including those identified below by the NMJD. In addition to this, Koidu Holdings had exported a total of 33,381 carats of Kimberlitic diamonds valued at US$7,098,120 by June 2004 (Newsletter of the National Movement for Justice and Development October 2004) and were expected to continue to develop this.

Table 5.1 Sierra Leonean Artisanal Diamond Production Exports, October 2004

Exporter	Value (US$)	Percentage	Total (US$)
H.M. Diamonds	28,047,299	46%	68,282,702.49
Andre' T. Hope	11,743,542	19	
Sarahdiam	9,081,766	14	
Kassim Basma	7,849,242	12	
Sima Star Co (SL) Ltd	3,252,277	5	
Others	1,210,456	4	

Source: *Newsletter of the National Movement for Justice and Development* October 2004

Smuggling: tricks of the trade

The smuggling and illegal export of diamonds is so deeply embedded in Sierra Leone's diamond industry that there is both an expectation and acceptance by those who have a vested interest in perpetuating this state of affairs. Smuggling has been an ongoing issue since diamond production began to be formally controlled in the 1930s when the SLST was granted exclusive rights to prospect, mine and deal in diamonds. Anyone else undertaking such activity was deemed to be acting illegally. Police reports and court cases at this time show a preponderance of Lebanese traders amongst others involved in illicit operations. They, along with European businesspersons, were ideally placed to trade diamonds because of existing overseas contacts. Many Lebanese smugglers declared their diamonds to customs after arriving in Beirut (Van der Laan 1965). Dealing in diamonds was made legal through the issuing of licences in 1956 (though illegal non-licensed dealers continued) under the Alluvial Diamond Mining Ordinance. Exports became tightly controlled through the DCSL, so the dealer acted as intermediary between the diggers and the exporter. In terms of those who became dealers at this time, some former diggers and employees of the SLST were identified alongside traditional traders like the Foulah, Lebanese and Mandingo. The latter groups were able to utilise their trading skills acquired in other businesses and apply them to diamond dealing. Initially this was more of a sideline to their main business but gradually it increased over time. The success of these groups led to government concerns and eventually restrictions in 1957 in terms of the number of licences permitted to these 'non-natives' as they were defined. There were also American and Belgium dealers operating as dealers at this time though it seems these were not subject to such restrictions (ibid.).

Despite moves to control legal diamond exports, illegal trading continued. Those diamonds exported to the Lebanon before 1956, which were by definition illicit, were then exported to Belgium and the US, where diamond-cutting industries were established. The Lebanon and Switzerland acted as transit countries (ibid.). In an attempt to shorten the route from Sierra Leone to the Lebanon and bypass the string of intermediaries, diamond cutters sent buyers to Africa (Monrovia) where direct transactions took place. What gradually emerged in the 1950s and 1960s were various routes through which illicit diamonds were smuggled out of the country. Those smuggled by air by Lebanese were taken to the Lebanon via Freetown. Diamonds were also smuggled across the border to Liberia by Lebanese and Africans. The buyers in Monrovia were Lebanese that had contacts with the Sierra Leonean Lebanese or were Africans employed by American and European cutters. The incentive to use Liberia as a route to export smuggled diamonds in the early 1950s partly stemmed from the fact that the Freetown police were becoming increasingly proactive in arresting diamond traders trying to smuggle out of Freetown. An alternative, less dangerous route was sought in addition to the Freetown route.

Another incentive for using Liberia related to the fact that diamonds were paid for in the international currency of US dollars and additionally, the export duty on diamonds related to the 'declared value'. Since there was no official valuation of exported diamonds, exporters could grossly undervalue these diamonds so that they would only pay an export duty of around 1 or 2 per cent instead of the official 9 per cent duty. Many were prepared to pay this to acquire official documentation for their exports. On the other hand, the limited number of export licences suggests that large amounts were exported illegally. Of known official exports the main countries to which these went were Belgium and the US (ibid.). Interestingly, official statistics in Liberia showed no diamond imports into the country. Therefore, diamond exports were passed off as domestic production, even though Liberia had a negligible diamond industry and it was recognised that Sierra Leone diamonds formed the bulk of Liberia's diamond exports.

Diamonds from other African countries like the Ivory Coast, Guinea and the Central African Republic also found their way to Monrovia during the 1950s, though many of these had a high proportion of industrial rather than gem diamonds (ibid.). Moreover, traders from Guinea, Mali, Senegal and the Gambia had been involved in diamond dealing, whilst diggers from Guinea had operated in Sierra Leone before their expulsion in 1956. Even those diamonds exported legally have often come through illicit channels. So for example, African illicit diggers often sell their stones to Lebanese or other dealers at a fraction of the value because of the fear of being caught with illicit diamonds. By the time they have passed through various dealers' hands, they eventually reach the larger dealers who have official export licences. Some diamonds will pass through these official channels though the export duty means many others avoid this route (Green 1984).

During the civil war in Sierra Leone, many of the legal diamond dealers fled, though some used the conflict to strengthen their interest here. Today, many internal incentives for continued smuggling relate to the low value received for diamonds from the diggers upwards. Those at the bottom end of the hierarchy may choose to bypass those 'above' and seek a better price through smuggling. Additionally, tax avoidance at the stage of exporting from Sierra Leone and importing into another country through undervaluation is another incentive for smuggling (directly by not declaring and indirectly through declaring undervalued stones). Diamonds can also be useful for money laundering since cash earned from illegal/criminal activities can be converted into tradable diamonds that can then be sold and converted back into 'white-washed' cash (see Chapter 6). Licensed dealers and exporters can also use their cloak of legality to pursue additional illegal activities. In 2002, of 35 licensed exporters who had purchased this for $5,000, around 15 had declared annual export volumes that amounted to less than the cost of their licence. The absurdity of paying for a licence that costs more than total exports is of course nonsensical. Legally mined diamonds then can still find their way into parallel illegal markets. This makes little difference to those at the bottom of the hierarchy who still receive next to nothing in absolute terms as well as in comparison to those higher up the chain. In addition, this provides no incentive for workers to declare all winnings and encourages the selling of diamonds 'on the side'. Until the benefits of legal mining and export outweigh those for illegal activities, it seems likely that the main players will pay lip service to government attempts to regulate the industry but will not give total commitment to such efforts. This is especially so when some of the 'hidden partners' of the country's diamond interest are also Sierra Leonean politicians (Even-Zohar 2003).[7]

Undervaluation

Historically, the incentive to smuggle both rough and cut diamonds by not declaring these goods at customs related to tax avoidance (though customs duties were stopped in the late 1970s between Common Market countries and from 1981 from the US) though VAT and income and profit tax was still payable. In cases where smaller dealers are involved, some operate through overseas family networks and wish to avoid formal procedures. In recent years, one way of trying to avoid customs tax has been by carrying an invoice with an address that is outside the country being entered so that if the person carrying diamonds is stopped, the invoice can be produced to show these goods are bound for elsewhere. If she or he is not stopped, then the diamonds can be delivered there. Fraudulent invoicing can also be used to undervalue the goods. There is much room for discretion when parcels of polished diamonds are made up since no two diamonds are the same and their valuation through the customs appraiser is open to interpretation.

Moreover, if for example 20 per cent of the value of the diamonds is paid for in cash and the remaining 80 per cent is invoiced and paid for by cheque this allows for tax evasion on the 20 per cent. If we consider that such parcels can amount to hundreds of thousands of dollars, the lost tax can amount to a considerable sum. Invoicing can also be used to overvalue goods and can be used to show that some buyers are getting their diamonds 'at cost'. For example, a retailer could buy at $4000 and ask that a memo/bill is given showing $6000 (Green 1984). Fraudulent invoicing can also be used to disguise the place of cutting and polishing of the stones since they can be bought in one place and taken and packaged elsewhere, though customs appraisers may be able to recognise the particular characteristics of some cutting centres. What is much more difficult to trace is the origin of rough diamonds once they have been cut and polished, especially if there is no such industry in the place of origin. This is especially so of African diamonds and less so of Russian diamonds where they cut and polish their own.

Those involved in couriering in the past have involved family, friends or strangers and have included schoolteachers recruited in Germany and

[7] In October 2010 the *Cocorioko International* newspaper reported that the current opposition SLPP Chairman, John Oponjo Benjamin Hirsh, Secretary General of the NPRC and former Minister of Finance in the Kabbah-Berewa SLPP, was involved in the 'Antwerp diamond deal'. Benjamin allegedly made arrangements for the sale of one of Sierra Leone's finest diamonds during the NPRC era. He is said to have personally transacted the 45 million dollars deal at Antwerp and shared the proceeds amongst himself, Karefa Kargbo, Maada Bio and Tom Nyuma. See 'SLPP Chairman John Ben has benefitted from corruption more than any Sierra Leonean politician' 16 October 2010.

airline captains ideally positioned to carry contraband. As well as the usual bizarre and imaginative places used pre-9/11 to hide diamonds (tubes of toothpaste, tins of fruit, aerosol cans, make up, false bottom suitcases, shoe heels) diamonds have also been known to have been smuggled on or in the body (mouth, ears, armpits, naval, rectum, vagina, between the toes and even swallowing) (Green 1984).

Research undertaken by Even-Zohar (2003) has argued that the value of Sierra Leone alluvial diamonds is grossly undervalued and can in part account for levels of smuggling. The nature of the product itself does not help in the valuation since no two diamonds are the same and therefore value or 'price discovery' can be problematic. This situation is in the interest of dealers who can be more reliably informed of value than government rough-diamond valuators (ibid.). If government valuators are underestimating the value of these rough stones, then this will translate into official diamond exports.

Whilst official diamond exports stood at $41 million in 2002, the value of the parcels exported was estimated to be closer to $125 million, an undervaluation of almost 60 per cent. This undervaluation relates to the process of classifying gem and industrials with the former fetching much higher prices than the latter. In 2002, 58 per cent of Sierra Leone's production was recorded as representing industrial by the GGDO. Even-Zohar (2003) explains this is highly unlikely given the high quality gem nature of Sierra Leone's diamonds and that Belgian experts accept that many more industrials from Sierra Leone are of gem quality than the GGDO currently certify. So, why this discrepancy which is clearly not in the interests of Sierra Leone? The GGDO use a classification system devised by De Beers which has the effect of reducing the value since there is a tendency to undervalue, but these are accepted in Belgium because the differences are considered small. In addition, in 2003 a 94–carat single gem was recorded by the GGDO as a 'parcel of mixed stones' at a very low per-carat value (Diamond Industry Review, Sierra Leone 2004).

There appears to be further evidence that the GGDO has undervalued Sierra Leone's diamonds by categorising gem stones as industrials or underpricing high quality gem stones. This resulted in the independent valuator being replaced in 2003 (Diamond Industry Review, Sierra Leone 2004). Recent investors in the county's Kimberlite reserves have made projections concerning the value of these which are estimated to be in the region of $240–$270 per carat (based on 2002 prices) with similar conclusions being made by those working on the Antwerp market (Even-Zohar 2003). However, official value as reported by the GGDO was alarmingly low in comparison at $116.94 per carat (2001) and $118.60 (2002). While Kimberlite production is more problematic than alluvial production, the quality of such stones would be at least as valuable as alluvial stones. (Even Zohar 2003). In the light of this, the Sierra Leone government have an interest in ensuring that GGDO valuators are more thoroughly trained in the future in methods of valuating rough stones so that the country's wealth is not needlessly and carelessly lost.

The GGDO valuators now come under the remit of the National Revenue Agency and not the Ministry of Mineral Resources as before. Valuations are carried out in the presence of Customs and Excise, a senior Mines Monitoring Office and an international Diamond Consultant. Various monetary incentives have been put in place to encourage trade. These include giving GGDO management 0.03 per cent of the value of diamonds to be exported and tax bonuses for high-performing exporters (Diamond Industry Annual Review, Sierra Leone 2004). Those who benefit from undervaluation are the exporters who in effect smuggle 'diamond value' through official channels.

Countries importing rough diamonds also lose government tax revenue since they tend not to verify valuation as there is no legal requirement to do so. Privately owned diamond businesses stand to gain the most. The bulk of Sierra Leone's official diamond exports, that is those that are certificated, end up in Antwerp (77 per cent in the 2000–2002 period) followed by the United States (8 per cent), United Kingdom (6 per cent) and Israel (3 per cent). Smuggled stones that have acquired certification en route may also end up here.

As much as three-quarters of the value of Sierra Leone diamonds end up in rough-diamond trading centres like Antwerp. The profits made from sales are transferred through bank credits to various intermediate companies located in places like Switzerland, Dubai and elsewhere. Worldwide, a dozen or so bank branches service the diamond industry by providing cash for diamond purchases. There is currently no system in place for checking that cash withdrawn from banks for use in Sierra Leone is used for this purpose. Nor are there procedures that allow matching the cash withdrawn with the actual value of diamonds imported (Even-Zohar 2003).

Conflict diamonds: present and future initiatives

Perhaps more worrying than the practice of undervaluation is the way diamonds have been and continue to be used in criminal networks and other serious illegal activities. This includes their use as international currency for money laundering; transferring undeclared income from one country to another and the selling of diamonds to purchase drugs (Green 1984). Such activities will be the subject of Chapter 6. Diamonds have also played a key role in various African wars. Their uses to fund arms deals and finance destructive civil wars like those in Sierra Leone, Liberia, Angola and the Democratic Republic of Congo raise important questions concerning the distribution and marketing of these conflict diamonds. Whilst the activities of rebel armies terrorising civilian populations in their quest for diamonds is well known, what is not so well documented is the role of multinational companies in the buying and marketing of such diamonds.

Throughout the 1990s, diamonds smuggled out of conflict zones like Sierra Leone and Angola were bought by the De Beers controlled Central Selling Organisation (CSO) in the full knowledge of where they had come from. Indeed, according to Global Witness 'De Beers spent time and money promoting the concept that it was "essential" to buy the conflict diamonds to maintain a steady world market place' (Global Witness 2000: 2). De Beers stated in 1995 that 'our outside buying operations are a vital ingredient of our management of the world market for rough gem diamonds' and 'The CSO buys diamonds in substantial volumes on the open market, both in Africa and in the diamond centres'. De Beers openly acknowledged that increased Angolan production of diamonds in the mid-1990s as a result of UNITA mining and selling diamonds on the open market (through De Beers CSO) had helped fund the civil war there (Global Witness 2000: 8). It is within this context that NGO organisations like British-based Global Witness have not only exposed the atrocities being committed against civilians in diamond conflict zones like Sierra Leone but have also been vocal in condemning the trade in conflict diamonds by multinational corporations like the De Beers Group. Business considerations then, not least the potential threats to consumer confidence that bad publicity could have on the demand for diamonds has prompted some action by this Group. Moreover, the company faced the additional burden of accumulated rough diamond stocks at a time when its share of the market was shrinking. This meant it could not control the supply of diamonds nor maintain high and stable prices by absorbing surpluses, as it had in the past. De Beers used the issue of conflict diamonds to recast itself as *the* legitimate trader of diamonds by deciding to support the UN embargoes on illicit diamond sales in Angola and Sierra Leone in 2000 and successfully distanced itself from unlawful trading. As Cowell states in the *New York Times* (August 2000):

> ...De Beers hit upon a way to use the controversy over blood diamonds to address its commercial problems. Turning necessity into a virtue with the same skill it has used for decades to promote diamonds as glittery icons of love and beauty, it recast and began promoting itself as the squeaky-clean crusader for guarantees across the industry that 'conflict diamonds' – as they are also called – be kept out of the world of luxury goods.... As it seeks to improve its image, De Beers is focussed on turning itself into what it calls the supplier of choice – a branded, high-value diamond trader looking to marketing to replace its old monopoly status and to maintain its leadership of the global market for uncut diamonds worth $7 billion to $8 billion a year. (New York Times 22 August 2000)

In March 2000 De Beers guaranteed that the CSO would not sell diamonds from rebel-held zones (*The Mail* and *The Guardian* 24 March, 2000). Moreover, the diamond industry sought to address the issue of conflict diamonds at the biennial World Diamonds Congress held in Antwerp July 2000 'galvanized by the threat of an anti-diamond campaign similar to the campaigns previously launched against fur and ivory.... (Goreux 2001: 9). Meanwhile in Sierra Leone, the signing of the Lome Peace Accord in July 1999 saw the creation of the *Commission for the Management of Strategic Resources, National Reconstruction and Development* to be headed by RUF leader Foday Sankoh as a gesture for peace. The US Office of Transition Initiatives (OTI) provided funds to assist in the establishment of national policies that would aid legitimate and efficient use of resources like gold and diamonds to aid the country's reconstruction and development. Under Sankoh, the Commission undertook to review all contracts and banned *all* diamond mining, though the Commission's intention had been to halt illegal diamond mining, which continued and did not form part of the UN mission in Sierra Leone (UNAMSIL) mandate (Global Witness May 2000).

De Beers has also had a problem with US antitrust laws since the company has been accused of fixing the prices of industrial diamonds and consequently cannot operate in the world's largest retail market for polished stones. De Beers has been forced to respond to external pressures (both ethical and commercial) in order that consumer demand and confidence is both created and nurtured. Without this, De Beers cannot hope to shift any stockpiles of surplus diamonds created today or in the future.

In its efforts to promote an ethical side, De Beers in recent years has made links with Global Witness and Partnership Africa Canada to look into ways of developing future sustainability in the informal alluvial mining sectors in Central and West Africa. This has no doubt come about because of the work undertaken by both these non-governmental organisations not only in bringing to light the whole issue of conflict diamonds, but also in their exposure of other issues. For example, widespread poverty and poor living conditions (including lack of basic amenities in some areas), the use of child labour, particularly in artisanal mining and general lack of development here despite the country's mineral wealth. Ultimately, De Beers is motivated by its ability to sell diamonds and has taken steps with this is mind to protect its interests. Gary Ralfe, De Beers Managing Director stated in March 2004:

> Potential threats to consumer confidence relating to the integrity of diamonds, especially unscrupulous practices deriving from treatment technology and synthetics, conflict diamond and child labour concerns remain a fundamental concern to the entire industry. The valuable work being done by the DTC to develop mechanisms by which to prevent such practices damaging our and industry reputation must be applauded. (De Beers 2004: 37)

Another development that De Beers and others have initiated is the Kimberley Process set up in 2000 and named after the famous De Beers mine in South Africa. Under this mandate, a certification system was established following UNSC resolution 1306 that stated:

Under the system, only diamonds that are legally mined are allowed to be exported. Legally mined means that they come only from areas under GOSL control, and are the product of a chain of legally authorised transactions, from use of land, permission to mine, purchase by authorised dealers and agents, and export by licensed exporters. (USAID-OTI 2001 in Global Witness 2002: 2)

This was implemented in January 2003 as an international certification and verification system for rough diamonds by around 45 diamond producing, trading and marketing countries, and the diamond industry (Global Witness 2002). Its aim, to certify clean or non-conflict diamonds to retailers and consumers. The initiative hoped that by recording all diamond sales, those conflict diamonds that continued to flood out of war torn areas like Liberia and the Democratic Republic of Congo could be curbed (*The News* 14 April 2003; Campbell 2004). The fact that diamonds had become embroiled in brutal civil wars in countries like Sierra Leone and elsewhere was in danger of provoking a consumer backlash. Media images of wars directed against civilians stood in stark contrast to the romantic symbolism that multinational companies like De Beers had created to sell their diamonds. As Greg Campbell eloquently explains:

> Civil wars are nothing new in Africa, but in Sierra Leone in particular the carnage was numbing and the direct involvement of diamonds was a serious threat to the business of romance. Images of civilians whose arms have been crudely hacked off with rusty blades didn't mesh well with television commercials featuring hand-shadows proudly displaying expensive jewellery. One diamond industry leader is said to have had nightmares in which the tag line at the end of such commercials read, 'Amputation is forever'... (Campbell 2004: 115)

De Beers maintains that more than 99 per cent of global rough diamond production falls under this initiative (De Beers 2004). However, the certification scheme introduced by the Kimberley Process is not without its problems and in particular illegal diamond smuggling from war-torn areas like the Democratic Republic of Congo continues, as indeed does the illegal smuggling of diamonds from post-civil war Sierra Leone.[8]

Once cutting and polishing has taken place, it is almost impossible to know the source of these stones making it extremely difficult to police conflict diamonds. Moreover, the Belgium Diamond High Council's policies on imports, (from where many of the world's diamonds are exported), require that only the diamonds' country of 'province' is listed, that is, its location before arriving in Belgium. Moreover, there still exist opportuni-

---

[8] During time in Sierra Leone in 2003 I noted the number of stories running in the local newspapers on the issue of diamonds and in particular diamond smuggling. Two headlines stand out, one from *For Di People* April 2003 that ran with the headline 'Blood Diamonds and the Lebanese Community', the other came from the *Midweek Spark* February 2003 with the headline, 'Mafia deal exposed...Lebanese bags 10 carat diamond'. Both point to the continuing problem of diamond smuggling, and both implicate the Lebanese community in this.

ties and incentives for corruption, even with a certification scheme. As Campbell points out:

> In a place like Sierra Leone, where the average monthly income for a customs official is less than the daily earnings of a minimum-wage employee in the United States, why not take a cut of the action in exchange for a certificate? (Campbell 2004: 132)

This it seems is the crux of the problem. Diamond mining in Sierra Leone does not benefit the country as a whole; it merely feeds the coffers of a minority of the country's elite (including Lebanese diamond dealers) who manage to siphon off a relatively small proportion in contrast to their eventual value. On a grander scale, diamonds benefit the likes of Branch Energy/Koidu Holdings (currently exploiting Kimberlite pipes in Sierra Leone) and others involved in their distribution like De Beers. De Beers and other international corporations are still able to mine or buy rough diamonds through whatever means, cut and polish them, and with the weight of their advertising and PR teams, invent a powerful image for consumers in the developed world. The cost involved in this finished product ensures that only the elite of Sierra Leone can afford to purchase this. Ordinary Sierra Leoneans will probably never see a finished diamond in their lives.

Diamond identification

In the case of conflict diamonds, there appears to be a lack of international provision or control to police country of origin. Certificates of Origin (CO) information contain a number of loopholes making it difficult to define true 'origin'. In 2000, diamonds entering the EU did not require a CO unless they were Angolan, and since October 2000 all Sierra Leone diamond exports must have a Certificate of Origin (Global Witness April 2001). Defining origin is the responsibility of the country from where they were mined and is dependent on the importer (when entering the EU) to declare this to Customs. Where this is unknown, country of consignment is given. Rough diamonds go to London's CSO for sorting while Antwerp imports and exports diamonds via the Belgium Diamond Office, and trades and re-routes diamonds. Countries of origin stipulations only apply to unsorted rough diamonds but because diamonds are routinely sorted in Freetown before being exported, the majority are excluded (Global Witness 2000).

In the following statement to Global Witness, De Beers refutes the claim that rough diamonds can be identified by source:

> If you are sitting in Tel Aviv or Moscow or New York whatever the potential for positive identification you have not a clue where they came from. Just to be clear if he [diamond seller] says they are Scottish diamonds

[there are no diamond mines in Scotland], you take his word for it…..they could be diamonds from the moon. (Global Witness 1998: 7)

However, elsewhere, De Beers claim to be able to identify the source of rough diamonds (see above). We know that Kimberlite and alluvial diamonds whilst sharing the same crystalline structure differ in terms of their surface appearance. The scattering of alluvial diamonds from their original volcanic pipe over wide areas by rivers and streams leaves them with distinct surface abrasions, differing patterns of chips and scratches and a general frosted appearance. Kimberlite diamonds have no such characteristics. Some diamond traders claim to be able to identify country of origin, though if diamonds are mixed, this makes it more difficult. (Global Witness 2000). Moreover, Global Witness (2000) has documented a number of scientific identification techniques that enables the provenance of diamonds to be identified. Indeed, the former president of De Beers' Canada Corporation explained in 2000 that 'It's very evident to our buyers what a parcel of Sierra Leone goods looks like. It's not rocket science' (Global Witness 2000:7).

Moreover, technologies exist that could be further developed like the use of lasers to mark or code both rough and cut diamonds to denote origin. This could aid in evaluation alongside the use of branding and grading to establish manufacturers' inventories and to trace lost and stolen

Fig. 5.3 Specimen *Certificate of Origin* document used in the export of rough diamonds (Government Gold and Diamond Office, Freetown, Sierra Leone), 2003

cut diamonds. De Beers already uses a type of branding or hallmark technology called the 'Marque' comprising an eight-digit serial number that 'is unique and personal to the buyer' and is invisible to the naked eye (De Beers 2004; Global Witness 2000: 22). As with all companies, De Beers is motivated by its desire to sell diamonds and in the context of all the bad press that conflict diamonds had received, felt it necessary to reassure the consumer of the high quality of their products. Of course, this is no guarantee that those rough diamonds entering the CSO are not from conflict zones or have not been involved in other unethical or illegal activities.

Global Witness has put a number of recommendations forward. These include the creation of a 'chain of custody' within the trade that is auditable from the mine to the consumer; the establishment of a regulatory framework in which governments of exporting and importing countries should have a main role alongside industry representatives. They call for greater transparency within the trade to stem the flow of conflict diamonds to some importing countries, a need to establish a clear infrastructure that breaks down some of the complexities involved in the transport of rough and cut diamonds (including the keeping of clear and centralised records in Freetown). There is also a need to tackle corruption in some producing countries. Global Witness believe that the international community has some responsibility in assisting producer countries like Sierra Leone to develop and improve on existing systems of export. Moreover, greater controls are called for at the point of production, especially in small-scale alluvial artisanal mining where greater financial incentives and penalties would aid control and transparency here. Such measures would go some way in generating localised wealth and increase government revenue. This would also control those buyers in Sierra Leone who smuggle diamonds out once they have paid very low prices to miners (Global Witness 2000). There also needs to be some accountability by large corporations like De Beers who wield much power and influence in the trade in diamonds:

> There is a clear role for De Beers and the CSO to take the lead in this process of transformation because given the scale of their involvement in, and control of the industry, no progress can be made without their willing participation. Indeed as the organisation which set up the CSO to deal with a crisis in production and supply in the late 1920s and 1930s, it is now time for it to face up to a new crisis in the diamond business; that of how to reform the industry to keep in step with the vital changes in the late 20th century in how corporates carry out their business. De Beers should endeavour to live up to its own rhetoric on corporate ethics. (Global Witness 1998: 9)

In the meantime, exploration companies like the Mano River Sources, Inc. and Africa Diamond Holdings Ltd (ADH) both Canadian, and Gondwana (Investments) SA (based in Luxembourg) continue to prospect for diamonds (alluvial and Kimberlite) and other resources in Sierra Leone (Sierra Leone Ministry of Mineral Resources February 2003).

6

Parallel Economies, Global Criminal Networks & Sierra Leone Diamonds

'Diamonds have been to Africa what cocaine has been to Latin America.' (Plaut 2002: 1)

Sierra Leonean diamonds form part of a much larger global trade in diamonds which in turn is an integral part of the wider global economy. In recent years economic growth across the globe has led to numerous parallel developments seen in the expansion in global trade and services that have become increasingly infused with corporatist ideology. Such moves reflect what some would call the hegemony of free-market economics. Indeed, as free-market economics has become the trade mark of global trade and services this has both encouraged and cultivated ever more patterns of privatisation, particularly of public services like defence and security once controlled by national governments and often paid for (in the developing world) with natural resources. The growth in private security firms is indicative of this. Moreover, economic globalisation has also witnessed selective wealth creation as seen in the growth in socio-economic disparity linked to resource predation and potential conflict. Such resources, whether oil, diamonds, timber or other sought-after resources tend to flow from the developing to the developed world. The struggle for such resources often leads to potential or actual conflict such as that witnessed in Sierra Leone.

Economic globalisation has also seen the emergence of co-existing 'parallel' global economies that display intricate, close and complex relationships with each other (Duffield in Berdal and Malone 2000). Such economies are symbiotic in nature and can be seen in the way those involved in criminal economic networks 'drift in and out of crime contexts [so that] crime networks span conventional distinctions between legitimate or illegitimate government, business and associations' (Findlay 1999: 144). Such parallel economies have created greater opportunities for global crime as the relationship between legal and illegal activities becomes obscured. In this way, criminal enterprise can utilise existing legitimate structures.

Against these global trends, there have also been developments that are specific to sub-Saharan Africa (excluding Botswana and South Africa). For more than two decades there has been a huge deterioration in Africa's trade, investment, production and consumption compared to the rest of the world. Structural adjustment policies have undermined efforts to diversify economies and have increased Africa's dependency on the export of primary products (Simon et al. 1995 in Castells 1998) and on international aid (government and humanitarian) and loans. At the same time, Africa continues to provide valuable metals and precious minerals that benefit not only global networks and companies involved in the buying and trading of these resources but also continue to benefit powerful national elites. As Castells explains:

> The problem is the use of earnings from these resources, as well as of international aid funds received by governments [...] The small, but affluent, bureaucratic class in many countries displays a high level of consumption of expensive imported goods, including Western food products and international fashion wear. Capital flows from African countries to personal accounts and profitable international investment throughout the world [...] for the exclusive benefit of a few wealthy individuals, provide evidence of substantial private accumulation that is not reinvested in the country where the wealth is generated [...] and the overwhelming majority of the population, are left to their own fate, between bare subsistence and violent pillage. (Castells 1998: 91)

Such processes form the broader backdrop to developments in Sierra Leone where the country's resources have been subject to both internal and external predation, particularly before and during the civil war there. This has occurred at three simultaneous and inter-related levels. First, resource predation has occurred at the level of the state, where government corruption and mismanagement of the nation's resources led to its eventual collapse. This paved the way for the second set of internal players – the rebels and insurgents that used their control of diamond resources to fund the war. The third set of players has involved external international interests that include foreign multinational mining companies and private security firms, including mercenaries, rebel groups from Liberia and other groups with links to the illegal/terror economy like al-Qaeda. Such groups operated within clearly defined corporate economic interests and their involvement was self-serving – to secure mineral wealth. The complex inter-relationships that exist between competing predatory elites, resource wealth and a host of other external 'players' that operate inside and outside global markets since the early 1990s will be discussed in the context of Sierra Leone.

Resource predation, conflict and competing interests

Civil wars in the post-Cold War era have had at their centre powerful economic drives with opportunities for business that benefit particular groups both inside the country and outside it and may include mineral wealth.[1] The millions amassed by the former Liberian dictator, Charles Taylor is estimated to have been in excess of US $400 million a year from the war in Liberia between 1992 and 1996 (Berdal and Malone 2000). The government backed Popular Movement for the Liberation of Angola (MPLA) strengthened its business interests during the war here through the selling of weapons to opposition UNITA forces. Such collusion between warring factions has occurred elsewhere including Cambodia, Liberia and Bosnia where conflict has in fact been perpetuated because of economic gains (ibid.). The role of international aid agencies in supporting humanitarian efforts can also create economic opportunities for local warring factions seen in reports of aid being diverted or stolen (Shearer cited in ibid.).

The end of the Cold War saw new political alliances being built between Sierra Leone's rulers and those foreign firms who had a mutual interest in natural resource wealth. Sierra Leone's rulers had used their political position to 'exploit and manipulate creditors and diplomatic partners [.......and] have applied these tools to pursue internal strategies that select, delegitimise, and economically marginalise rival politicians and deny them their own local power bases' (Reno 1998: 114). Such strategies emerged in conditions of crisis and while the country did not become embroiled in Cold War rivalries as others (notably Angola and Liberia) did, it did become dependent on more broad-based support. This was particularly so with reference to outside business and security interests when efforts to tackle widespread poverty and win back control during the civil war were high on the agenda. The complex inter-relationships that exist between predatory elites, resource wealth and a host of other external 'players' that operate inside and outside global markets since the early 1990s needs to be examined in the context of Sierra Leone.

Various theories have been posited to describe the position of Sierra Leone vis-à-vis global economic interests before the outbreak of civil war. One argument is that Sierra Leone's ruling elites had become agents of foreign economic interest, akin to what Rodney termed a 'comprador class' (1982). On the other hand, the country may have been afflicted by what Michael Doyle (1986) termed 'imperialism by invitation' involving the recruitment of foreign groups to support different factions inside the

---

[1] See Indra de Soysa (2000) 'The Resource Curse: Are Civil Wars Driven by Rapacity or Paucity?' 5, 6; Collier, P. (2000) 'Doing Well out of War: An Economic Perspective'; Reno, W. (2000) 'Shadow States and the Political Economy of Civil Wars', all in Berdal, M. and Malone, D.M. (2000) *Greed and Grievance – Economic Agendas in Civil Wars*.

country (Reno 1998). Whether Sierra Leone had become the pawn of external interests or not, Sierra Leone's ruling classes had been looking after their own personal interests in the interim, seen in what some theorists have termed the 'politics of pillage'. Fatton's (1992) theory of 'predatory rule' argues that this emerged after the county became independent in the 1960s and this idea is supported in other works by Davidson (1992), Leys (1994) and Lewis (1996) (See also Castells 1998). Bayart's (1989) notion of the 'politics of the belly' on the other hand is said to have been a strategy pursued by Sierra Leone's political elite since pre-colonial times.

The pillage of Africa through predatory rule for personal aggrandisement appears to have afflicted many African states (with the exception of some) in the 1990s and is characterised by various patterns (Castells 1998). These include a tendency for resources (international or domestic) to become part of personal accumulation rather than being for the benefit of the economy and the people. Different political elites compete for state power as this is synonymous with wealth and provides further opportunities for pillage and future wealth. This in turn leads to state instability and enables the military to have a greater role. Finally, political support operates through a system of patronage whereby political allegiance has to be given in order to secure and have access to services, jobs and favours. Clientelistic support can be based on a combination of ethnicity, economics and territoriality as a means of maximising political support which in turn relies on the maximisation of resources to pay for such support (Castells 1998).

Reno (1995) terms this (in the context of Sierra Leone), *shadow rule* as a way of describing how wealth accumulated from natural resources like diamonds is used to 'buy' political support or provide subsidies or access to state assets. Payouts might also include the discretionary use of power to turn a blind eye to law breakers by not prosecuting. The personal or private use of state funds to buttress political support instead of investing such resources in services like welfare provision, leads to the creation of shadow rule, that occurs outside of the formal state (Reno cited in Bernal and Malone 2000). Political patronage works by undermining sovereign economic and political stability to the majority of the population who are then compelled to seek personal favours from those in power. As Reno explains:

> .... the ruler seeks to impose negative externalities – that is, costs or hindrances on subjects-while distributing relief from these burdens on the basis of personal discretion in return for compliance or loyalty. Thus there can be no civil rights because there is no rule of law in the shadow state, since relations with authorities are subordinate to the personal discretion of those authorities. Personal security, protection of property, and economic opportunity (in lieu of public services or security) are subject to the personal discretion of a superior, rather than as a consequence of impersonal institutions. (Reno 2000: 47)

Clapham (2000) argues that with independence, those societies with a pre-colonial tradition of statehood were more able to implement effective governments and sustain structures of government. For those that did not (Somalia, northern Uganda, southern Sudan, Liberia and Sierra Leone) the cost of running the state was greater than state revenues. This weakness led to compensatory strategies, in particular the development of patronage so that political allegiance was 'bought'. However, as this became difficult to maintain, this undermined support for the state. For Clapham (ibid.) such structural factors were exacerbated by the dependence of African states on one or two primary products that were vulnerable to world fluctuations in demand and price. The corrupt practices of individuals further undermined the state but did not cause this structural weakness.

During the 1960s and 70s, diamonds made up around 61 per cent of Sierra Leone's foreign exchange (Bangura, 2000). From the late 1970s to the early 1990s, there were clear connections between diamonds and international political and criminal interests. Hizbullah for example, the Shiite Muslim group with links to Lebanese activists, used the Lebanese Diaspora in Western and Central Africa to fundraise through diamonds (BBC 20 Feb 2003). Various Lebanese militias (including Hizbullah) from the continuing civil war there looked to Lebanese Sierra Leoneans for financial support. It has been argued that the Lebanese civil war was 'played out' in Sierra Leone as Lebanese here gave financial support through their involvement with diamond dealing and trading that acted as an informal tax base for various factions and militias (Global Witness 2000). Moreover, 'Israeli investors' with links to Russian and American crime families in the late 1970s and 1980s have also been implicated. Indeed many of the weapons supplied to rebel forces in Sierra Leone and Liberia were Russian (Smillie et al. 2000).

Parallel global economies: war, 'entrepreneurship' and criminal dealings

The predatory kleptocracy that emerged and flourished in Sierra Leone must bear some responsibility for the ten year civil war there. Those who became disillusioned, disenfranchised, alienated and excluded from the free for all of the nation's wealth, mobilised (with the support of Charles Taylor and others) against this. The war economy that emerged provided many opportunities for all kinds of 'business', particularly as this related to diamonds. Diamonds became integral to the various competing factions who were either directly involved in the conflict like the RUF or who were there for purely commercial exploits. Rebel RUF paid international weapons dealers in diamonds and diamonds were used to pay for the mercenaries who provided services on both sides of the fence. Other players inside Sierra Leone were also involved in illegal diamond trading including government soldiers, corrupt officials and some Lebanese traders. If diamonds did not initiate the war, the demand for these precious stones certainly perpetuated it.

During the chaos of war, state collapse led to the criminalisation of Sierra Leone's economy as various commercial-political interests were attracted here from outside as well as within the country. Internally, state collapse resulted from the lack of regulation of a resource dependent economy and years of endemic corruption. This in turn paved the way for economic stagnation as profits from diamonds and other resources went into the pockets of those in power. This was also extended to other 'state personnel' during the war. Illegal mining and smuggling of diamonds was also found amongst sections of the Sierra Leone Armed Forces (SLAF) (the *sobel* – soldiers by day and rebels by night) as well as corrupt police officers and some UNAMSIL peacekeepers (Mitchell 2005). Diamonds and other concessions were bartered for arms or security by both the elected government and by rebel factions. Such illicit activity also involved the Nigerian-led ECOMOG forces. Its commander Brigadier General Maxwell Khobe was known as 'Ten Million man' after allegedly receiving $10 million for allowing RUF rebels to mine diamonds (Bourne 2001). Additional interests in Sierra Leonean diamonds include its neighbour Liberia, where dealings in illicit stones have been an issue since the 1950s. However during the course of the conflict, Liberia's involvement became integral to this conflict as more than 60,000 Liberian fighters came across the border supplying arms to RUF and AFRC factions who fought for control of the diamond areas (Bangura 2000). Such activity was not only common knowledge to the Liberian state, it was sanctioned by it. Smillie et al. have argued:

> What was different and more sinister after 1991 was the active involvement of official Liberian interests in Sierra Leone's brutal war – for the purpose of pillage rather than politics. By the end of the 1990s, Liberia had become a major centre for massive diamond-related criminal activity, with connections to guns, drugs and money laundering throughout Africa and considerably further afield. In return for weapons, it provided the RUF with an outlet for diamonds, and has done the same for other diamond producing countries, fuelling war and providing a safe haven for organised crime of all sorts. (Smillie et al. 2000: 8)

After the signing of the Lome Peace Accord in 1999 between the Sierra Leone government and RUF rebels, 'armed gangs [were now] rewarded with power by the international community without the benefit of a democratic mandate' (Bangura 2000: 565). Foday Sankoh, the rebel leader was made chair of the Board of the Commission for the Management of Strategic Resources, National Reconstruction and Development[2] in which they agreed to relinquish control of the mines to UN forces. Yet diamonds continued to be mined and smuggled. Between 1998 and 2000 the value of official annual diamond exports by Sierra Leone halved to $30m, whilst

[2] According to Bangura (2000: 565) 'this effectively put [Sankoh] in charge of diamonds'.

Liberian diamond exports rose dramatically to $300m, even though Liberia possesses relatively few diamond resources (BBC World News 15 May 2000). Indeed Liberia's former leader Charles Taylor had historical links with the RUF and whilst diamonds continued to cross the border into Liberia, he had a vested interest in prolonging the war in Sierra Leone.

Charles Taylor's role in Sierra Leone and in particular his activities around diamond production and looting, which enabled him to amass huge personal wealth, 'highlights the special role that natural resources play in facilitating violent entrepreneurial strategies and the positive aspects of warfare for shadow state elites' (Reno 2000: 56). In such a situation, war is perpetuated since it serves the economic and political needs of certain elites – to control land and resources like diamonds in the case of Sierra Leone. Moreover, President Kabbah's use of private security (such as Executive Outcomes) and the awarding of mining licences to private firms like Branch Mining allowed him to curry political support outside of Sierra Leone and rely less on local 'strongmen' (Reno 1998). The pacifying of the diamond mining areas through private security attracted smaller foreign investors here who could also be involved in other activities. According to Reno:

> Small firms learned that they could milk outsiders for themselves if they created and financed closely associated 'NGOs' to attract money and political support from overseas donors. In joint venture arrangements with favoured local politicians, 'social service' spending by firms through 'NGO' fronts encouraged local people to associate benefits with the firm's and the politicians' presence. (Reno 1998: 136)

During the RUF's occupation of the diamond areas, Lebanese traders among others were targeted in a bid to mobilise popular support against these outsiders, who were seen as privileged and wealthy, in the hope of receiving protection money. Some collaborated with the rebels. Lebanese migration to Sierra Leone had increased during the Lebanese civil war (circa 1975–1991) since they already had Lebanese contacts there. By the early 1980s the Lebanese population of Sierra Leone reached 13,000 representing an increase of 230 per cent. In Kono, this community grew at the same rate between the years 1967 and 1985, with many becoming involved in the retail trades, aided by family support (Reno 1995). This community came to dominate commerce and continued to enjoy success in the diamond industry. In both cases, trade avoided the prohibitions in force against 'stranger' ownership of Kono land (ibid.). Lebanese business success in the diamond industry can be seen in the distribution of dealer licences.

The Lebanese were able to occupy an economic niche as entrepreneurs able to utilise family contacts both inside and outside the country. While they were seen as receiving preferential treatment because they could pay a bigger 'dash' or bribe to local official, they did contribute to the bulk of local government revenue.

In 1987, Lebanese business was estimated to have paid around 90 per

Table 6.1 Distribution of Dealer Licences, 1973–1982

	Lebanese (heritage)		African		Shared addresses	
	No.	%	No.	%	No.	%
1973	107	78	30	22	–	–
1974	152	75	52	25	–	–
1975	134	79	36	21	–	–
1976	110	65	57	35	22	13
1977	88	64	49	36	22	17
1978	99	70	42	30	37	26
1979	139	66	72	34	96	46
1980	102	56	79	44	92	51
1981	104	62	63	38	74	44
1982	96	73	36	27	90	68

Source: Reno, W. (1995) *Corruption and state politics in Sierra Leone* (Cambridge, University Press)

cent of Koidu/Safadu tax receipts in 1987, whilst revenues collected from chiefdom subjects was taken and used by the chiefs for themselves. Moreover, local officials involved in diamond dealing favoured these non-African businessmen over African ones since additional payoffs could be had through official toleration of their connections with diamond-dealer relatives (Reno 1995). The Lebanese community had become firmly embedded in diamond production and trading in Sierra Leone before the outbreak of the civil war. This meant they were strategically placed (alongside other players) to continue with 'business' during the war.

Opportunities could also be had for other non-government players both inside and outside Sierra Leone. These included international mining firms like Branch Energy that the Kabbah government approached as an investor. Branch Energy was created when Executive Outcomes (EO) underwent corporate and military expansion between 1993 and 1995. Based in London with registered branches in Africa, Branch Energy would manage EO mineral concessions in gold, diamonds and others acquired during security operations in Angola, Uganda, north-eastern Kenya, Sierra Leone, Mozambique and Tanzania.[3] DiamondWorks Limited was formed in late 1996 with links to Branch Energy (Pech 1999).

In 1996, the British military company Sandline International was formed and headed by retired Lieutenant-Colonel Timothy Spicer, a distinguished war veteran in Northern Ireland, the Falklands campaign, the Gulf War and Bosnia. Although registered in the Bahamas, Sandline shared its headquartered offices in Chelsea with Branch Energy and Heritage Oil and

[3] For a fuller and detailed account of Executive Outcomes development and business interests see Pech, K (1999) 'Executive Outcomes – A corporate conquest' in Cilliers, J. and Mason, P. (eds) *Peace, Profit or Plunder? The Privatisation of Security in War-Torn African Societies*. Institute for Security Studies, South Africa.

was known to subcontract work out to Executive Outcomes (Pech 1999). RUF rebels also made contracts with various (US) mining firms[4] (see Perz-Katz 2002). Such companies received in return for their support of one side or the other, long-term mining concessions. They operated outside of normal and legal working practices, free from tax and were able to engage in the unfettered exploitation of Sierra Leone's mineral wealth (Mitchell 2005). Other groups involved in the pillaging of Sierra Leone during the civil war included international drug cartels, regional rebels, terrorists groups[5] and various other private security firms from Armenia, America, Bulgaria and Russia (Reno 1998). The arms deals, money laundering, human trafficking and the smuggling of the county's mineral wealth also attracted an array of small foreign mining companies (Smillie et al. 2000).

Private security

The presence of private soldiers was indicative of the increasing global privatisation of public services that were once controlled by national governments. This 'war entrepreneurship' as Lilly (2000) describes it, emerged from the creation of surplus military personnel (including ex-combatants) that grew as Western governments made defence cuts. Mercenaries also have the protection of international law (Article 47 Geneva Convention 1977). Whilst there have been moves to curb their activities (Organisation of African Unity adopted a Convention for the Elimination of Mercenarism 1985; UN banned mercenaries in 1989) the problem of definition has allowed for their unfettered use as soldiers in national forces (for example in Sierra Leone, Zaire, Angola and outside Africa). Their increased availability and use not only mirrors the trend towards a privatisation culture but in the wider context of market-led globalisation, actually cultivates it.

In West Africa, mercenary activity continued after the war ended in Sierra Leone with ex-combatants from Sierra Leone, Liberia, Guinea, the Gambia, Ghana and Burkino Faso offering their 'services' in this volatile region. For one organisation: 'the mercenary industry is leading the privatisation of conflict in Africa and throughout the world' (Global Witness 2003). Iraq has become particularly salient as an important testing ground for this growth industry where huge financial opportunities are up for grabs. Moreover, Iraq has provided the single biggest boost to the growth of such organisations (Howden and Doyle 2007).

---

[4] These included BECA Company, Lazare Kaplin International and Integrated Mining. See U.N. Panel of Experts, 2000: 4–5 cited in Mitchell (2005): 7–8.

[5] Terrorist groups are defined by the UN General Assembly (1994) as those who commit 'criminal acts intended or calculated to provoke a state of terror in the general public, a group of persons for particular purposes are in any circumstances unjustifiable, whatever the considerations…that may be invoked to justify them.' Napoleoni (2004) discusses the way 'terror' has become privatised as seen in financial extortion, resort to illicit economic activities and self-financing armed struggles.

Many private security companies avoid terminology like 'military' adopting instead more corporate language like 'security'. As organisations structured along business lines, the industry is estimated to be worth up to $120bn annually with operations spanning at least 50 countries (Howden and Doyle 2007). Indeed many such organisations are legally registered businesses and are advertised as multinational corporations. All have close ties to mineral assets such as diamonds and oil and span the globe from Africa to South America and the South Pacific. Such organisations meet the approval of IFI and Western governments because 'they supposedly make Africa safe for investment' by protecting mineral assets for corporate establishments (Francis 1999: 323). Between 1995 and 1996 various UK- based security companies and operations were directly involved in Sierra Leone. These included the Gurkha Security Guard (GSG), who was employed to train the Sierra Leone army (RSLMF). Others, such as Defence Systems Ltd (DSL), Control Risk, Group 4, J & P. Security Limited and Rapport Research and Analysis Limited were there seeking business opportunities (Hooper 1996 cited in Vines 1999). The South African based Executive Outcomes arrived in April 1995 when the GSG left.

The roles of such companies like EO and Sandline International in Sierra Leone throws into sharp focus the many difficult dilemmas faced by the besieged government here. These relate to short-term and long-term effects. EO involvement had some short term impact on the defence of the civilian population (regarded by many as liberators) against rebel atrocities when the international community was reluctant to get involved. Amongst the civilian population there is no doubt that EO was a lifeline during a period of extreme terror. In the words of Hinga-Norman (former deputy Defence Minister): 'Our people have died, lost their limbs, lost their eyes and their properties for these elections. If we employ a service to protect our hard-won democracy, why should it be viewed negatively?' (1996, cited in Rubin 1999). During the siege of Freetown in 1995, EO intervention and their working alongside the Republic of Sierra Leone Military Force (RSLMF) was successful in pushing the rebels from Freetown and forcing them to withdraw 100 kilometres into the interior (Douglas 1999, Cilliers & Cornwell 1999). Moreover, their intervention enabled some 300,000 refugees to return home and within a year stability had been restored, though atrocities resumed after their withdrawal. The company had agreed a sum of $15 million and lucrative diamond mining concessions for their work (Rubin 2007). In total, it cost the Sierra Leone government $35 million for the 21 months of EO operations (Francis 1999).

The operation of private security firms like EO[6] in Sierra Leone made

[6] Executive Outcomes is part of a wider consortium or EO group that includes security and mineral companies with common shareholders and paymasters who were closely affiliated with EO military operations. Between 1994 and 1998, the 'group' included between 30–50 companies. See Pech, K (1999) 'Executive Outcomes – A corporate conquest' in Cilliers, J. and Mason, P. (eds) *Peace, Profit or Plunder? The Privatisation of Security in War-Torn African Societies*. 1999, Institute for Security Studies, South Africa.

it easier for those involved in commercial and non-commercial interests here to do their work. This includes NGOs, diplomats and others involved in foreign aid organisations and development projects. Indeed, humanitarian agencies in most war zones today are dependent on private military firms or companies (Howden and Doyle 2007). Whilst these projects may benefit the people they are aimed at, at the same time such 'benefits appear to be coincidental to their proximity to essentially private commercial operations' (Reno 1998: 135). EO was hired by the NPRC under Strasser in 1995 to take the diamond areas from RUF hands and place them in the hands of Branch Mining (a British subsidiary of Branch Energy) (Mitchell 2005). Sierra Leonean political figures (like the military leader Brigadier Julius Bio who overthrew Strasser in 1996 and the civilian president, Tejan Kabbah) believed that EO was a positive force. Moreover, there appears to be a link between EO weakening the RUF militarily and the opportunity for elections to be held in Sierra Leone (Shearer 1998 cited in Francis 1999). In addition, EO provided training and armaments to the civilian defence force, the Kamajors and during successful Kamajors' attacks on RUF bases, had provided helicopter gunship cover as well as tactical advice and logistic support. Yet EO was not the only force bolstering the military strength of the government. There was the additional 30,000 strong *Kamajors* who proved invaluable in bush warfare and who became the 'eyes and ears of EO' (Douglas 1999: 183). Also, ECOMOG forces and Nigerian battalions proved important to the military operation against the RUF (Francis 1999).

In the long term, the role of such companies raises numerous ethical and political dilemmas since they offer no long term solution to political instability and state security. Indeed such companies thrive on their ability to exploit political instability and violence for private gain and profit (Francis 1999).

There is a growing body of research that suggests that the activities of mercenaries and private military companies (PMCs) is having a damaging and detrimental impact on the long-term stability of host states by undermining their authority (see Cilliers and Mason 1999, Musah and Fayemi 2000, Serewicz 2002 and Brayton 2002 cited in Whyte 2003). According to Francis:

> The guise of providing national security for collapsing, but mineral rich developing states, [and this serves to] only accentuate their international exploitation and marginalisation. The argument here is that this corporate mercenarism – in search of strategic minerals – represents the 'new face' of neo-colonialism, operating under the guise of neoliberal market policies. Through this privatisation of security, mercenary companies therefore provide viable foreign policy proxies for Western governments in the pursuit of national interests. (Francis 1999: 319)

Moreover, for Ruggiero (2003) the process of globalisation itself undermines structured hierarchies of social control as these are increasingly given over to 'networks'. He explains:

Power relationships tend increasingly to be embedded not in organisations and institutions but in networks in which instructions are processed. While globalization implies the weakening of localized sovereignty and structures (Beck, 2000), contemporary networks of capital, production, trade, science, and communication by-pass the nation-state. (Castells, 2000 cited in Ruggiero 2003: 173)

Whether the role of private military companies poses a threat to the political sovereignty of the state (Francis 1999) or not (Whyte 2003), such companies are not a long-term solution to the future political stability of African or other states. Their use in wresting mineral resources from RUF rebels in Sierra Leone ultimately exacerbated the international exploitation of that country (Francis 1999). At the same time, there was genuine support in Freetown and elsewhere for the role of EO and Sandline in bringing respite and stability from RUF attacks on civilians (Peel 2004). Their involvement and the controversy surrounding these did more to raise the profile of this war in Britain than the daily atrocities had ever done (Douglas 1999). Moreover, as O'Brien (2003) has argued, the debate concerning the pros and cons of private military companies is dependent on which perspective is employed, as a mercenary to one can be a military adviser to another.

Increasingly, African rulers in recent years have sought military solutions to what are essentially political issues. The 'militarisation of politics' and the 'privatisation of the state' have been mutually reinforcing and can be seen in the expansion of private security firms in Africa and beyond (Cilliers & Cornwell 1999). Yet, the commercialisation of state functions whilst creating economic opportunities for private security and opportunities for a whole range of criminal economic activities, has done little to alleviate corruption and political instability nor aided economic growth (Cilliers & Cornwell 1999). Moreover, the control of certain state assets and services by global corporations has undermined the legitimacy and ability of some African states to function. Such developments have been seen as part of the growth in organised crime in Africa. Where predatory economic exploitation of resources by organised criminals enters the political process or as Bayart et al. (1999) argues: 'the political arena is invaded by criminal practices' what occurs is the 'criminalisation of the African state' (ibid. cited in Cilliers & Cornwell 1999: 231). Moreover, concern has been raised about the practice of the British government allowing private security and mining firms to dictate and implement foreign policy, as occurred in the case of Sierra Leone (*Africa Confidential* 1998 cited in Cilliers & Cornwell 1999). Of equal concern is the ability of such companies to force political change by playing a direct role in influencing the outcome of particular power struggles (Pech 1999). Yet as Clapham (cited in Herbst 1998) notes, the use of mercenaries and private security in Africa is indicative of the deep-seated security problems in Africa rather than the causes of it.

Established criminal and underground networks involved in Sierra Leonean diamonds meant that when rebel factions took control of various diamond areas during the duration of the war, there were many willing to do business and exchange these *blood diamonds* for arms. During the war, diamonds were extracted in Kono and Tongo by locally recruited miners and youths who were forced to mine by the RUF and AFRC in return for armed protection (Bangura 2000). Diamonds from occupied areas were used by rebels to buy arms, drugs and in some cases the services of foreign mercenaries. Press reports have revealed the capture of various individuals and groups involved in supporting rebels through mercenary activities. These included Ya'ir Klein in early 1999, a lieutenant colonel in the Israeli army who had been previously involved in supplying arms and military training to the Colombian Medellin drug cartel. There were also reports of several hundred Ukrainian mercenaries and similar numbers of soldiers from Burkina Faso who had been recruited to fight with the rebels. Additionally, a criminal South African neo-Nazi group was also reported to be involved (Bangura 2000). Indeed the nature of mercenary activity meant that there was competition for their services on both sides of the war. Mercenary organisations like British based Sandline International, pushed for mining concessions in return for supplying arms to the civil defence force in breach of a UN embargo. Private security firms like the South African EO had been employed by the military NPRC government in 1995. It was paid $1.5 million a month to defend the diamond mines from rebel forces. Mining concessions were also given to the British company, Branch Energy to continue mining in areas under rebel control[7] (Bangura 2000, Hayward 1997).

Mercenary organisations like EO have been at the forefront of increasing privatisation of military markets and their increased use around the globe in recent years. Moreover, their monetary cost for struggling impoverished underdeveloped states is less than that associated with more permanent military forces (Whyte 2003). EO was formed when a former officer of the South African Defence Forces brought together around 2000 former military and intelligence personnel who had served the apartheid regime. This included the Civil Coordination Bureau. These forces were used against anti-apartheid organisations like the African National Congress (ANC) including the carrying out of covert assassinations of ANC and other anti-apartheid activists. EO used its 2000 strong company of men from superfluous and demobilized South African military units previously involved in surveillance, anti-insurgency and bush warfare inside and outside South Africa. EO had also provided 'security' to the Angolan government during its resistance to the National Union for the Total Independence of Angola. They have little use in post-apartheid

[7] SEE UNHCHR 55th session 1998 'Report on the question of the use of mercenaries as means of violating human rights'.

South Africa and have been outlawed along with all such organisations. Consequently, their services in military, technical and organisational expertise have been offered around the globe, particularly in Africa. The company specialises in oil drilling, arms sales and refurbishment, diamond mining, transportation, engineering and land mine detection and clearance. Essentially they are a private military force who work for state officials and private-firms (Reno 1998). In the light of peace-keeping failures in Somalia and Rwanda, organisations like the OAU and the UN have considered using the services of private military companies to enforce regional peace-keeping (Pech 1999). Indeed, ex-SAS officer, Colonel Tim Spicer had secured a contract worth $293 million for his firm Aegis Defence Services to supply security to US companies in Iraq. This includes those involved in reconstruction projects around oil and gas fields as well as electricity and water services, in addition to the several dozen private security firms involved in anything from body guarding of key personnel to guarding oil pipelines (Chatterjee 2004). Moreover, in the summer of 2003 the Department for International Development (DFID) entered into a contract with the South African firm Meteoric Tactical Solutions (MTS) to protect British personnel in Iraq, the same company accused of an attempted coup in Equatorial Guinea later in 2004 (Barnett, Hughes and Burke 2004). Before EO became involved in Sierra Leone under the NPRC in April 1995, mercenaries made up of Nepalese Ghurkas who had served in the British army were used to form the Ghurka Security Group. This group provided training to the Sierra Leone army in 1993–1994 but the losses it endured saw its withdrawal in 1995 (Hirsch 2001).

EO sought the support of local societies, including hunting and initiation societies that had formed civil militias (Kamajors) for self-protection. This served to aid the acceptance of a foreign mercenary organisation among local people who was employed to work on behalf of the government under Strasser. In April 1995, Freetown was cleared of rebels in this combined effort, followed by the diamond areas between July and August in the same year (Reno 1998). All of this was paid for with mineral concessions since the bill of several million dollars a month to enlist their services did not exist in terms of government revenue. EO were given a free hand to mine and market Sierra Leone's diamond wealth and found a willing partner in Branch Energy (a British diamond mining firm, part of a group of companies owned by a South African firm with links to EO – Reno 1998). Branch Energy arranged for Branch Mining, its Sierra Leone subsidiary to mine diamonds in Kono in 1996 under the protection of EO. The presence of security firms in Sierra Leone has attracted other foreign investors, including small mining operations (Reno 1998).

Small businesses

By the early 1990s, small mining firms known as 'juniors' became involved in Sierra Leone diamond mining. Three were known to trade on the Canadian stock exchanges. One of them, Rex Diamond, with its HQ in Antwerp holds Sierra Leonean concessions in Zimmi and Tongo Field. This company had been involved in arrangements to supply the Sierra Leone government with engines, parts and ammunition worth US$3.8 million after losing its only combat helicopter in 1998.[8] Rex's managing director – Zeev Morgenstern – and the company's president – Serg Muller – explained to the Washington Post '...the arms deals were unrelated to Rex's mining activities' (Smillie et al. 2000: 6). A second company – AmCan Minerals, based in Toronto, held various exploration licences in Sierra Leone and acquired the South African owned firm ArmSec International. This has links with the diamond and security industries. Moreover, AmCan's Sierra Leone lawyer was chairman of the Government Gold and Diamond Office (GGDO). This body oversees the monitoring valuation and taxation of the diamond industry. A third company, Diamond-Works with its HQ in London, acquired Branch Energy Ltd in 1995. Both these private companies have been seen to have connections with two major international security firms – EO and Sandline. In 1995, EO were engaged by the Sierra Leone government to push the RUF from Freetown and to clear the diamond areas around Kono, which they did. EO took control of the diamond areas, whilst Branch Energy was given a 25-year-lease on Sierra Leonean diamond concessions (Smillie et al. 2000).

The intimate relationship that these small 'juniors' or mining companies have with private security firms like EO and Sandline can be explained first by the inability of successive Sierra Leonean governments to police the diamond areas which dates back to the 1950s. Since the setting up of the Sierra Leone Selection Trust (SLST) Diamond Protection Force, Sierra Leone governments had required foreign investors to make their own security arrangements. Second, these small companies came to Sierra Leone when the civil war was in full force and when formal state structures were being undermined or had collapsed. The use of private security forces enabled such companies to do business in difficult circumstances, though their use raises a number of issues. Whilst EO were employed to protect the legitimate government of Sierra Leone and the 'Sandline deal' involved supplying the Sierra Leone government (under Tejan Kabbah) with weapons in breach of a UN embargo, one must ask why was Sierra Leone abandoned by the international community and forced to 'bargain' to survive? The situation where a poor nation like Sierra

---

[8] This had been an effective weapon against RUF rebels. However, defective parts supplied by Russia marred the deal. See Smillie, I. et al. (2000) 'Getting to the heart of the matter: Sierra Leone, diamonds and human security. *Social Justice* 27 (4).

Leone is forced to pay with future mineral concessions has been described as being more akin to a 'protection racket' (Smillie et al. 2000).

EO not only aided the Kabbah government in expunging rebel forces from Freetown and the diamond area of Kono, they also unearthed the coup plots against him and were instrumental in blowing these out. Moreover, the company was involved in mediation between the civil militia force, the Kamajors and the regular army in October 1996 during which 100 troops had been killed. The contract that EO had with the Sierra Leone government ended in January 1997 and was not renewed, no doubt influenced by IMF disapproval of government money being used to fund mercenary activity (Reno 1998). Of course the RUF had its backers and from 1996 to 2000, deals were done with international mining firms like Integrated Mining. Such firms had experience of Kimberlite mining in remote areas and were additionally able to diversify into other forms of mining such as rutile and bauxite (Mitchell 2005). The undertaking of 'business' by these small enterprises during the chaos of war when formal state structures had collapsed calls into question the legitimacy of such 'business'. In a country where the mores of the 'wild west' operate in peace time with reference to diamond production, such companies were mercenary in their exploitation of the utter and absolute chaos brought about by war. Full advantage was taken of the opportunities for 'business' made possible through the purchasing of protection provided by private security forces. It seems likely that the diamonds exploited and exported by such companies during this period entered the realms of grey or even black parallel global economies since the legal-illegal boundaries of diamond business became blurred and intricately close.

Criminal groups

In addition to the criminal activities undertaken in Sierra Leone by internal players (including sections of the Sierra Leonean elite and RUF rebels), big time criminals from outside have orchestrated drug smuggling, money laundering, diamond smuggling and weapons deals. Russian and Ukrainian syndicates are a case in point as they are thought to have operated *shell companies* in areas around Kono and Makeni even though the specific areas occupied were known to have no diamonds. Claims of between US $1–10 million per month have been circulated through such laundering businesses (Mitchell 2005). In addition, arms deals involving ex-Soviet weapons have been known to exchange hands in return for Sierra Leonean diamonds.

In 2001, Leonid Minin an Israeli businessman originally from the Ukraine who had links with the Odessa Mafia in the Ukraine was charged with weapons trafficking and supplying the RUF. Another individual involved in criminal business deals was Victor Bout (arrested in March

2008), born in Tajik and an ex-KGB linguist. Bout received several million dollars in Sierra Leonean diamonds and several Liberian diamond mines in return for supplying Charles Taylor with weapons. Bout had been a major arms supplier to Africa and Afghanistan in violation of international embargoes and had links with the RUF leader Foday Sankoh, as well as al-Qaeda, the Taliban and other suspect characters like Jonas Savimbi, Mobutu Sese Seko, Muammar Gaddafi amongst others (see Farah 2004 cited in Mitchell 2005).

In recent years, details have emerged of the links between diamonds and international terrorism.[9] In a report researched and published by Global Witness (2003) *For a Few Dollar$ More: How al Qaeda Moved into the Diamond Trade*[10] it details how al-Qaeda carried out a ten-year strategic move into the unregulated diamond trade and infiltrated diamond trading networks by taking advantage of weak governments and illicit trading structures. The report shows how Liberia's government under President Charles Taylor allowed al-Qaeda access into Sierra Leone and Liberia to buy diamonds from rebels (including RUF) in exchange for weapons. The report states that criminals and terrorists buy rough diamonds in order to launder money because such diamonds are impossible to trace.

In the post-September 11 world, groups like al-Qaeda have accelerated their involvement in the trade in African gold and gems because of the crackdown on the group's financial assets. 'Front companies and individuals' have enabled such groups to hide its assets, continue to earn money and evade financial sanctions and freezes. It has been alleged that al-Qaeda began to transfer cash and weapons for precious stones as early as 1993 and that this continued in the aftermath of the 1998 US embassy bombings in Kenya and Tanzania (BBC News 20 Feb, 17 April 2003; Global Witness 2003; Mitchell 2005). Napoleoni (2004) has shown how al-Qaeda exploited oil and money markets in the run up to the attacks on the Twin Towers and the Pentagon in 2001 and how it converted many of its resources into more liquid assets like gold and diamonds post 9/11 in the knowledge of impending financial crackdown. Global Witness (2003a)

[9] See various news reports: Sherman, J. 'Al Qaeda Cash Tied to Diamond Trade' and "Blood Diamonds" Fund More than Terrorism' in *The Washington Post* 1 and 7 November 2001; Hill, A. 'Bin Laden's $20m African "Blood Diamond" Deals: How the terror network financed its operations with stolen gems' in *The Observer* 20 October 2002; Leppard, D. & Nathan, A. 'Al-Qaeda tried to sell gems in UK' in *The Sunday Times* 5 January 2003; Rosenbaum, A. 'Diamonds to die for – Terrorist groups and African rebel armies are funding their atrocities through the rough diamond trade, particularly in Antwerp. So what is the industry doing about it?' *The Times* 20 February 2003; Jones, L. 'Al Qaeda traded "blood diamonds"' *BBC News Online* 21 February 2003 accessed 25 June 2004; Roberts, J. 'Diamonds in the rough' *New Internationalist* Vol 36, 7 May 2004; Lamont, J. 'Diamond nations try to restore industry's sparkle' in *Financial Times* 5 November 2002.

[10] Global Witness is a British based non-governmental organisation that monitors the role natural resources play in funding conflict and aiding corruption and brought the issues of conflict diamonds to the world's attention in 1998. The full report can be found at www.globalwitness.org/reports/

estimated that al-Qaeda had laundered $20m through the purchasing of diamonds alone by 2003.

Napoleoni (2004) has identified three types of 'terror economies' that parallel traditional capitalist economies. The first she identifies as state sponsored terrorism as seen during the cold war when the two super-powers (and others) funded and trained terrorist organisations.[11] The second type of terror economy was more privatised in that financial inde-pendence and self-sufficiency gave such groups economic independence and freedom from state control. This development emerged during the wars in Chechnya, Afghanistan, Bosnia and Albania. So called 'shell states' emerged where resources became integral to war economies controlled by terrorists groups. The third type of terror economy is that utilised in more recent years by globalised terror organisation like al-Qaeda. Napoleoni argues that terror groups operate by exploiting global financial markets made possible by the deregulation of international economic and financial markets. The ability to operate more freely across national boundaries has allowed armed groups across the globe to forge economic links with one another. Such developments have allowed for even closer links and mutual dependence between traditional capitalist economies and terrorist controlled economies. This resembles the 'parallel' global economies identified by Duffield (2000) whereby legal and illegal (criminal) economies become closely intertwined so much so that many western corporations are only too well aware that they are conducting business with groups that are closely linked with criminal /terror economic activities (Napoleoni 2004). During Sierra Leone's civil war period, elements of the second and third type of 'terror economy' were apparent though linkages between legal and illegal economic activity was apparent before this.

'Legal' and criminal economies in diamond trading

Increasingly, academics and others have noted the intricate and complex relationships that have developed between not only legal and illegal global economies, but also between these and resource predation and conflict. *Conflict diamonds* have brought together the international diamond market with various transnational networks that have links with rebel groups in this regionally based African trade (mainly Sierra Leonean and Angolan). This is paralleled by the trade in illicit drug production and trafficking networks that remain dominated by the 'golden crescent' and the 'golden triangle' respectively (Bourne 2001). The complexity of such

[11] A good example of this was the support the Reagan government gave to Nicaraguan Contra rebels to fight the Sandinista government in the 1980s. The Soviet Union provided military training, arms and ammunition to Western European groups such as the Italian Red Brigades and the German Baader-Meinhof gang. See L. Napoleoni (2005) 'The new economy of terror' openDemocracy, www.opendemocracy.net/node/2321

relationships can be accounted for by the fact that criminal trafficking in diamonds, arms and drugs for example often takes place alongside other legitimate transactions and therefore 'criminal activity and legitimate commerce act in mutually complementary ways' (Naylor 2003: 50). Moreover, it is not the commodity in itself that is at issue (the same illegal weapons, diamonds or drugs are also sold legitimately) but rather the 'boundaries of permission' to use Findlay's term (1999: 54 cited in Whyte 2009). It is the particular form regulation takes that will influence the existence of legal and illegal markets – so while both markets are trading in the same commodities, regulation and policing will deem one market illegal, the other legal. Ruggiero (2000 cited in Whyte 2009) argues that this scenario mirrors that of the organisations that produce and distribute these commodities since whilst there is no intrinsic difference in the commodities themselves, their legal or illegal status during the buying and selling of such commodities will depend on the 'boundaries of permission'.

The coexistence of parallel global economies (legal and illegal) has been shown to overlap, especially when resources like diamonds and their association with conflict is involved (Duffield in Berdal and Malone 2000). The trade in conflict diamonds could not exist without the legal wholesale and retail markets to absorb and move these illicitly mined stones often supplied by international criminal networks and rebel groups or 'terrorists'[12]. Aside from the use of private security to secure resources like diamonds, the movement of illicit Sierra Leonean diamonds during the civil war relied on various external and internal players who could access both *legitimate* and *criminal* networks (Duffield cited in Berdal and Malone 2000, Gamba and Cornwell cited in Berdal and Malone 2000).

In global terms, various 'middlemen' have been identified as providing an important link between illicitly mined stones and legal markets. According to *Le Monde* (June 2000), these include Lebanese in West Africa, Israelis in Southern Africa and Belgians in the Great Lakes region (Bourne 2001). The involvement of such middlemen in the trading process makes accountability difficult since it is near impossible to accurately trace the movement of diamonds across the globe (Global Witness 1998). Historically, Lebanese business used their contacts with the Middle East and Europe to market diamonds and raise capital. Individual Lebanese like Yazbeck and Jamil[13] had allowed the former leader of Sierra Leone, Siaka Stevens, access to these business links with Lebanon that dated back to illicit trading pre-1973 when the need to finance illegal activities had

---

[12] 'Terrorist' is a loaded and contested term, and open to debate. Interestingly, Hezbollah, the Lebanese paramilitary group is designated as a 'terror' group by the US State Department while the European Union does not define them in such terms.

[13] Jamil Mohammed was an Afro-Lebanese diamond dealer born in Port Loko who had been active in Kono since the 1960s. He had been the co-director of the GDO with Stevens in the 1980s and became one of the largest private exporters of diamonds in Sierra Leone. He had also acted as managing directors of NDMC 1979 to 1985. Jamil fled to London in 1987 after being implicated in a failed coup plot against President Momoh. See Reno, W. (1995) *Corruption and State Politics in Sierra Leone*, Cambridge University Press.

compelled them to contact overseas banking services. Such contacts proved useful to Stevens and other politicians as ways of financing private diamond exports that circumvented the official government's contract with the DeBeers' Central Selling Organisation (CSO). By the early 1980s, Lebanese banks like Byblos Bank and Jammal Bank were used to finance illicit exports. The establishment in Freetown of the International Bank of Trade and Industry in cooperation with Byblos Bank and the Bank of Credit and Commerce International dealt with private export financing that was considered to be illicit by other banks like Barclays who had refused credit to those who went outside of the official CSO (Reno 1995).

Israel's involvement with Africa has been steadily increasing since the 1980s through its intelligence training and as a supplier of military hardware, especially since the end of the Cold War. Israel continues to have links with various sectors in Africa that include government, private and surreptitious organisations (Smith 2003). In 1988 the Israeli N.R. SCIPA Group under Nir Guaz entered Sierra Leone's diamond industry through the alleged financing of legal and illegal export of local diamonds. SCIPA agreed to import rice with the profits (legal and illegal) from diamond exports. In 1989, SCIPA claimed to have imported 27,000 tons of rice and promised a further 80,000 tons in 1990. SCIPA's presence in Sierra Leone rivalled that of the Lebanese and was used by some politicians to gain greater independence from Lebanese business to market diamonds. President Momoh himself saw the benefits of SCIPA's rice imports that could be used to buy presidential clients who speculated on the rice market. This also gave Momoh alternative resources outside rival Lebanese control (Reno 1995). SCIPA stepped in to aid Momoh's Government on more than one occasion. In 1989 for example, SCIPA reportedly paid the ministry of works three months overdue salaries in return for the use of their heavy equipment in the diamond fields. Moreover, in the same year SCIPA made two arrears payment to the IMF of $500,000 and $5 million (Reno 1995). Yet the low level of formal-sector export of diamonds (around $6 million) by the company convinced Momoh that SCIPA was doing business with the president's political rivals and had Guaz arrested on Christmas Eve, 1989 for 'economic sabotage'. He was later released (Reno 1995).

When civil war broke out in Sierra Leone in the early 1990s, opportunities for 'business' in what was to become a 'criminalised war economy' were indeed strengthened. This served to:

> [...] create opportunities for building covert strategic alliances between warlords, politicians, regional leaders, multinational companies and even peacekeepers. These alliances form the networks that allow the trading in diamonds and the return trade in arms and ammunition. They operate at different levels from within the conflict state to regional or global networks. (Bourne 2001: 10)

In 2000, Partnership Africa (a Canadian NGO) published its damning report '*The Heart of the Matter*' that was highly critical of the deep seated government corruption in Sierra Leone and blamed this for encouraging illicit mining and becoming involved in criminal or near criminal activities. The report also targetted De Beers, the diamond buying processes in Belgium and the role of Liberian warlord and President Charles Taylor who 'acted as banker, weapons supplier, trainer and mentor to the RUF' (Smillie and Gberie 2001: 2). Initial reactions to the report from the diamond industry and some governments were not only hostile and uncooperative but were dismissive of some of its claims. It took unfolding developments, including a report from the UN on Angolan blood diamonds (UN Fowler Report, March 2000) that precipitated discussion on Sierra Leone, and legislation in the US (2000) aimed at halting the flow of illicit diamonds there, that eventually saw the industry and respective governments embracing initiatives like the Kimberley Process. The adverse publicity that came out of such reports as the *Heart of the Matter* (Partnership Africa Canada 2000) could threaten to disrupt the profits and the reputation of this industry, as had happened with the fur industry several years before. It was this fear that prompted De Beers by the middle of 2000 to withdraw from buying diamonds in Africa and to deal only with those mines and companies that it owned or partly owned (Smillie and Gberie 2001).

Findlay (1999) provides a broader context within which clandestine trading operations and their links with the formal economy can be understood. He argues that global economic development results in socio-economic disparity that opens up greater opportunities for global crime. The growth of international crime can be seen as 'a natural response to the pressures of development' since a close relationship exists between international interests in certain or selective forms of development and the growth of certain forms of criminal activity (ibid.: 59). Crime then can be promoted through what he calls the 'politics of development' since regulated market structures are not always as profitable as illegal commercial enterprise. Findlay explains:

> Where profit opportunities exist under regulated conditions which favour restricted access to profit opportunities, and where the accountability of regulators is limited or highly conditional, then criminal enterprise (because of its structure) will have a competitive edge over legitimate business. This is because criminal enterprise is also not bound by the legitimate regulations of the market. (Findlay 1999: 80)

For Findlay, criminal economic enterprise thrives in market conditions where some form of regulation exists since this in turn minimises who can and cannot participate. Where criminal enterprise is regulated and controlled, for example in the case of conflict diamonds, this has consequences for the diamond market in terms of supply, distribution and price. In other words, attempts to control illicit enterprise in turn influences market conditions and creates further opportunities for criminal enterprise. Findlay (ibid.) uses the example of drug trafficking to illustrate this point:

> Where the law generally prohibits trade in a particular drug, but law enforcement concentrates on the lower end of the distribution chain, small-time drug dealers are squeezed out of the market to the benefit of the better-organised and capital-resourced traders. (Findlay ibid.: 142)

Controlling criminal enterprise is a double edge sword since attempts to reduce opportunities for some creates openings for others. Findlay (ibid.) advocates crime control strategies that work against profitable market conditions. This is based on the premise that in undermining the market profitability of a particular illegal product this will work against profit as an incentive for future criminal activity. If the profit motive is undermined, this will in turn diminish the incentive of those ready to take over from previous criminal organisations. Moreover, undermining the profit motive of a particular trade or industry will additionally weaken the link between organised crime and corruption since the former relies on a degree of corruption within government and criminal justice agencies to regulate the market. Weakening the links between criminal organisations and corruption will also serve to weaken the links between corruption and legitimate business (ibid.).

Castells' (1998) concept of a 'global criminal economy' demonstrates how international ethnic/cultural networks are utilised by global criminals in their trades in drugs, illegal weapons, migrants, sex workers, money laundering, nuclear materials, oil and natural resources. Profits made here are reinvested or 'laundered' in legal economic activities (ibid.). The flexibility of these networks enables such activities to bypass state controls and national regulation. If money is used in such transactions this occurs through computerized exchange systems. Moreover, Castells alerts us to the potential for criminal networks to bribe and intimidate government officials and other law enforcement agents and of the threat such groups pose to democratic politics itself. Criminal gangs can give much needed support (financial and otherwise) to politicians during political campaigns. Naylor (1995) explains how:

> Today, however, clandestine business activities of all sorts have broken through the traditional constraints, and have developed rapidly in terms of technical and commercial sophistication. From 'recreational drugs' to counterfeit credit cards, from fake designer watches to stolen diamonds, it is no longer the operation of this or that individual black market. Rather, there has emerged a veritable underground economy consisting of a set of interrelated black markets supported by their own sources of supply, their own systems of information, their own distribution networks and their own modes of financing. This does not add up to a monolithic criminal conspiracy. Modern black markets are complex, but they are not integrated into neat monopolies or cartels. If they were, they would be easier to control. Instead of an organizational hierarchy one finds a series of arms-length commercial relationships. (Naylor 1995: 20)

'Arms-length commercial relationships' (including corrupt business and political practices) hit the headline news in 2005. A senior British Tory MP, Tony Baldry was exposed in the *Sunday Times* (27 March 2005) for attempting to use his position (as Chairman of the Commons International Development Committee that aims to alleviate poverty in the Third World) to make up to £1.5m for his own company. Baldry received payment by a diamond firm – Milestone Trading (a UK-registered company owned by two Israeli's) to lobby the Sierra Leone government to secure diamond concessions during two visits there in 2005.[14] In addition, Baldry used House of Commons notepaper to write to the International Development Minister – Hilary Benn – asking for Milestone Trading to be given a 'best practice' seal of approval. For his efforts, £40,000 was paid into Red Eagle Resources plc, of which Baldry is a non-executive chairman and a one-third shareholder. Baldry also brokered a deal for his firm to take a 3 per cent share in Milestone (estimated to be worth £1.5m.) when the company was floated later in 2005, though this was not declared. As alarm bells were set off in the Foreign Office, they decided to look into the company's involvement in Sierra Leone and unveiled a series of alleged human rights abuses at two of its alluvial diamond mines in the areas of Sandoh and Nimikoro. Moreover, the United Mineworkers Union in Sierra Leone claimed that workers in these mines were paid only £1 per day and were denied adequate water and accommodation (*Sunday Times* March 27 2005).

Five years earlier in December 2000, the UN found that despite imposing an arms and diamond embargo with Sierra Leone, international criminal networks were being used by the governments of Liberia and Burkino Faso to contravene this. Aircraft owned by Russian businessman Victor Bout delivered arms from Europe to Liberia. The same Victor Bout had also supplied UNITA rebels in Angola and opposition groups in the Democratic Republic of Congo (Amnesty International 2002). By the beginning of the twenty first century, it would seem that West Africa was powerless to stem such developments:

> Armed opposition groups receive arms and ammunition through interlinked networks of traders, criminals and insurgents moving across borders. Systematic information on the smuggling of arms and ammunition in the region is non-existent, and information which could be used to combat the problem on a regional scale, through ECOWAS or through bilateral exchanges, is generally not available. Few counties in the region have the resources or the infrastructure to tackle smuggling. (Amnesty International 2002 3)

What was true of arms was also true of diamonds. During the civil war, large amounts of diamonds from Sierra Leone were disguised as Liberian,

---

[14] Tony Baldry is reported to have extensive commercial interests and long-standing links with Sierra Leone, forged during his time in London with former colleague and barrister President Ahmad Kabbah. Baldry was also head of chambers that acts for the Sierra Leone government in Britain. See the *Sunday Times*, 27 March 2005, 'Tory MP in £1.5m diamond mine row'.

Guinean and Gambian in origin and were traded through 'legitimate' channels in Europe in the full knowledge that these were conflict diamonds. An Antwerp diamond trader admitted to Amnesty International in October 2000 (after the ban on non-certified stones from Sierra Leone):

> If someone offers me a diamond at 30 percent discount, will I suspect something? Of course. It is probably a conflict diamond. Will I buy it? Of course. I'm here to do business. Have I done it? I can't tell you that. (Amnesty International 2002: 4)

By 2003, a small group of dealers and merchants whose economic positions had been strengthened during the civil war there now controlled around 85 per cent of the Sierra Leone diamond market. Their increased economic power has enabled them to influence domestic economic and political agendas that have significant political ramifications for democratic processes in Sierra Leone. These are not necessarily the 'criminal networks' that Castells has identified , but such individuals (many of them Lebanese) do have strong ties to other countries and networks that enable them to dispose of hundreds of millions of dollars through an 'invisible' or parallel economy. Representatives of Freetown's Lebanese community have denied allegations of links (direct and indirect) with Hizbullah, Hamas and Fatah in recent years (Even-Zohar 2003, Gberie 2002). However, according to Global Witness (2000) between the late 1970s and early 1990s, different factions in the Lebanese civil war were being supported through diamond revenues accrued by Sierra Leone's Lebanese community.

There is also evidence to suggest that individuals with links to al-Qaeda (as agents or otherwise) have been involved in the buying of Sierra Leone rough diamonds in the recent past (See *Washington Post* cited in Even-Zohar 2003). Mitchell (2005) argues that a group of around five Lebanese families dominate the diamond industry in Sierra Leone today, including the Mackie family who control an estimated 40 per cent. Mitchell (ibid.) argues that the majority of Lebanese in Sierra Leone operate legitimate businesses though the existence of a minority that have been involved with Hizbullah or criminal activities has served to unfairly blame the whole community for criminal behaviour.

Other so-called 'legitimate' channels are flouting measures like the Kimberley Process in their dealings with diamonds. Large companies likes De Beers, which controls about 65 per cent of the total rough diamond trade claims that all of its stock is Kimberley compliant (*The Times* Feb 20, 2003). However, the head of Britain's diamond office, Clive Wright believes the Kimberley Process lacks the ability to monitor itself, especially when some countries do not raise enough tax from diamond exports to make implementing the scheme worthwhile. (*BBC News Online* Feb 21, 2003). Moreover, as Christine Gordon (part of a United Nations monitoring programme in Angola) explains: 'Some companies are honest but other companies want to buy diamonds and where they come from is of little or no concern' (*BBC News Online* Feb 21, 2003).

In a another recent report, *Broken Vows* published by Global Witness (March 2006) this shows that the American diamond jewellery retail sectors (which accounts for over half of global diamond jewellery retail sales) are not implementing basic measures of self-regulation. Nor, it has been shown, is the World Diamond Council (the body responsible for coordinating industry's efforts to combat conflict diamonds) monitoring compliance with self-regulation.[15] Whilst the Kimberley certification scheme committed prominent and key players in the diamond industry to ensure that only legally mined rough diamonds would reach the market, evidence suggests this has been flouted. In the US for example, it was found in 2004 that the diamond jewellery sector (that accounts for over half of all retailed diamond jewellery) was inadequately self-regulated. Moreover, the World Diamond Council – the body invested with this responsibility was not adequately monitoring compliance with self-regulation. As Global Witness stated in their report on this:

> As the public face of the industry, diamond jewellery retailers have a special responsibility not just to comply with the self-regulation but also to ensure that their suppliers are in full compliance. [...]Anything less means that diamonds can continue to fuel conflict, human rights abuses and terrorism. (Global Witness 2004: 1)

In a recent survey of UK diamond jewellery retailers undertaken by Global Witness and Amnesty International UK (May 2007), it was found that lack of effective policies are failing to combat the trade in conflict diamonds. More than three-quarters (79 per cent) of those who responded to the survey reported having no auditing procedures in place to combat this trade. It would seem that:

> After all the promises the diamond industry has made it is very disappointing to find that retailers here in the UK are still not taking the necessary steps to ensure the diamond supply chain is cleaned up from mine to shop counter. (Nick Dearden, Amnesty International UK Business and Human Rights Campaigner – See Global Witness & Amnesty International UK, June 2007)

Part of the problem appears to be the lack of rigorous regulation within the industry itself. Therefore, whilst many jewellery retailers show evidence of adhering to systems of warranties and self-regulation, these are not stringent enough. Calls for companies to go beyond existing standards by enforcing third-party auditing measures are seen as crucial if existing warranty systems are to be credible and effective in combating conflict diamonds (Global Witness & Amnesty International 2007).

A UN Expert Panel's report (2000) noted that import procedures had facilitated not only the funding of UNITA but other rebel groups like the RUF in Sierra Leone. In the three major diamond trading centres

---

[15] Global Witness see www.globalwitness.org/report/show.php/en.00050.html for copy of full report.

(Antwerp, London and Tel Aviv) lack of regulation and a tradition of dealing through 'honour and trust' allowed for the entry of conflict diamonds into the legal retail and wholesale markets. Moreover, the self-monitoring of the industry through the Diamond High Council results in a conflict of interests since neutrality cannot be assured. Indeed, Antwerp has become one of the world centres for Russian organized crime attracted by lax controls and opportunities for fraud and corruption (Bourne 2001, Smillie et al. 2000).

The Kimberley Process Certification Scheme (KPCS) emerged out of such concerns in January 2003. Whilst this has meant the introduction of tamper proof certificates of origin for sealed packets of diamonds, this still relies on the co-operation of importing states. International pressure has led to some co-operation in Antwerp but not in Tel Aviv (Bourne 2001). The issue is whether existing systems of controls can ensure accountability and prevent conflict diamonds entering the 'legal' retail trade. A system of standardised global certification and monitoring has been endorsed by many, but some countries and large companies like De Beers continue to flout such procedures and trade in illegal diamonds. Counterfeit certificates are also easily available in places like Cote D'Ivoire and Togo (Mitchell 2005). As recently as December 2006, conflict diamonds from the rebel-held areas of the Ivory Coast were finding their way to international diamond markets. This was in contravention of a UN embargo on all diamonds from here (Global Witness & Amnesty International 2007). The United Nations reported that up to \$23 million of conflict diamonds from here entered the legitimate trade in diamonds through Ghana and Mali. Diamonds also continue to be used by crime networks, for money laundering and tax evasion (Global Witness Nov 2006).

In October 2007, a newly elected government came to power in Sierra Leone under President Ernest Bai Koroma. The newly appointed minister of mines, Alhaji Abubakarr Jalloh announced soon after that in a review of all mining agreements, corrupt and illegal mining firms operating under the pretence of 'exploration permits' while illegally mining would be rooted out. In addition, with the aid of the British government's development department, the overhaul of Sierra Leone's mining sector would also include the targeting of corrupt government civil servants (Reuters 1 November 2007).

Conclusion

The war in Sierra Leone and the continued decline in the socio-economic position of the majority of its people have to be understood in broader global terms and in particular, resource predation, especially of diamonds. However, the conflict here also has to take into account specific internal conditions, like patrimonialism and mismanagement of the country's resources by sections of the elite (as well as the role of other players inside the country).[16] The brutality of the RUF reflected the brutality of life in Sierra Leone but in a far worse and twisted form. The acquisition of diamonds became increasingly central to the RUF as a currency to pay for weapons supplied by foreign backers. The supply of foreign arms in return for diamonds enabled the RUF at certain points of the war to strengthen and perpetuate their control of the diamond areas (through killings, mutilations, abductions and other atrocities). Indeed the war became a struggle for the control of the country's resources, particularly diamonds. In so doing they could supply their foreign backers with these sought after precious stones. Such commodities did not then disappear but entered the global market through various avenues.

Conflict and other illicit diamonds from Sierra Leone and elsewhere have become an integral part of the global economy through transnational networks linking rebels and criminal networks with the international diamond market. The intricate relationships that exist between civil wars, state collapse and the global political economy including criminal networks has to be acknowledged in the first instance if such issues are to be seriously addressed. Underdevelopment, resource predation and state collapse opens up important economic opportunities for international criminal groups. Here, the boundaries of economic activity move from the informal to the formal and from the illegal to legal. Therefore, any future development of states such as Sierra Leone has to be committed to economic stability, regional security and an engagement with state strengthening if future criminal international predation and civil war is to be avoided (Mitchell 2005). Moreover, because of the intricate and symbiotic links that the global political economy exhibits, developments in one part of the world have ramifications on the rest. As Mitchell states:

A neglected war in a neglected region on a neglected continent still has international repercussions. In a globalised economy, with globalised organised crime and globalised insurgents such as al Qaeda, no corner of the world can be ignored as Sierra Leone was. (Mitchell 2005: 31)

---

[16] Talking to activists from MOCKY in Kiodu town against illegal diamond smuggling, Lebanese and *Maracchas* from Banjul and Mali were seen to be the worst offenders.

Conclusion: The New 'Scramble for Africa' | Diamonds: 'A Blessing or a Curse'?

> Our approach to the continent is riddled with contradictions. We pour in billions in aid while erecting trade barriers that squeeze out African firms. We encourage land tenure in Africa, then drive farmers out of business by dumping cheap produce. We pay lip service to good governance, then prop up repressive regimes, do deals with despots and allow our banks to launder their plunder. We retain prohibitive drugs laws that are spreading chaos through some West African states, having wrecked parts of South and Latin America already. Then we complain when migrants flee the consequent poverty and unrest. (Birrell 2009)

This work began by examining the social, economic and political role that diamonds have played in Sierra Leone's development since the 1930s. A main conceptual question implicit in attempting to understand this history is the extent to which diamonds here represent what Ross (1999) has termed a *resource curse* – used more generally to explain the position of countries rich in mineral resources yet afflicted by extreme poverty and underdevelopment. Despite over 80 years of diamond exploitation (alongside other resources and minerals), Sierra Leone continues to exist on the margins of global development. For much of this history, diamond production formed part of what has been described as 'a dual economy' 'composed of a developed and isolated export sector and an underdeveloped economy in general' (Bangura and Dumbuya 1993: 91).

We have seen that the early years of diamond discovery and exploitation began under British colonial rule and continued during independence. After several decades of political misrule followed by economic collapse, the ensuing civil war would see diamonds becoming an integral part of this conflict. The war in Sierra Leone became part of a wider regional conflict here that was largely ignored by the international community and only became news headlines as controversy over *blood diamonds* entering the legitimate global trade in rough stones was gradually exposed.

The illicit nature of this trade appears to have been a consistent pattern present throughout the history of Sierra Leonean diamonds which began many decades before the civil conflict. Indeed, since its very inception in the 1930s, the diamond industry has been characterised by illegal and illicit practices. Indeed initially under the British, the colonial authorities made it illegal for Sierra Leoneans to be in possession of diamonds and became increasingly preoccupied with trying to police the diamond areas. At the same time many Sierra Leoneans believed that a foreign colonial power like Britain had no moral or legitimate right to take the wealth contained in the land that belonged to Sierra Leoneans. Controlling illicit digging and dealing set a precedent for future patterns of exploitation that continued throughout this nation's history in various different guises. At the same time, Sierra Leone's emerging ruling class continued to exploit the nation's resources post independence partly for its own personal aggrandisement and partly to buy political power.

This work has largely been about Sierra Leone but it has demonstrated that this trade goes beyond the borders of this tiny state. Indeed, any analysis of this industry necessitates a broader examination of the structures and conditions within which the industry operates both inside and outside Sierra Leone. A number of characteristics relating to Sierra Leone's historical economic and political development have been identified that may help us understand the position it occupies today. This includes the emergence of patterns of economic dependency that mainly relate to agents external to the country as well as political relationships based on patrimony inside the country. Since independence, Sierra Leone has continued to rely on external capital in relation to extractive industries like diamonds and which subsequently feed into 'development' issues more generally. Moreover, we have seen how political relationships emerged from within the parameters of what has been termed a shadow state – spawned during the colonial era and sustained by an internal elite who in turn drew sustenance from the corrupt proceeds of diamond production. As the elite continued to serve the needs of the former colonial power, it simultaneously looked after its own political and economic interests. In the meantime, the mass of Sierra Leoneans endured deeper levels of impoverishment, inequality and disenfranchisement, made worse by structural adjustment policies (SAP) that were implemented in many developing nations throughout the 1980s (Killick 1994). SAP policies undermined economic diversification and further increased dependence on primary products (Simon et al. 1995 cited in Castells 1998). This in turn reinforced economic dependency on IFI and aid, perpetuated a liberal model of development (as pursued by the IMF) whilst simultaneously and inadvertently strengthening the shadow state inside Sierra Leone. Taken together, these factors helped sow the seeds of civil conflict that produced and sustained for at least a decade, an economy of blood diamonds. Such economic dependency on the IFI continued throughout the war period. Between 1992 and 2002 Sierra Leone received in excess of £150m in aid from Britain in part to tackle corruption.[1] According to Dowden (2002) this made Sierra Leone one of the highest recipients of British aid in 2002 with promises of further aid and funds for peacekeeping.

Since then and despite having an abundance of mineral wealth, the story of Sierra Leone has been a continuous cycle of debt and aid seen in an array of initiatives that have come from the IFI like the World Bank and the IMF. Therefore any analysis of the diamond industry in Sierra Leone today is integral to wider questions of development. By 2006, the World Bank and the IMF agreed that Sierra Leone had sufficiently progressed under the Enhanced Heavily Indebted Poor Countries (HIPC) initiative that further debt relief[2] could be given (World Bank 2007). In 2007, the United States cancelled a debt of $58 million out of a share of $363 million owed by Sierra Leone to the Paris Club group of donor countries (*The Independent* 2007). The World Bank's 'Country Assistance Strategy' 2006–2009[3] (2005) was part of its Poverty Reduction Strategy Paper for Sierra Leone (SLPRSP) (World Bank May 2005) and both of these came out of the *Millennium Development Goals* (MDGs). Some successes have been reported by DFID since the end of the conflict in 2002 including the maintenance of peace and security; declining child mortality rates from 284 per 1000 in 1999 to 265 per 1000 in 2004 and the doubling of primary school enrolment rates since 2003 following the abolition of fees in 2002 (DFID November 2005). Former Secretary of State for International Development Hilary Benn explained in 2005:

> Our commitment to Sierra Leone remains strong. The country has made significant progress in rebuilding the general machinery of government and in introducing reforms to help sustain peace, stability and encourage further economic growth. The government has demonstrated its commitment to combat corruption by creating an Anti-Corruption Commission and introducing new procurement rules. But more work is needed to tackle corruption and ensure that services reach the poor, progress which is essential if the Poverty Reduction Budget Support Programme is to be realised. Although good progress has been made in some areas such as increasing school enrolments rates, Sierra Leone is

[1] However, it soon became apparent that the work of the anti-corruption commission (ACC) was being undermined by the then newly installed Kabbah government that returned to power in May 2002. Evidence emerged that the head of the ACC was instructed to drop a case against a government minister who was in possession of approximately £25,000 worth of illegal diamonds. Moreover, the practice of warning government personnel of ACC intentions to raid offices or accounts so that evidence could be removed, have also surfaced. See Dowden, R. (2002) 'Sierra Leone locked in shackles of corruption' *The Guardian* 12 October.
[2] Debt relief was given from the IMF, World Bank's International Development Association (IDA), and the African Development Fund (AfDF) under the Multilateral Debt Relief Initiative (MDRI) World Bank 2007.
[3] The fragility of Sierra Leone's post-conflict recovery and the continuing deep-seated issues of poverty (around 70 per cent of the population fall below the poverty line); severe gender inequality, high unemployment (especially affecting urban youth), weak governance and poor infrastructure was recognised by the World Bank and informed policy here.

still a way off Millennium Development Goal targets in others, such as maternal mortality... (DFID November 2005)

There have been various ongoing initiatives that have attempted to regulate the international diamond trade and promote peace and development. This includes the Diamond Sector Reform Programme (DSRP) that initiated a strategy for ensuring that diamonds are used to promote peace and economic development and to prevent their use in future conflict. The main thrust of this initiative is to effect change in the structures and processes of the Kono diamond industry through involvement of various key sectors. These include donors (USAID, DFID and the World Bank), the Government of Sierra Leone, the Peace Diamond Alliance (PDA, composed of traditional leaders, international NGOs, industry and community-based organisations) and a US development consultancy organisation, Management Systems International (MSI)[4] (Levin 2005). Other initiatives include the establishment of an anti-corruption commission and the enforcement of the Kimberley Process to regulate diamond exports. The anti-corruption commission was established to begin the process of exposing and then tackling corruption amongst government officials, namely civil servants and ministers. While diamond trade revenue has increased in past years, at the same time, continued smuggling has led to a decrease of official exports from US$140 million in 2005 to US$120 million in 2006. Two main groups benefit most from illicit diamond dealings – sections of the nation's elite who benefit at the expense of the poor, and commercial interests who have no qualms about being involved in what has been described as 'organized illegality' in the global economy (Ferguson 2006). Extractive industries appear to be especially prone to such corrupt practices (AAPPG 2006).

Although it is no longer appropriate to use the term *blood diamonds* with reference to Sierra Leonean stones, by the end of 2006, six years after the Kimberley Process scheme was introduced to regulate such stones, there were clear indicators that this was being flouted internationally. Not only have *conflict diamonds* come out of rebel-held territories in Ivory Coast (despite a UN embargo on all diamond from here), but it would seem the Kimberley Process Certification Scheme (KPCS) has been violated through the smuggling of diamonds from Zimbabwe into South Africa and through the illegal smuggling of Venezuelan rough diamonds into the US, Belgium, Guyana and elsewhere (Global Witness & Amnesty International June 2007). Indeed, despite controls and Kimberley Process regulations operating in Ghana for example, evidence suggests that this country has become a repository for conflict diamonds from neighbouring Ivory Coast. According to Amnesty International (2006), a report of a UN Group of Experts on Côte d'Ivoire (October 2006) concluded that conflict diamonds

[4] Management Systems International became involved in Sierra Leone under the auspices of USAID to assist peace building. It has been involved in the Peace Diamond Alliance; the Diamond Policy and Management Project and the Integrated Diamond Management Model of Resource Governance. See Levin, E, A. (2005).

from Côte d'Ivoire were infiltrating the legitimate diamond trade through Ghana, a Kimberley Process participant. Conflict diamonds worth up to $23 million have been smuggled from the rebel controlled areas in northern Côte d'Ivoire into Ghana where they have been certified as conflict-free due to Ghana's weak system of internal controls (Amnesty International 2006 cited in Hilson and Clifford 2010).

As well as the KPCS's inability to regulate the supply of conflict diamonds from Côte d'Ivoire and elsewhere, an additional weakness is the scheme's failure to regulate illicit gems from Sierra Leone and elsewhere that enter the legal and illegal global trade in diamonds. Instead, the scheme has focussed on the marketing side of the industry rather than the supply side (Hilson and Clifford 2010). Having said that whilst diamond retailers have adopted minimum standards of self-regulation and warranties, it is far from clear how such warranties are implemented and how far these are effective. In a survey carried out by Global Witness & Amnesty International (2007), only 21 per cent of respondents reported having auditing measures in place to ensure supplies of diamonds are responsibly sourced over and above the written warranty. The report concludes:

> The diamond industry must go beyond the voluntary standards agreed upon to eradicate conflict diamonds. The survey results show that there are few industry leaders in the UK jewellery retail sector working to achieve this, but that most large companies are not doing enough. It also calls into question how seriously other sectors of the diamond industry further up the chain are implementing policies to combat blood diamonds. (2007: 9)

This has led to calls for the need for all sectors of the diamond industry to introduce 'third party auditing measures and responsible sourcing policies' as well as greater enforcement of the Kimberley Process by the EU and the UK Government (Global Witness & Amnesty International 2007: 9).

How far then have such initiatives led to improvements in Sierra Leone's position today? To what extent has nearly 80 years of diamond exploitation, millions of dollars of aid and loans, and numerous strategies aimed at poverty reduction, reconstruction and political stability helped Sierra Leone's development? The picture that is emerging is both alarming and depressing as Sierra Leone continues to depend on international aid and borrowing for its survival despite its mineral wealth. Today, only around 58 per cent of this nation's urban population and 21 per cent of the rural population have access to safe water. An estimated 220 per 1000 children in Sierra Leone will die before their fifth birthday. Those that survive will invariably suffer from malaria and the secondary infections that can follow. Many do not have access to continuous primary school during their developing years nor proceed to continuous secondary education. Those who do are fortunate, as indeed are those who benefit from basic primary health care. It is little wonder that life expectancy in Sierra Leone is one of the lowest in the world at 48 years for males and 49 years for females.[5]

In a broader global context, Sierra Leone's position is merely one of many where the picture is equally alarming. In the global South more generally, over 1 billion adults are illiterate and the same number live in absolute poverty. Many are deprived of primary health care (one and a half billion) (UNDP, *Human Development Report* 2007/2008). In addition, the South is dependent on the North for investments, for access to markets in the North, for technology transfer, and for consultants. At the same time, the North contains approximately a quarter of the world's population, consumes 70 per cent of the world's energy; 60 per cent of its food; 75 per cent of its metals and 85 per cent of its wood. This then is the wider context within which marginalised nations like Sierra Leone operate and where the free market in mineral wealth has resulted in increasing inequalities rather than greater wealth.

An important characteristic of this is the intensification of capital accumulation – part of a broader process of globalisation. This includes an unrestricted 'free market', the promotion of universal and uniform economic growth and a process of homogenisation (as seen in the undermining of local diversity and its replacement with carbon copy uniformity through consumption patterns and behaviour). Many of the natural resources to fuel this economic growth come from the developing world (the coffee beans for retail outlets like Costa and Starbucks or the diamonds used in engagement rings sold in Europe and America). The cultivation of coffee or the mining of diamonds for the export market often has adverse effects. Price fluctuations make such markets unstable. Moreover, production for the export market can often lead to a distortion of production patterns for local consumption (for example turning over prime agricultural land for diamond mining). Such developments prioritise corporate interests over local needs as increased levels of economic exploitation and profiteering becomes the order of the day. Sierra Leone has become part of a wider pattern of corporate neo-colonialism that operates through the financial clout of the corporation as power is secured through trade, production and financial contributions to political friends.

It was Nkrumah (1968) that first developed a concept of 'neo-colonialism' in the aftermath of political independence in Africa in the 1960s. He described it in the following terms:

> The essence of neo-colonialism is that the State which is subject to it is, in theory, independent and has all the outward trappings of international sovereignty. In reality its economic system and thus its political policy is directed from outside. (Nkrumah 1968: ix)

Indeed, a 2010 BBC report for *Newsnight* (23 June 'Can Britain lift Sierra

---

[5] UN Statistics (2011) Social Indicators, based on figures for 2010–2015 – http://unstats.un.org/unsd/demographic/products/Soclnd/

Leone out of poverty?') found British influence in Sierra Leone to be far greater today in terms of direct political involvement than it has been since British colonialism ended in the early 1960s. This could be seen in the way British officials monitor the main offices of state in Sierra Leone through the scrutinising and supervision of ministers' activities and through the influence of European-style governance (Little 2010). However, in the new world order that has developed in recent years, a new 'scramble' for Africa's resources is taking place. The exploitation of Sierra Leonean diamonds has to be seen as part of this wider scramble for Africa's precious resource that includes amongst others, oil. Indeed, the continuing influence of corporate neo-colonialism can be seen in the example of the 'oil-for-infrastructure' deals that have been noted involving Chinese state companies brokering deals for Angolan oil (*The Times* 12 Nov 2009). Indeed, it is expected that the US will receive a quarter of its crude oil imports from West Africa by 2015 (Simms 2009).

A number of key issues have emerged that relate to the struggle for resources, particularly oil. First, the fight against terrorism has become a major preoccupation of Western governments. The 'war on terror' strategy, that emerged out of the attacks on the US in 2001 and elsewhere, saw Washington's relations with Africa (previously dominated by Cold War rivalries) now being influenced by this anti-terror stance. A central feature of this is the fear that failed African states could become breeding grounds for terrorists. This is particularly pertinent given the US need to secure future 'non-Islamic' oil and essential minerals (for military, political or economic purposes) in the light of the 2001 attacks (Royal Africa Society 2005). Second, the salience of corporate neo-colonialism in this new world order has seen a series of 'resource wars' as the pressures of global economic expansion compel corporations to search the globe for resources like oil (Tombs & Whyte 1998). Many conflicts in Africa (and elsewhere) have largely been concerned with controlling the supply and profits to be made from natural resource wealth (particularly minerals and including diamonds). Whilst resources or minerals like diamonds may not have been the initial cause of such conflicts, they have quickly become embroiled in such struggles. There are numerous examples where huge profits have been made out of the 'business of war'[6] including the many 'business opportunities' that arose during the conflict in Sierra Leone. The pursuit of profits became responsible for both financing (through illegal diamond trading) and sustaining this conflict through arms trading and private security. Finally, this 'new scramble' for resources is like history repeating itself as Africa's historic colonial role as provider of raw materials for the

---

[6] Thus in Angola, the government backed Popular Movement for the Liberation of Angola (MPLA) strengthened its business interests during the war here through the selling of weapons to opposition UNITA forces. Such collusion between warring factions has occurred elsewhere including Cambodia, Liberia and Bosnia where conflict has in fact been perpetuated because of economic gains (Berdal, M. and Malone, D.M. (eds) (2000), *Greed and Grievance – Economic Agendas in Civil Wars*, Boulder, Lynn Rienner: 5, 6).

developed world is now satisfying increased demand from the BRIC (Brazil, Russia, India and China) countries (Ferguson 2006).

A number of large multinational companies have ventured into sub-Saharan Africa in search of future oil reserves. These have involved oil-backed commercial loans between Western banks (like the Royal Bank of Scotland, Standard Charter and Barclays), and state owned oil companies like those in Angola, the second biggest oil producer in Africa (*The Guardian* June 2005). Africa has become 'a cornucopia of natural wealth to be mined, harvested, picked, squeezed and taken' (Simms 2009) as a whole host of natural resources are extracted. An additional feature of this is the large-scale transnational land acquisitions and leases or 'land-grabs' of Africa, spearheaded by wealthy nations in an attempt to secure future food reserves and bio fuels (Simms 2009). Such moves threaten to further undermine Africans' food security that is already precarious and represents an additional attack on the symbolic importance of land in Africa. As one Zimbabwean agricultural consultant explained: 'In Africa, far from being perceived as a mere economic resource, land has cultural, sentimental and political meanings and represents one of the strongest symbols of dispossession during the colonial era' (cited in Howden 2009). Indeed one UN official from the Food and Agricultural Organisation (FAO) explained such 'land-grabs' as: 'in the worst cases it's fair to say we are looking at neo-colonialism' (Hallam cited in Howden 2009). The 'scramble' for natural resources, whether oil, wood, land or precious stones like diamonds is being fuelled by consumption patterns in the developed world, with scant concern of the consequences of this on the developing world.

Contrary then to what the World Bank (1996) has claimed in past years that the issue of corruption and economic mismanagement have deterred foreign investors in Africa,[7] recent global interest in Africa's minerals and natural resources suggests the opposite. Foreign direct investment in Africa has significantly increased, especially in the last few decades (Mines and Communities May 2004). In Sierra Leone alone increased mining activity between 2007 and 2008 saw over 50 (non-artisanal) mining companies registered with the Ministry of Mineral Resources (February 2008 – see Maconachie 2008). This is the context within which Sierra Leone's diamond wealth has to be seen. Indeed, the pattern that is emerging throughout Africa and particularly in relation to oil is one of enclave development. Here, resources are not developed by the state for the benefit of the country but are exploited by private capital and safeguarded with private

[7] In past decades the World Bank blamed corruption and economic mismanagement for deterring foreign investors in Africa. Thus, in 1994, Africa contributed a mere 1,4 per cent of world trade compared to 3 per cent in the early 1960s. Between 1990 and 1995, external investors accounted for $830 million annually in comparison to $38 billion invested in China in 1995. Global agricultural exports from Africa stood at 17 per cent in 1970 and fell to 8 per cent in 1990. See World Bank, World Debt Tables, 1996 Washington DC: World Bank, 1996; M. Barrett-Brown & P. Tiffen (1992) *Short-Changed: Africa and World Trade* Statistical appendix. Both cited in Reno (1998): 50.

security, who represent companies in their own right. Such developments occur with the collusion of the political elites who continue to accrue personal wealth (Ferguson 2006) and buy political patronage. The wealth created from Angolan oil or Sierra Leonean diamonds has not been used for the betterment of those societies as both countries continue to occupy lowly positions in the UN Human Development Index.[8]

Sierra Leone today continues to be heavily dependent on extractive industries more generally, yet mining appears to be unpredictable and volatile. A World Development Report (2008) noted that official diamond exports were increasing, particularly with reference to Kimberlite reserves (that rely on foreign mining firms for extraction).

> With regards to diamonds, full-scale Kimberlite mining is on going in Koidu. This has contributed to the increase of official diamond exports from $121 million in 2004 to $149 million in 2005, with Kimberlite accounting for $113 million while alluvial mining accounted for the rest. (World Development Report 2008 – Annual Progress Report Sierra Leone Poverty Reduction Strategy Paper September 2006)

However, more recent reports suggest that industrial diamond mining has ceased in the country whilst alluvial mining appears constant. In 2004, diamonds accounted for 88 per cent of Sierra Leone's exports and 20 per cent of GDP (World Bank 2005) whilst mining more generally accounted for 30 per cent of the country's GDP in 2008, though much of this was artisanal and illegal (Extractive Industries Transparency Initiative EITI 2008).[9] By the beginning of 2007, alluvial mining accounted for 90 per cent of Sierra Leone's official diamond exports. However, in Kono, an area most affected by the war and the largest diamond producer in Sierra Leone, rural poverty stood at 79.6 per cent compared with 59.6 per cent in rural Pujehun District – a mainly agricultural area which also produces diamonds (Global Witness Oct 2007). This is in spite of a poverty reduction strategy that was incorporated into the country's Peacebuilding Commission launched in October 2006 that sought to address the cause of the recent conflict and to put in place strategies for future development and sustainable peace. Sierra Leone's mineral sector has been seen as key to the future stability and sustainable development of the country, yet claims that the effective management of this sector has been omitted from the Peacebuilding Commission's strategy has been criticised as a 'dangerous oversight' and undermining of peacebuilding efforts (ibid.). This is of particular concern in light of reports of persistent youth margin-

---

[8] Angola was rated 161 out of 173 in 2003 (Ferguson 2006: 198) and Sierra Leone 177 out of 177 based on 2005 data. See UNDP Human Development Index 2007. According to 2007 data, Sierra Leone ranked 180 out of 182 in the UN Human Development Index

[9] The Extractive Industries Transparency Initiative (EITI) is composed of a coalition of governments, companies, civil society groups, investors and international organisations. Its declared aim is to strengthen governance in resource-rich countries through publication of company payments and government revenue from oil, gas and mining. See http://eitransparency.org

alisation, 'low level conflict and increasing frustration amongst youth' in diamond areas and continuing tension surrounding corrupt management of diamond production.

Corporate neo-colonialism sustains a diamond economy in Sierra Leone today either through the (limited) industrial mining of these stones or, more significantly, through the buying and processing of artisanal rough diamonds. We have noted how the mark up value from one end of the diamond chain (remuneration paid to diggers) to the other (price of retail jewellery) can be as much as 500 per cent. This occurs in a context where Sierra Leone continues to have significant numbers of men and children involved in artisanal diamond digging (as opposed to industrial mining),[10] who live in absolute poverty with lack of electricity and decent homes. Many earn less than a dollar a day and work in dirty and dangerous conditions (Global Witness 2006). The artisanal diamond industry is dependent on men and children who sell any winnings for around a fifth of the worth when it leaves the country. The World Trade Organization (WTO) has reported on the alarming levels of child labour in Sierra Leone where long hours and harsh conditions were found in artisanal mining areas. Children involved in the digging and sifting of gravels worked in conditions that resembled slave labour. The review observed that: 'The overall statistics show that an overwhelming 71.6 per cent of children between the ages of 5 and 14 are working under unpaid conditions' (Seibureh 2005: 1). The International Labour Organisation (ILO 2003) had previously found the highest incidence of child work (between the ages of 5 and 14) was in sub-Saharan Africa where a total of 29 per cent worked.

Opportunities for crime

Both internal and external factors lie at the root of Sierra Leone's illicit mining and smuggling of diamonds. Internally, diggers and licensed miners have little incentive to hand over their winnings since prices paid by their financial supporters are too low[11] (Even-Zohar 2003). This is clearly not a deterrent to small-scale local smuggling. However, more serious are the external factors that actively facilitate large-scale smuggling in return for huge profits. As we have seen, economies like Sierra

[10] Many African countries are involved in artisanal mining where thousands are involved in digging out alluvial diamonds using crude picks, shovels, and sieves. This includes Sierra Leone, Liberia, Guinea, Côte d'Ivoire and the DRC. Botswana and South Africa mine their diamonds on an industrial scale. In the case of Botswana, diamonds here are concentrated in one location and are easy to secure. In South Africa, deep mining of Kimberlite diamonds necessitate the use of heavy plant machinery and explosives. See Global Witness (2006*) The Truth About Diamonds: Conflict and Development* November. Also Global Witness (2007) '*Peacebuilding Omission?'* October.
[11] Local diamond prices are set by the diamond cartel. See Even-Zohar (2003) 'Sierra Leone Diamond Sector Financial Policy Contraints', USAID.

Leone continue to rely on external capital that has links with both legal and illegal markets. Complex relationships involving private enterprise and national elites can be forged where legal and illegal boundaries are obscure and porous. As Duffield explains:

> There are many structural similarities between mafia organizations and private protection agencies, arising both from the qualification of nation-state competence and, especially, from its declining ability to enforce the rule of law. They both answer the growing needs of elites to protect themselves from internal rivals and, at the same time, to forge new linkages with the global economy. In relation to the politico-commercial nexus, the Russian mafia plays a similar role, for example, to private security companies concerning weak state rulers in Africa. Both couple the use of violence with extensive parallel and grey international networks of intermediaries and contacts. In this respect, there is an affinity between the networked, mutable and covert organisation of money laundering and the opaque and flexible corporate structure of international private protection. Mafia groups and private protection are symptomatic of the blurring of legality and illegality in the new international order. At the same time, they are powerful expressions of a defining feature of global liberal governance: the need to control processes and markets rather than territories. (Duffield 2005: 187)

We have seen (in Chapter 6) how private security companies are often offshoots of larger corporate organisations (particularly with respect to mining firms) or represent corporate bodies in their own right. Either way, the research presented here has shown how 'parallel global economies' obscure the boundaries between legal and illegal commercial activities. This has led to opportunities for criminal enterprise to utilise 'legitimate' or legal structures whilst at the same time 'legitimate' enterprise can stray over into illegal activities. Consequently, the disposing of illicit diamonds from Sierra Leone relies on access to legitimate markets and networks. In this way, the boundaries between one and the other necessarily become blurred. The role of corporations in illegal diamond activity then is part of the problem and not just in terms of the mining of African diamonds. The De Beers Group for example, whilst withdrawing from the mining of African diamonds in recent years, continues to be involved in other aspects of this trade. The following observations are still relevant:

> De Beers is part of the problem. In its efforts to control as much of the international diamond market as possible, it is no doubt purchasing diamonds from a wide variety of dubious sources, either wittingly or unwittingly. The breadth of its control, however, is also its major strength, and is part of the solution to the problem. If De Beers were to take a greater interest in countries like Sierra Leone, and if it were to stop purchasing large amounts of diamonds from countries with a

negligible production base, much could be done to end the current high levels of theft and smuggling. (Smillie, Gberie and Hazleton 2000: 9)

Campaign groups like Global Witness have been pro-active in exposing the diamond industry's role in encouraging organised crime, and in particular the role of diamond traders:

> Attempting to blame only the African diamond producing nations for the failures and weaknesses of the diamond industry is unacceptable. A significant proportion of the responsibility lies with diamond traders who continue to buy diamonds from unknown sources and by default are aiding and abetting the financing of terrorism, drug money laundering and organised crime. (Yearsley 2002)

The criminality involved in the diamond trade has to be seen as part of a wider pattern of organized crime in West Africa that often transits this area rather than originates here. This involves cocaine trafficking from Latin America to Europe and illegal oil 'bunkering' (theft or smuggling) particularly in the Niger Delta. West Africa has also become a dumping ground for weapons, waste and fake medicines (including electronic waste from old computers and mobile phones, toxic waste and counterfeit medications). Indeed, the volume of illicit income generated from illegal oil bunkering or cocaine trafficking (approximately $1 billion each) rivals the GNP of Cape Verde or Sierra Leone (UNODC 2009:1). According to the United Nations Office on Drugs and Crime (UNODC) Executive Director Antonio Maria Costa:

> West Africa has everything that criminals need: resources, a strategic location, weak governance and an endless source of foot soldiers who see few viable alternatives to a life of crime [...]. Organized crime is plundering West Africa – destroying governments, the environment, human rights and health [...]. This makes West Africa more prone to political instability and less able to achieve the Millennium Development Goals [he added]. A powerful minority, all the way to the top, is profiting from crime in West Africa, at the expense of the many. [He warned that] democracy and development will falter, while crime and corruption will flourish. (UNODC 2009:1)

The continued involvement of companies like De Beers in the retail of potential conflict or smuggled diamonds from non-conflict areas led Global Witness and Amnesty International UK to commission a survey (June 2007). Their findings are symptomatic of continuing problems here. Of 42 top British diamond retailers, it was found that 79 per cent of retailers who responded reported having no auditing procedures in place to combat the trade in conflict diamonds. Thirty one per cent did not respond to repeated requests to provide information on their policies (including Cartier, House of Fraser and John Lewis) and two per cent did not give any information about their policies on conflict diamonds. Many of those surveyed admitted to following the industry's minimal systems of self-regulation but only a handful (including Signet and subsidiaries Ernest Jones, H. Samuel and Leslie Davis, and Tiffany & Co) have reported putting more robust measures in place to combat conflict diamonds (Global Witness & Amnesty International UK May 2007). Indeed, many in the polish and retail sectors of the industry had opposed government regulation during the establishment of the Kimberley Process, preferring instead to police themselves. It would seem that any attempts to enforce a robust tracking system to ensure diamonds are conflict free have failed. Undoubtedly, the trade in conflict diamonds has declined in recent years, but this is due in large part to the ending of conflicts in Angola and Sierra Leone rather than the success of policing this by the industry itself. Moreover, investigations by Global Witness have found that:

> In November 2005 [....] diamonds mined in West Africa are regularly smuggled and given Kimberley Process certificates by countries other than their country of origin. Some of these are blood diamonds, and they are being certified as conflict-free. (Global Witness November 2006)

In a recently released press statement entitled 'Blood Diamonds – Time to Plug the Gaps', Global Witness reported how a number of civil society organisations (including the Freetown based *Network Movement for Justice and Development)* claimed that the Kimberley Process Certification Scheme (KPCS) (designed to regulate the trade in rough diamonds) was failing. Claims of non-compliance, smuggling, money laundering and human rights abuses in alluvial diamond areas continued (19 June 2009). Several days later *The Independent* ran with a front page headline 'The return of blood diamonds' in which it was reported that the original architect of the Kimberley certification Scheme – Ian Smillie – (Partnership Canada Africa) had quit amid the failure of governments and the industry to tackle gross violations and allow 'all manner of crooks off the hook'. The slaughtering of hundreds of Zimbabwean diamond miners by the government-backed military in 2008 was a case in point. While these diamonds had not come out of conventional 'civil conflict', nevertheless Smillie insisted these were indeed 'blood diamonds' as in his words, 'they have blood all over them' (*The Independent* 25 June 2009).

There have been attempts in Sierra Leone to enforce legal artisanal digging and trading in diamonds. In December 2001 for example, the Diamond Area Community Development Fund (DACDF) was established to support legal diamond mining and to allocate a percentage of mining revenue to the local chiefdom for small-scale community development. Donors match funding for social and infrastructural development (Temple 2005). Such funds are based on the number of mining licences issued and the value of diamonds recovered. The scheme has been used for educational, health and training, as well as infrastructural development (ibid.). By the end of 2004, 54 chiefdoms had benefitted from this initiative though alarmingly a government committee found in the same year that the scheme suffered from a lack of transparency and community involvement in decision-making of the fund. The establishment of Chiefdom Development Committees (CDCs) to oversee this have not been successful in ensuring decision making is fair, accountable and inclusive of groups such as youth and women. In many cases the decisions made by such committees have remained in the hands of the traditional rural (often conservative) elite that have been accused of misuse of funds in the Sandor and Lower Bambara chiefdoms[12] (Maconachie & Binns 2007a, Temple 2005, Jackson 2007).

There is a broader national and international context within which the business of Sierra Leonean diamonds operate and in particular the issue of corrupt practices. While corruption is something that afflicts most nations to some degree or another, according to the Transparency International Corruption Perception Index (PCI) for 2005, out of 20 countries rated most corrupt, 10 are in Africa. Countries recovering from conflict like Sierra Leone are particularly vulnerable since efforts to secure future security and economic sustainability can be undermined. Moreover, compared to the amount of debt relief Africa receives (estimated to be around $25 billion a year), the problem of illegal capital flight where the proceeds of corruption are banked in Western coffers, is huge in comparison and is estimated to be in the region of $100–200 billion (Africa All Party Parliamentary Group [AAPPG] 2006). Moreover, around 80–90 per cent of illegal capital flight out of Africa is permanent, that is, it does not re-enter the continent and for those African elites who have a hand in this, collectively they hold around $700 to $800 billion in overseas accounts (ibid.).

Future trends

The role of international mining companies like the Sierra Leone Diamond Company (SLDC) and Koidu Holdings (formerly Branch Energy) has caused a degree of contention in Sierra Leone. Their involvement has seen in recent years increased moves towards industrial scale mining in Sierra Leone. Internationally, the International Labour Organisation (ILO) reports that the mining industry is moving away from a labour intensive industry towards a capital intensive one leading to the loss of jobs as it comes to rely on a core of highly skilled workers. This of course has implications for Sierra Leone's employment problems and particularly the future employment of existing artisanal miners. Moreover, such companies have been linked to an increasing pattern of 'land grabbing' after concessions had been granted by government. In some cases this has led to mining

---

[12] See Maconachie, R. (2008) 'Diamonds, governance and "local" development in post-conflict Sierra Leone: Lessons for artisanal and small-scale mining in sub-Saharan Africa?' *Resources Policy* for a greater discussion of this.

licence holders not having these renewed or even having them withdrawn without any or little recompense.

The recent proliferation of mechanised mining companies, has led to an increase in competition for land between artisanal diggers and mining companies. There is a diminishing need for the massive labour force employed in the artisanal sector, and there is growing friction around environmental and property rights. All of this suggests an increased role for government, the need for a joined-up approach that extends far beyond the Ministry of Mineral Resources, and standards of a significantly higher level than has been the case historically (Global Witness and Partnership Africa Canada 2008).

In addition, the involvement of mining companies has led to the use of explosives to blast for Kimberlite deposits which involve the temporary evacuation of communities and in some cases permanent relocation.[13] Such operations are adding to existing tensions as local communities feel they have little control over the operations of these companies and any economic benefits to the communities affected are not apparent (Global Witness 2007). Indeed, a number of organisations involved in social activism have emerged as a result (directly or indirectly) of a range of issues thrown up by the diamond industry in Sierra Leone. This includes such factors as democracy and governance, and gender and youth. Community based organisations like the Movement of Concerned Kono Youth (MOCKY) and the Network Movement for Justice and Democracy (NMJD) have attempted to link up with broader based organisations like the Peace Diamond Alliance in an attempt to have some input and influence into the decision making surrounding diamond governance.

Much of the existing deep mining of Kimberlite diamonds in Africa is controlled by international mining companies who utilise bank transfers to deal with sales. Alluvial mining in Sierra Leone and elsewhere in Africa tends to be cash based and relies on family and business ties to other African diamond markets and the use of non-traditional remittance systems in diamond trading. This makes monitoring extremely difficult and can account for the circa $300 million in diamond value smuggled out of the country in 2002 (Even-Zohar 2003). Recommendations have been made by such organisations as USAID that relate to greater control over money laundering and reforms to the credit, production and marketing systems, (particularly as this relates to indigenous miners) but there is little evidence of enforcement.

---

[13] Those refusing to move have joined together to form the Affected Property Owners Association. They claim that housing provided by Koidu Holdings was substandard and insufficient for the numbers affected. Others in the community feel resentful that government has made decisions involving their land without consultation and complain that facilities promised by Koidu Holdings such as schools and roads have come to nothing. See Global Witness (2007) 'Peacebuilding Omission?' October.

Conclusion

Diamond revenues in Sierra Leone have not been effectively utilised for the development of that country. There is now a broad consensus that globally, artisanal/small-scale mining (ASM) such as that which exists in Sierra Leone is driven by poverty. Poverty here continues to be concentrated in the rural and urban areas outside of the capital Freetown. Underemployment is a huge problem especially amongst young urban men between the ages of 20 and 24. In 2006, three out of ten in this age group were unemployed or not in education or training (World Bank 2008). The World Bank's and United Nation's use of a $1 a day to measure income or consumption against basic material needs for food, shelter and clothing does not take account of the cumulative impact of other factors that affect the poor including lower life expectancy, undernourishment, higher infant mortality, illiteracy and disease (ILO 2003).

Sierra Leone's Poverty Reduction Strategy Paper (SL-PRSP 2005), found lack of food or hunger was considered by Sierra Leoneans as the strongest indicators of poverty. This relates to income poverty that is determined by the employment status of the household head, their level of education and the sector they are employed in. A poverty rate of 58 per cent among the youthful working population demonstrates limited employment and economic opportunities for the most potentially productive part of the labour force. Income levels are very low for women, especially in rural areas and school attendance is higher among males than females in both poor and non-poor households. In addition, human development indicators such as illiteracy rates, infant and maternal mortality, access to education, health care and safe drinking water reflect low levels of human development. Such indicators are particularly poor for women who endure extremely high maternal mortality, infant mortality and fertility rates. Sierra Leone's are amongst the worst in the world (SL-PRSP 2005).

The debilitating effects of poverty also impact on more qualitative factors like the loss of dignity, self-respect, weakening of family and community relationships and feeds a cycle of poverty that is passed on from one generation to the next (ILO 2003). Sierra Leone is among the poorest countries in the world, where recent adult literacy rates (aged 15 and older) stood at 34.8 per cent and life expectancy at birth stood at 41.8 years (UN Development Report 2007/2008). In addition the Human Poverty Index for developing countries (HPI–1) measures human development using the same criteria as the HDI (living a long and healthy life, access to education and a decent standard of living). This represents a more complete and multidimensional measure of deprivation than the $1 a day criteria. For Sierra Leone, the HPI-1 in 2004 was 51.7 giving it a ranking of 102 out of 108 developing countries (UN Human Development Report 2007/2008). In addition, the gender-related development index

(GDI) that measures gender inequality and forms part of the value of its GDI found that out of 156 countries measured in this way, Sierra Leone had 152 countries with a more favourable GDI-HDI ratio. (UN Human Development Report 2007/2008).

Diamond mining and other natural resources in Sierra Leone should in theory have aided development. Instead, the history of this small West African state has been marred by ineffective state regulation of the mining and trading of diamonds (artisanal and Kimberlite). The lack of control over illicit production and trading alongside legitimate diamond production has produced a pattern of 'parallel' economic activity that forms part of a 'shadow' state. While sections of the political elite have gained socially, economically and politically from this state of affairs and have little incentive to challenge this, at the same time such developments have meant that those at the bottom of the 'diamond chain' (the artisanal diggers, miners and small licence holders), have little incentive to deter illicit activity here since they do not share in the benefits of this wealth. Gross exploitation seen in terms of unfair remuneration and prices merely perpetuates this pattern. Whilst official diamond exports in previous years (2004–2005) had increased with Kimberlite accounting for the bulk of this (see World Development Report 2007/2008), artisanal mining more recently has formed the bulk of diamond exports. In 2007, Sierra Leone officially exported $141 million worth of diamonds and over $100 million of this was produced by artisanal miners (Global Witness & Partnership Africa Canada 2008). Better regulation, challenging corruption from the top down and fair prices for those working at the diamond face is one strategy for making this rich resource work to benefit the country. Government has a huge role and responsibility here.

The government has primary responsibility for ensuring that communities where diamonds are mined benefit from the process. It must ensure that the country as a whole benefits as well. Government must take the lead in establishing policies and standards that encourage developmentally sound investments which protect and enhance local infrastructures and land use. The government must also develop systems for project monitoring and evaluation to ensure that diamond mining, whether on a large or small scale, protects the rights and interests of all Sierra Leoneans (Global Witness & Partnership Africa Canada 2008).

Future poverty alleviation as pursued through the World Bank's policy of sustainable development should be dependent on pro-poor and government initiatives that support effective social and environmental policies. This includes the creation of greater employment opportunities particularly for artisanal/small-scale mining (but also more widely) as this is driven by a lack of alternative economic opportunities and poverty. Indeed, the global problem of artisanal mining has forced a general rethink on how illicit mining per se should be dealt with. Cooperation with illegal operators is seen to be preferable to confrontation as too is the idea of providing alternative and diverse employment in rural areas in an effort to reduce illicit activity. Agricultural seasonality encourages illicit mining activity in the absence of alternative livelihoods during the rest of the year, though a number of alternative livelihood projects have recently been endorsed by donor bodies, government and mining companies (see Maconachie and Binns 2007 in Hilson and Banchirigah 2009). Improved terms of trade and investment between developing and developed countries would also support sustained economic growth. Such changes are dependent on the political willingness of those in positions of power to support real and sustainable change. Only future developments will determine whether this happens or not.

An additional strand that has become increasingly important in developing nations is the role of the third sector, particularly the use of NGOs in partnership with the state, business and civil society to provide services that would otherwise be provided by the state.

New partnerships like the *Kono Peace Diamond Alliance* (disbanded by 2008)[14] have emerged in Sierra Leone involving government, business (for example Koidu Holdings Limited) and civil society. It would seem that some NGOs in their capacity to act as *advocates* on behalf of the poor are at the same time acting as 'subcontractors' of the state in their capacity as service providers, especially of welfare services that the state will not or cannot provide. Such action neatly fits the neo-liberal discourse espoused by the IMF, the World Bank and others that the free market rather than the state should provide welfare to the poor. However, the promotion of laissez-faire market economics and liberal concepts of freedom not only legitimise huge social and economic inequalities, but they help reinforce diverse forms of exploitation in the world economy (Brown cited in Thomas in Evans 1998). In addition, economic liberalisation as in the cases of Angola, Sierra Leone, Rwanda and Sudan has also according to Hoogvelt (1997:166), 'directly contributed to the descent into anarchy and civil wars'.

The government of post-conflict Sierra Leone had begun to embrace a pro-market policy through its encouragement of private sector investment in the mineral industry in preference to investing state assets here. The adoption of a mining policy that is 'in accordance with international best practice' is testimony to the universal legitimacy of Western liberal values that are presented as universal, inevitable and 'natural' (see Thomas and Wilkin 1997). The issue of course is whether 'best practice' and universalist policy is favourable to local diversity and conditions or whether as some would argue, this undermines and weakens this? (Thomas and Wilkin 1997). What cannot be disputed is that such discourse is based on the premise that global wealth as generated from economic and political liberalisation will provide enough for all. Whilst the 'market' does indeed

[14] According to Maconachie, the Peace Diamond Alliance (PDA) had been disbanded by 2008. See Maconachie, R. (2008), 'Diamonds, governance and "local" development in post-conflict Sierra Leone: Lessons for artisanal and small-scale mining in sub-Saharan Africa?' *Resources Policy*.

create surplus wealth that could potentially benefit all, in reality, 'free markets' have resulted in increasing inequalities not only between the developed and developing world but within national boundaries in nations like Sierra Leone (Falk cited in Dunne and Wheeler 1999).

Grass roots organisations like MOCKY; the Network Movement for Justice and Development (NMJD) its affiliate the Campaign for Just Mining (CFJM) have been important in articulating the views of those excluded from development policies through their calls for greater government regulation of mining companies, as well as more open and democratic consultation with those communities affected. Many of these grass-roots organisations who are involved in lobbying for greater local empowerment, participation, and transparency and equity within diamond mining are also involved in NGOs as a means through which broad-based social organisations can build alliances. Moreover, some key members of MOCKY have taken positions as Councillors in Kono District Council, Koidu-New Sembehun Town Council and even positions in the Office of the Vice-President (Fanthorpe and Maconachie 2010). While such moves encourage greater civil society participation, at the same time such developments can uphold existing political and economic structures (a kind of democratising capitalism according to Ungpakorn 2004) and can even be seen as symptomatic of party political manipulations. At the same time, there is evidence that grassroots associations (focused around sport, religious activity and entertainment) are also challenging the hold of traditional rural elders, leading to greater empowerment of both women and young men (Richards, Bah and Vincent 2004 cited in Fanthorpe and Maconachie 2010). Nevertheless, the tensions inherent in moves by global mining corporations to disregard the views and demands of local communities do come to light on occasions as they did in Sierra Leone in 2007. Here civil unrest erupted in the town of Koidu-Safadu, in which several hundred protesters came out to demonstrate against the environmental and social damage being inflicted on this area by the mining company Koidu Holdings. Local police used live ammunition and tear gas to disperse the protesters in which eight people were injured and two were tragically killed (Gonzalez, 2007). Indeed, if future localised conflict is to be avoided it is important that such voices be heard and acted upon, as this has major implications for more widespread future civil conflict. Indeed, the United Nations Peacebuilding Commission (2007) reported that: 'Many of the dire conditions that gave rise to the conflict in 1991 remain in 2006, with many youths unemployed, marginalized and lacking hope for the future' (cited in Fanthorpe and Maconachie 2010: 255). Moreover, according to a World Bank report (Collier et al. 2003) those marginalised countries whose economic characteristics conform to low income, economic decline and dependence on primary commodities, the risks and incidence of civil war tend to increase. Sierra Leonean diamonds have been linked to the wider regional instability of nations like Guinea, Côte d'Ivoire and particularly Liberia and we have seen how various studies have established a causal relationship between a reliance on natural resources and an increased risk of conflict (Collier and Hoeffler, 2001, Elbadawi and Sambanis, 2002 cited in Maconachie and Binns 2007b).

As this work comes to a conclusion, Sierra Leoneans and others witnessed the sentencing of the former Liberian war lord Charles Taylor to 50 years in prison for war crimes and crimes against humanity (*The Guradian* 30 May 2012). When we consider the brutality of the civil war, and the continuing high levels of poverty, inequality and social injustice, diamonds have not been a blessing for the majority of Sierra Leoneans. Rather, they have brought misery, conflict, corruption and greed. Only those who have benefitted would disagree, including the powerful kleptomanic minority within the country itself, as well as those external interests that have benefitted, including criminal networks and corporate interests involved in different sections of the *diamond chain*, notwithstanding the overlapping and symbiotic ties that exit between these. The one positive that comes out of all of this is the resilience of the human condition, witnessed in huge quantities in Sierra Leone itself. Indeed, the patience, hope, pride and dignity that many Sierra Leoneans express, despite the odds stacked against them and the challenges they face on a day-to-day basis, gives some optimism for the future. However, the pace of change here needs to move up a gear. Sierra Leone's diamonds have to be utilised more equitably for the benefit of the poor and marginalised. Otherwise, like the volcanic energy that created these rich diamond deposits millions of years ago, and the carnage created by the recent civil war, Sierra Leone will erupt again with equally or even greater devastating consequences.

Appendix A – The Diamond Chain/Pipeline

Source: DiamondFacts.org

Table A.1 Diamond Pipeline: Value Added

Percentage of GVC	% (of original value)
Producer Selling Value	100
Sorting	115
Polishing	127
Polished Dealing	133
Jewellery Manufacturing	166
Retail	320

Source: 'Value Chain' Commodity Focus – Diamonds. The Mining Journal Ltd, 27 October 2006

Appendix B – A note on methodology

This work has utilised a variety of qualitative research methods to illustrate different aspects of the diamond industry in Sierra Leone. It includes secondary sources such as published academic books, journal articles and papers; reports and investigations carried out by organisations and activists, NGOs and pressure groups (inside and outside Sierra Leone) as well as newspapers (British and Sierra Leonean) and documentary sources such as official reports (UN, World Bank, IMF, Commission For Africa, DIFID). These secondary sources were used alongside historical and archival primary sources and include Colonial Office (CO), Colonial Secretary's Office (CSO), Ministry of Mineral Resources and Statistics Sierra Leone (1985–2004). Such sources have been combined and cross-referenced as far as possible with other methods in a process of triangulation. Thus, in addition to the above written and documentary sources, ethnographic research methods such as observation, semi-structured and unstructured interviews undertaken during field trips to Freetown and Kono in 2003 have been used. The use of long and informal unstructured interviews and other ethnographic tools such as informal conversations and observation to explore qualitative and more intimate features of social life help enrich and bring into focus more mundane and formalised documentary sources.

Access to the Government Gold and Diamond Office (GGDO) and Ministry of Mines personnel in Freetown (as well as other key personnel who had interests in Sierra Leone's diamonds) was both fascinating and enlightening in terms of seeing sizable quantities of rough diamonds and observing both the informality and buzz during negotiations between a diamond dealer and GGDO personnel. Contacts made in Freetown were invaluable in smoothing the way to contacts in Kono, including trips to non-mechanised diamond fields, often out of bounds to visitors. The gendered and ethnic nature of these interactions (all Sierra Leoneans and male in the majority of cases but some interviews were conducted with women in Kono), said much about the predominance of men in this industry. In this situation, perhaps my position as a white Western woman was an advantage? In a patriarchal society where women have few rights, perhaps some informants (for example government officials in Freetown) felt a paternal-like obligation to aid me in my work? Moreover, for those activist groups who were trying to get their message of injustice and inequality across, as a white Westerner perhaps I stood a better chance of conveying this to the outside world. Indeed, if the research process itself becomes a tool to further the cause of injustice by those subjects being studied, then such research serves a valuable and positive political purpose.

Kono is a rural area in the south east of Sierra Leone that borders

Guinea and takes almost a day to access by road from Freetown (approximately 200–250 miles) because of intermittently poorly maintained roads. The destruction of bridges over rivers also meant added miles to the journey. On visiting this area in 2003, many of the dwellings and buildings here (that are never more than two-storeys high because I was told of the problem of subsidence due to decades of digging) had been damaged by the devastation of the rebel occupation. Water wells had been contaminated and satellite telecommunication (of the kind used in war zones) was the only access (from one of the Lebanese shops) to the outside world. As night fell, the area was in almost total darkness except for the odd lights that came from those lucky enough to own generators. Otherwise the majority relied on kerosene lamps and candles. There was a real sense of isolation here, a feeling of being cut off from the outside world, though there was a significant UN military presence (mainly Pakistani and African) here. UN peacekeepers brought additional advantages to the researcher, including resources like photocopying facilities that were hard to come by in the town. My privileged position as a white female Westerner opened doors that were closed to Sierra Leoneans as I was given access to the invaluable photocopier despite a sign that read *Do not ask to photocopy.*

The ethnographic research undertaken in the Kono area was overt and based on informed consent. Thus the nature of the research was explained to the subjects, why it was being undertaken and what it would be used for. Gaining access to some of the diamond fields involved in one or two cases going through a 'gatekeeper' in this case the local Town Chief. This appeared to be relatively straightforward as I had arranged (through another contact) to stay in one of his properties. There are few hotels or guest houses in Koidu Town and many of the buildings there had been damaged during the rebel occupation. Through the 'gatekeeper' I was able to visit several areas where diamond digging was taking place. However, the practicalities of interrupting diggers during their work in addition to the problem of age (some were children under 16 years of age) meant I had to change tack and concentrate on observing the processes involved in digging and asked more casual questions about this. I was painfully aware of my presence as a white female Westerner and the effect this might have. Also, using an interpreter added to the sense of detachment and distance between myself and these workers. I was also aware of the effect of having the presence of the Town Chief – a figure of authority and power. All this appeared to unnerve these young diggers so such visits were kept brief. Instead, I later interviewed those who had once been involved in diamond digging as well as those who had never undertaken this but lived in the area and had an opinion. Such informants were more willing to be interviewed and recorded. During my time here I was also able to observe, engage in informal conversations with people (sometime in bars) ask questions, take notes and record interviews.

Appendix C – Hidden Voices – Selection of Interviewees

Those interviewed for this work were chosen from of a very small cohort of people that were deemed appropriate for the purpose of the research. All were in some way connected with the subject being documented. Whilst the author makes no claim of representative sampling of subjects here, nevertheless the views given, from a qualitative and ethnographic perspective, are nevertheless significant and help to shed some light on different aspects of Kono life. In this sense purposive or snowball sampling was employed. Those who contributed to the interviews used here have been anonymised where this has been requested through changing names to protect their identity and confidentiality. In such a sensitive industry and where diamonds became embroiled in civil war, awareness and sensitivity towards ethical and political issues is paramount. This research has adhered to the following BSA guidelines to:

> … ensure that the physical, social and psychological well-being of research participants is not adversely affected by the research. They should strive to protect the rights of those they study, their interests, sensitivities and privacy, while recognising the difficulty of balancing potentially conflicting interests. (BSA Ethical Practice Guidelines)

The method used here for interviewing adopts what some scholars have referred to as 'theoretical sampling' (Munck and Rolston 1987). This involves searching out those interviewees more likely to have something to say on the subject matter being researched either because s/he is involved directly in the industry or has some involvement in social organisations. Such people might also wish to highlight other factors deemed significant that the interviewer did not ask or know about. This form of selection allowed Munck and Rolston (ibid.) in their study of Belfast to look for 'people who were likely to be the most fruitful and revealing for the questions we were interested in'.

Those 'selected' for interview in Kono were in many cases amongst the most articulate and politicised. Yet, during informal conversations with other Sierra Leoneans I was inspired and impressed with their levels of analysis and understanding not only of Sierra Leone, but Africa and the developing world more generally. Many adopted a critical stance towards inequality and poverty and displayed a wider knowledge and understanding of global politics, and of the nature of 'race' and class structures in Britain and the US. Of course, such communities cannot afford to be complacent and apathetic since they have a higher investment in the political process, even if it does let them down. Their everyday experience of life and struggle in the developing world has served to radicalise and politicise many. Conditions of extreme and absolute poverty, hunger, inadequate education and health care systems, unemployment, lack of state welfare, limited economic opportunities, human rights abuses, inequality and political corruption and instability has meant that people more generally articulate their concerns and take an active interest in current affairs. The trauma of civil war has added to the political debating and activism in rights based organisations that have emerged at the grass roots and elsewhere.

'Access' to my informants initially began through a friend that I had met during doctoral research in Freetown in 1989–1990 and with whom I had intermittently stayed in contact, throughout the civil war period. He introduced me to a Kono activist who was a student at the university in Freetown and was president of the Kono students union. He would become my 'guarantor' in Kono, introducing me to other activist, taking me to meetings of various organisations that were trying to articulate the concerns of the youth, arranging trips to see and talk with diggers, and setting up (unstructured) interviews with individuals who had previously worked for foreign companies like Branch Energy before they left when war broke out. The interview questions varied considerably though for the purpose of the chapters (Chapters 3 and 4), the emphasis was on the nature of work in the diamond sector. Questions for discussion related to social organisations and in particular why such organisations were set up and what they hoped to achieve. Moreover, where possible cross-referencing with other sources has been used to either provide a wider context and/or confirmation of oral testimonies, including cross-referencing with other oral testimonies.

The exploitative nature of interviewing is something that immediately confronts the interviewer. Thus, it seems that the interviewer 'takes' knowledge and information from such communities and fails to give anything back. This raises the issue of remuneration, or paying interviewees to be interviewed. In such circumstances offering payment may lead to knowledge being compromised and the interviewee giving the answers they believe the interviewer wants to hear. The people I spoke with were not motivated by money (even though many occupied precarious socioeconomic positions) but by anger and frustration at the injustices inflicted on their society. They wanted those outside Sierra Leone, indeed outside Africa to have knowledge of their suffering and in particular, to rectify the obscene juxtaposition of a country endowed with mineral wealth, yet the majority afflicted with absolute poverty and few economic opportunities. Such people wanted their plight, their feelings and perspectives recorded and made available to a wider public in the developed world (notwithstanding the limitations of academic work in wider disseminations) so that their voices might be heard in the hope that future positive changes can be brought about. One final point to note is that those who spoke at length during informal conversations and semi-structured/unstructured interviews represent the real 'experts' on diamonds in Sierra Leone. The chapters that reproduce this material merely capture a snapshot of that experience and attempt to place it in a wider political and economic arena.

Appendix D – Movement of Concerned Kono Youth (MOCKY)

The hand written document (prepared by Aiah A.Y. Aroana, Secretary General on 19 April 2003) reproduced below explains the background and the aims and objectives of the movement:

'The Movement of Concerned Kono Youth known as MOCKY came into being in Freetown in November 1999. It was formed by disgruntled Kono youths who were then resident in Freetown as a result of the occupation of Kono district by the combined RUF and AFRC junta forces in February 1998. Secondly, the general status quo of the entire Kono displaced population within and outside Freetown was rather different from those from the Southern, Northern and some parts of the Eastern provinces and, virtually there was nobody to talk on behalf of the district, not even its people to tell [the] powers that be.

Above all, neglect and marginalisation was another factor that precipitated the formation of MOCKY. From its inception in November 1999 to December 2001, all the issues or problems affecting Kono people in Freetown and outside Freetown were championed by the organisation. The organisation (MOCKY) gained legal recognition (registered) with the government of Sierra Leone through the Ministry of Youths, Education and Sports on 23rd December 1999. Upon receipt of the certificate of registration from the Ministry, MOCKY there and then took up an agitation campaign to adequately inform the government of Sierra Leone and the international community about the plight of the Kono people.

First and foremost, on 4th March 2000 MOCKY organised a peaceful demonstration in Freetown which almost brought together all the Konos resident in Freetown and its immediate environs to demonstrate against the RUF occupation of the Kono district. Besides, in April 2000, the organisation again organised another demonstration referred to as "Black Monday" (ie Konos to dress in black attire) to mourn for the destruction of Kono district. The demonstration in question was observed both by Konos in Freetown and those in the diaspora. The organisation equally undertook other significant activities besides the aforementioned.'

Aims and Objectives of the organisation:

- To foster unity and cooperation amongst all Kono youths of Kono district and Sierra Leone in general
- Develop the land through collective participation
- Educate youths of their roles, responsibilities and civil rights
- Collectively oppose all acts inimical to the interest of Kono district and Sierra Leone at large

- Promote and sustain skills training and micro-enterprises for self-reliance and economic development
- Promote games and sports for the building of soul, body and mind and to help eradicate the use of harmful drugs among youths
- Females to be granted equal opportunity to hold executive positions and contribute to decision making

Primary Sources

Archives

Colonial Secretary's Office (Government Archive, Freetown)

CSO Confidential Series – Diamonds, Special reports on activities in mining – Allocation of Crown lands and mining sites. File Gold in the Central Provinces. Letter 3rd Feb 1930

CSO Confidential Series ibid File: Report to Governor from the Managing Director SLST Feb 1935

CSO Confidential File S/29/35

CSO Open Policy Files – Allocation of Crown Lands and Mining Sites File: Summonses and convictions under the Minerals legislation 1935

CSO Confidential Series – The Suppression of Illicit Diamond Dealing in Sierra Leone 1935

CSO Confidential Series – Diamonds, special reports on activities in mining – allocation of crown lands and mining sites. File: The Suppression of Illicit Diamond Dealing in Sierra Leone 6 March 1935

CSO S/19/35 Protection of Mining

CSO Confidential Series Feb 1935

CSO Open Policy Files – Allocation of Crown Lands and Mining Sites, File, SLST

CSO Confidential Series – Diamonds, Special reports on activities in mining

CSO Confidential Series – Allocation of crown lands and mining sites.

CSO Confidential Series –Agreement of SLST with certain chiefs

CO/029/63 Transcript of Legislative Council Dec 1952

CSO Confidential Series – Diamonds, Special reports on activities in mining – Allocation of crown lands and mining sites. File; Agreement of SLST with certain chiefs

CSO Sierra Leone – Geological Survey and Mines Annual Report for 1938

Colonial Office (Public Record Office, Kew)

CO/029/63

CO/029/63) Transcript of Legislative Council Dec 1952

CO/029/63 1953
CO/029/64 Letter to the Governor from four Sierra Leonean Ministers, 31 Oct 1953
CO/029/63 1954
CO/029/63 Letter from Acting Gov of Sierra Leone to Rt Hon Oliver Lyttelton MP, Sec of State for the Colonies File No S.F. 3630/3. Despatch No. 287 Secret

Interviews

Koidu Town, Kono District April 2003
Mocky Executive 1 (Anonymous) 18 April
Mocky Executive 2 (Anonymous) 18 April
Mr Abdullah (Mocky) 18 April
Mr Abnoa (fictious name) (Mocky) 19 April
Mr Aiah, A.Y. Aroana (Secretary Mocky)
Mr Amida ('supporter' and member of Mocky) 19 April
Mr Sahr Bendu (Mocky and President of Kono Students' Union) 18 April
Mrs Memuna Boya 19 April
Ms Esther Fasuluku ('supporter') 19 April
Ms Fasuluku (business woman – 'Supporter' and bar owner, Freetown) 19 April
Mr Fayie 18 April
Mrs Gladys Gbonda (Mocky and teacher for *Forum for African Women Educationalists* [FAWE]) 18 April
Mrs Jackson (Kono Women's Task Force) 18 April
Mr Mohammed (Mocky) 17 April
Chief Bondu (Town Chief Koiqema and 'supporter') 20 April
Vice President Mocky (name withheld) 18 April
'Victoria' Full name withheld (business woman and supporter) 17 April

Freetown April 2003
Mr Usman Kamara, Deputy Director of Mines (Ministry of Mineral Resources)
Mr Lawrence Ndola-Myers (Manager of the Government Gold and Diamond Office)

Secondary Sources

Books and articles

Abdullah. I. (1998), 'Bush path to destruction: the origin and character of the Revolutionary United Front /Sierra Leone', *The Journal of Modern African Studies*, 36, (2) 203–235
Abdullah, I. (ed.) (2004) *Between Democracy and Terror: the Sierra Leone Civil War*. Dakar: Council for the Development of Social Science Research in Africa

Abdullah, I. & Bangura, Y. (eds) (1997) 'Special Issue: Lumpen Culture and Political Violence: the Sierra Leone Civil War', *Africa Development*, Vol. XXII, Nos. 3–4: 171–216

Abdullah, I., Bangura, Y. Blake, C., Gberie, L., Johnson, L., Kallon, K., Kemokai, S., Muana, Rashid, P.K., Zack-Williams, A. B. (1997) 'Lumpen Youth Culture and Political Violence: Sierra Leoneans Debate the RUF and the Civil War', *Africa Development*, Vol XXII, Nos 3/4

Abdullah, I. & Muana, P. (1998) 'The Revolutionary United Front of Sierra Leone: A Revolt of the Lumpenproletariat' in Clapham, C. (1998), *African Guerrillas*, Oxford: James Currey.

Adeleke Adeeko, (2002) 'Bound to violence? Achille Mbembe on the Post-colony' *West Africa Review*

Adedeji, A. (1993) (ed.) *Africa within the World – Beyond Dispossession and Dependence*, London: Zed Books

Africa All Party Parliamentary Group (AAPPG) (2006) *The Other Side of the Coin: The UK and Corruption in Africa*, March: London, House of Commons

Africa Confidential (1998) 'Private Armies, Public Relations' 39 (11) 29 May cited in Cilliers & Cornwell (1999) 'Africa – 'From the privatisation of security to the privatisation of war?' in Cilliers, J. & Mason, P. (eds) *Peace, Profit or Plunder? The Privatisation of Security in War-Torn African Societies*, Institute for Security Studies: South Africa

Africa Confidential (May 2009) 'Rich resources, little investment' 20 February Vol 50 No 4

Ajayi, J.F. Ade (1976) (2nd edition), *History of West Africa*, London: Longmans

Alao, A. (2007) *The Tragedy of Endowment*, New York: University of Rochester Press

Ali, T.M. & Matthews, R.O. (eds) (1999) *Civil Wars in Africa – Roots and Resolutions*, Montreal & Kingston London: McGill-Queen's University Press, Ithaca

Amnesty International (2002) 'The Terror Trade Times' June Issue No 3

Amnesty International (2006) 'Kimberley Process: an Amnesty International position paper' in Hilson, G. & Clifford, M.J. (2010) 'A "Kimberley Protest": Diamond Mining, Export Sanctions and Poverty in Akwaitia, Ghana', *African Affairs* Volume 109 No 436 July

Appadurai, A. (1986) *The Social Life of Things – commodities in cultural perspectives*, Cambridge: Cambridge University Press

Archibald, S. & Richards, P. (2002) 'Converts to Human Rights? Popular Debate about War and Justice in Rural Central Sierra Leone', *Africa* 72 (3) 339–367

Arrighi, G. & Saul, J.S. (1973), *Essays on the Political Economy of Africa*, New York, Monthly Review

Arrighi, G. (2002), 'The African Crisis', *New Left Review* 15, May/June

Baker, B. & May, R. (2004) 'Reconstructing Sierra Leone', *Commonwealth & Comparative Politics,* Vol. 42, No 1, March

Bangura, A. K. & Dumbuya, M. S. (1993) 'The Political Economy of Sierra Leone's Mineral Industry since Independence' in *Sierra Leone Review* Vol. 2 Winter

Bangura, Y. (2000) 'Strategic policy failure and governance in Sierra Leone', *The Journal of Modern Africa Studies*, 38, 4: 551–577

Bangura,Y., (1997) 'Understanding the political and cultural dynamics of the Sierra Leone war: a critique of Paul Richards' *Fighting for the Rainforest*, in Abdullah, I. & Bangura, Y. (1997) (eds) Special Issue: Lumpen Culture and Political Violence: the Sierra Leone Civil War, *Africa Development* Vol. XXII, Nos. 3–4: 171–216

Barnett, A., Hughes, S., & Burke, J. (2004) 'Mercenaries in "coup plot" guarded UK officials in Iraq'. *The Observer* 6 June

Barrett-Brown, M. & Tiffen, P. (1992) *Short-Changed: Africa and World Trade* Statistical appendix in Reno, W. (1998) *Warlord Politics and African States*, Boulder, CO: Lynne Rienner, p. 50

Baudrillard, J. (1981), *For a Critique of the Political Economy of the Sign.* St. Louis, Mo.: Telos Press, cited in Appadurai, A. (1986) *The Social Life of Things – commodities in cultural perspectives,* Cambridge: Cambridge University Press

Bayart, J. F., Ellis, S., & Hibou, B., (1999) 'From Kleptocracy to the Felonius State' in Bayart, J. F., Ellis, S., & Hibou, B., *The Criminalization of the State in Africa*, Oxford: James Currey

Bayart, J. F., (1989), *The State in Africa: the Politics of the Belly*, London: Longman.

Berg Report (1981) World Bank: Washington

BBC News Online 'IMF unblocks aid for Sierra Leone 13 March 2002

Beare, M.E. (ed.) *Critical Reflections on Transnational Organized Crime, Money Laundering, and Corruption,* Toronto: University of Toronto Press

Berdal, M. & Keen, D. (1997) 'Violence and Economic Agendas in Civil Wars: Some Policy Implications', *Millennium Journal of International Studies*, 26, No 3

Berdal, M. & Malone, D.M. (eds) (2000), *Greed and Grievance – Economic Agendas in Civil Wars,* Boulder, Lynn Rienner

Binns, J.A. (1982) 'The changing impact of diamond mining in Sierra Leone', *Research Papers in Geography* No: 9, University of Sussex

Birrell, I. (2009) 'Why are repressive regimes given the succour of British aid?' *The Independent Online,* Thursday 17 September 2009, accessed 17 September 2009

Blomstrom, M. & Lundhal, M. (eds) (1993) *Economic Crisis in Africa: Perspectives and Policy Responses,* London: Routledge

Boahen, A. Adu (1987) 'The Colonial Impact' in Collins, R.O, McDonald Burns, J, Ching, E.K. (eds) (1994) *Historical Problems of Imperial Africa*, Princeton: Markus Wiener Publishers

Bourdieu, P. (1984) *Distinction: A Social Critique of the Judgement of Taste*, Cambridge, Mass: Harvard University Press, cited in Appadurai,

A. (1986) *The Social Life of Things – Commodities in Cultural Perspectives*, Cambridge: Cambridge University Press

Bourne, M. (2001) 'Conflict Diamonds: Roles, Responsibilities and Responses', *Peace Studies Papers* 2.1 Fourth Series, Department of Peace Studies, University of Bradford.

Braidwood, S.J. (1994) *Black Poor and White Philanthropists: London's Blacks and the Foundation of the Sierra Leone Settlement, 1786–1791*, Liverpool: Liverpool University Press

Brayton, S. (2002) 'Outsourcing War: mercenaries and the privatisation of peacekeeping', *Journal of International Affairs* 55

Brewer, A. (1980) *Marxist Theories of Imperialism: a Critical Survey*, London: Routledge and Kegan Paul

BBC News Online (2001) 'Blair Promises to Stand by Africa' 2 October

BBC News Online (2003) 'Angola Profile' 21 Feb

BBC News Online (2012) 'Liberia ex-Leader Charles Taylor gets 50 years in jail' 30 May

British Sociological Association (BSA) (2002) *Statement of Ethical Practice* March (Appendix updated May 2004)

Brown, T., Fanthorpe, R., Gardener, J., Gberie, L., Gibril Sesay, M., (2006) 'Sierra Leone: drivers of change. The IDL Group, Brockley Combe, Backwell, Bristol' in Maconachie, R. & Binns, T. (2007a) 'Beyond the resource curse? Diamond mining, development and post-conflict reconstruction in Sierra Leone', *Resources Policy* (32) 104–115

Burke, L.J. (1959) 'A Short Account of the Discovery of the Major Diamond Deposits' in *Sierra Leone Studies*, December New Series No. 12

Busumtwi-Sam (1999) 'Redefining "Security" after the Cold War: The OAU, the UN and Conflict Management in Africa' in Ali, T.M. & Matthews, R.O. (eds) (1999) *Civil Wars in Africa – Roots and Resolutions*, Montreal & Kingston London Ithaca: McGill-Queen's University Press

Campbell, G. (2004) *Blood Diamonds: Tracing the Deadly Path of the World's Most Precious Stones*, Boulder: Westview Press

Castells, M. (1998), *The Information Age, Economy, Society and Culture: End of Millennium Volume III*, Oxford: Blackwell Publishers

Chatterjee, P. (2004) 'Controversial Commando Wins Iraq Contract', *Corporate Watch* 9 June

Cilliers, J. & Cornwell, R. (1999), 'Africa – From the privatisation of security to the privatisation of war?' in Cilliers, J. & Mason, P. (eds) *Peace, Profit or Plunder? The Privatisation of Security in War-Torn African Societies*, Institute for Security Studies, South Africa

Cilliers, J. & Mason, P. (eds) (1999), *Peace, Profit or Plunder?: The privatization of Security in War-torn African Societies*, Institute for Security Studies, South Africa

Clapham, C. (1998) *African Guerrillas*, Oxford: James Currey

Clapham, C. (2000) 'Failed States III: Globalization and the Failed State' paper presented to *Failed States and Non-States in the Modern International Order*, Florence, Italy April 7–10

Cleeve, A. (1997) *Multinational Enterprises in Development. The Mining Industry of Sierra Leone,* Aldershot: Avebury

Clemens, M. & Moss, T. (2005) 'What's Wrong with the Millennium Development Goals?'
Center for Global Development Brief, September

Collier, P. (1995) 'The marginalization of Africa' *International Labour Review,* 134 (4–5); 541–57, cited in M. Castells (1998) *The Information Age, Economy, Society and Culture: End of Milennium Volume III,* Oxford: Blackwell Publishers

Collier, P. (2000) 'Doing Well out of War: An Economic Perspective' in Berdal, M. & Malone, D.M. (eds) (2000), *Greed and Grievance – Economic Agendas in Civil Wars,* Boulder: Lynn Rienner

Collier, P. & Hoeffler, A. (2001), 'Greed and grievance in civil war', *Policy Research Working Paper* No 2355. Washington DC: World Bank

Collier, P. et al. (2003) *Breaking the Conflict Trap – Civil War and Development Policy* A World Bank Policy Research Report, Washington DC and Oxford: Oxford University Press

Collins, R.O., McDonald Burns, J., & Ching, E.C. (eds) *Historical Problems of Imperial Africa,* Princeton: Markus Wiener Publishers

Commission for Africa (2005) *Our Common Interest: Report of the Commission for Africa,* March

Commission for Africa *(2010) Still Our Common Interest,* Executive Summary

Concilliation Resources (1997) 'Gender and Conflict in Sierra Leone' ACCORD September/October http://www.c-r.org/pubs/occ papers/briefings5.htm cited in Corporate Watch (2005) 'The Commission for Africa and Corporate Involvement' June. www.corporatewatch.org.uk/?lid=1535 cited in Mines & Communities (2005) 'Edinburgh G8 summit and mining companies' www.minesandcommunities.org/Action/press662.htm accessed 18 October 2005

Conway, H.E. (1968) 'Labour Protest Activity in Sierra Leone during the Early Part of the Twentieth Century', *Labour History* 15 (Canberra) 49–63

Cramer, C. (2006) *Civil War is Not a Stupid Thing. Accounting for Violence in Developing Countries,* London: Hurst & Company

Crowder, M. (1968) *West Africa Under Colonial Rule,* Evanston: Northwestern University Press

Davidson, B. (1992), *The Black Man's Burden: Africa and the Crisis of the Nation-State,* New York: Times Books

Dearden, N. (2007) 'Amnesty International UK Business and Human Rights', May, www.globalwitness.org.

De Beers Group (2004) 'From the Worshipful Company of Goldsmiths', (London 1513) *Annual Review* London

De Beers Group (2009) 'De Beers Launches Novel New Marketing Campaign' Press Release September; De Beers Group www.debeersgroup.com.

De Soysa, I. (2000) 'The Resource Curse: Are Civil Wars Driven by Rapacity or Paucity?' in Berdal, M. & Malone, D.M. (eds) (2000), *Greed and Grievance – Economic Agendas in Civil Wars*, Boulder, Lynn Rienner

Department for International Development (DFID) (2005) Press Release 'Continued progress in Sierra Leone brings further UK support' November, www.dfid.gov.uk/news/files/pressreleases/additional-support-sierra-leone.asp

Department for International Development (DFID) (2006) 'Millennium Development Goals', www.dfrid.gov.uk/mdg/

Diamond Development Initiative International (2008).

Douglas, I. (1999) 'Fighting for diamonds – Private military companies in Sierra Leone' in Cilliers, J. & Mason, P. (eds) *Peace, Profit or Plunder? The Privatisation of Security in War-Torn African Societies*, Institute for Security Studies: South Africa

Dowden, R. (2002) 'Justice goes on trial in Sierra Leone', *The Guardian Online*, October 3, accessed 30 October 2003

Dowden, R. (2002) 'Sierra Leone locked in shackles of corruption', *The Guardian*, October 12

Doyle, M. (1986) *Empires* Ithaca: Cornell University Press

Doyle, M. (2002) 'Sierra Leone diamonds "fuelled" Lebanese war', BBC News Online, www.news.bbc.co.uk 13 November, accessed 6 November 2007

Duffield, M. (2000), 'Globalization, Transborder Trade and War Economies' in Berdal, M. & Malone, D.M. (eds) (2000), *Greed and Grievance – Economic Agendas in Civil Wars*, Boulder: Lynn Rienner

Duffield, M. (2001), *Global Governance and the New Wars. The Merging of Development and Security*, London: Zed Books

Duffield, M. (2001) 'Governing the Borderlands: Decoding the Power of Aid' in Wilkinson, R. (ed.) (2005) *The Global Governance Reader*. London: Routledge

Ekholm-Friedman, K. (1993) 'Afro-Marxism and its disastrous effects on the economy; The Congolese case' in Blomstrom, M. & Lundhal, M. (eds) (1993) *Economic Crisis in Africa: Perspectives and Policy Responses*, London: Routledge

Elbadawi, I., & Sambanis, N. (2002) 'How much war will we see? Estimating the prevalence of civil war in 161 countries, 1960–1999'. *Journal of Conflict Resolution*, 46 (2): 307–334

Engineers Against Poverty (2004) *The Extractive Industries Review* www.engineersagainstpoverty.org, accessed 9 February 2009

Epstein, E.J. (1982) *The Rise and Fall of Diamonds*, London: Simon & Schuster.

Even-Zohar, C. (2003) *Sierra Leone Diamond Sector Financial Policy Restraint* Peace Diamond Alliance (Management Systems International), Under USAID Cooperative Agreement No. 636–A-00–03–00003

Extractive Industries Transparency Initiative (EITI) (2008) Sierra Leone

Fanthorpe, R. & Maconachie, R. (2010) 'Beyond the "Crisis of Youth"? Mining, Farming and Civil Society in Post-War Sierra Leone', *African Affairs*, Vol. 109, No. 435, April

Farah, D. (2002) 'African diamonds finance Al Qaeda', *The Washington Post*, 29 December

Farah, D. (2004) *Blood from Stones: The Secret Financial Networks of Terror*, New York: Broadway Books

Farlam, P. (2005) 'Working Together. 'Assessing Public-Private Partnerships in Africa' February. *The South African Institute on International Affairs*

Fatton, Jr, R. (1992) *Predatory Rule: State and Civil Society in Africa*, Boulder: Lynne Rienner.

Fearon, J. (2004) 'Primary commodity exports and civil war', *Journal of Conflict Resolution* 49 (4): 483–507

Feis, H. (1935) *Europe: The World's Banker*, 1870–1914 Yale, cited in Harman, C. (2003) 'Analysing Imperialism', *International Socialism Journal 99*, Summer

Ferguson, J. (2006), *Global Shadows – Africa in the Neoliberal World Order*, Durham and London: Duke University Press

Findlay, M. (1999) *Globalization of Crime: Understanding Transitional Relationships in Context*, Cambridge, Cambridge University Press

Fowler, R. (2000) 'Final Report of the UN Panel of Experts on Violations of Security Council Sanctions Against UNITA', *The Fowler Report*

Francis, D.J. (1999) 'Mercenary intervention in Sierra Leone: providing national security or international exploitation?' *Third World Quarterly*, Vol. 20, No. 2: 319–338

Frost, D. (1999), *Work and Community among West African Migrant Workers*, Liverpool: Liverpool University Press

Fyfe, C. (1962), *A History of Sierra Leone*, London: Oxford University Press.

Gallagher, J. & Robinson, R. (1953) 'The Imperialism of Free Trade', *The Economic History Review*, Second Series, Vol. VI, No. 1

Gamba, V. & Cornwell, R. (2000) 'Arms, Elites and Resources in the Angolan War' in Berdal, M. & Malone, D.M. (eds) (2000), *Greed and Grievance – Economic Agendas in Civil Wars*, Boulder: Lynn Rienner

Gamble, D.P. (1964) 'Kenema – a growing town in Mende country' *Bulletin of Sierra Leone Geographical Association*, 7/8 in Binns, J.A. (1982) 'The changing impact of diamond mining in Sierra Leone'; *Research Papers in Geography*, No. 9. University of Sussex

Gberie, L. (2002) *War and Peace in Sierra Leone: Diamonds, Corruption and the Lebanese Connection*, Partnership Africa Canada Occasional Papers

Gellar, S. (1995) 'The Colonial Era' in Martin, P.M. & O'Meara, M. (eds), *Africa*, Bloomington and London: Indiana University Press and James Currey

Global Witness (1998) 'A Rough Trade: The Role of Companies and Governments in the Angolan Conflict', London: Global Witness, www.globalwitness.org

Global Witness (2000) 'Conflict Diamonds: possibilities for the identification, certification and control of diamonds : a briefing document'

Global Witness (2002) 'Resources, Conflict and Corruption'

Global Witness (2003) 'For a Few Dollar$ More: How al Qaeda Moved into the Diamond Trade'

Global Witness (2006) 'Broken Vows: The diamond industry's failure to deliver on combating blood diamonds', November

Global Witness (2006) 'The Truth About Diamonds: Conflict and Development', November

Global Witness (2007) 'Peacebuilding Omission?' October

Global Witness & Amnesty International UK (June 2007) 'Results of Global Witness and Amnesty International UK Survey on Top Retailers' Policies to Combat Blood Diamonds'

Global Witness and Partnership Africa Canada (2008) 'Loupe Holes: Illicit Diamonds in the Kimberley Process', November Global Witness and Partnership Africa Canada

Gonzalez, R. (2007) 'Constant blasting for diamonds, low wages are one firm's legacy', *Western Catholic Reporter*, Edmonton 22 October

Goreux, L. (2001) 'Conflict Diamonds', Africa Region Working Paper Series No. 13, Washington DC: The World Bank

Green, T. (1984) *The World of Diamonds: The Inside Story of the Miners, Cutters, Smugglers, Lovers and Investors*, New York: William Morrow & Co.

Greenhalgh, P. (1985) *West African Diamonds 1919–1983: An Economic History*, Manchester: Manchester University Press

Hallam, D. (2009) in Howden, D. (2009) 'UN attempts to slow the new scramble for Africa', 7 November, *The Independent*

Harman, C. (1999) *A People's History of the World*, London: Bookmarks

Harman, C. (2003) 'Analysing Imperialism' *International Socialism Journal 99*, Summer

Harrell-Bond, B.E., Howard, A.M & Skinner, D.E. (1978) *Community Leadership and the Transformation of Freetown (1801–1976)*, The Hague: Mouton Publishers.

Hassan, S. (2004) 'Corruption and the Development Challenge', *Journal of Development Policy and Practice*, www.acdi-cida.gc.ca cited in Royal African Society (2005) 'A Message to World Leaders: What About the Damage We Do to Africa?' June, SOAS: London

Hayward, F.M. (1987) (ed.), *Elections in Independent Africa*, Boulder: Westview Press

Herbst, J. (1998) *Contemporary Efforts at Regulation: A Local and International Perspective,* paper read at the conference 'The Privatisation of Security in Africa', South African Institute on International Affairs, Johannesburg, 10 December 1998: 2, cited in Cilliers & Cornwell (1999) 'Africa – From the privatisation of security to the privatisation of war?' in Cilliers, J. & Mason, P. (eds) *Peace, Profit or Plunder? The Privatisa-*

tion of Security in War-Torn African Societies, Institute for Security Studies: South Africa: 240

Hibou, B (2004) *Privatising the State,* New York: Columbia University Press

Hilson, G. & Banchirigah, S.M. (2009) 'Are Alternative Livelihood Projects Alleviating Poverty in Mining Communities? Experiences from Ghana', *Journal of Development Studies* Vol. 45, No. 2: 172–196, February

Hilson, G. & Clifford, M.J. (2010) 'A "Kimberley Protest": Diamond Mining, Export Sanctions and Poverty in Akwaitia, Ghana', *African Affairs* Vol. 109, No. 436, July

Hirsch, J.L. (2001), *Diamonds and the Struggle for Democracy,* Boulder: Lynne Rienner

Hobson, J.A. (1902), *Imperialism, A Study,* Ann Arbor: University of Michigan Press

Hodkinson, S. (2005) 'Do stars really aid the cause?' 26 October, *The Independent Online,* accessed 26 October

Hoffman, D. (2004) 'The Civilian Target in Sierra Leone and Liberia: Political power, military strategy and humanitarian intervention', *African Affairs,* 103: 211–226

Hoogvelt, A., (1997) *Globalisation and the Postcolonial World: The New Political Economy of Development,* London: Macmillan

Hoogvelt, A., (2002) 'Globalisation, Imperialism and Exclusion: The case of Sub-Saharan Africa', in Zack-Williams, A.B. et al. (eds) *Africa in Crisis: New Challenges and Possibilities,* London: Pluto Press

Hooper, J. (1996), *Sierra Leone – The War Continues, Jane's Intelligence Review,* January 1996 in Vines, A. (1999) 'Gurkhas and the private security business in Africa' in Cilliers, J. & Mason, P. (eds) *Peace, Profit or Plunder? The Privatisation of Security in War-Torn African Societies,* Institute for Security Studies: South Africa

Howden, D. & Doyle, L. (2007) 'Making a Killing: how private armies became a $120bn global industry', *The Independent* 21 September

Howden, D. (2009) 'UN attempts to slow the new scramble for Africa', *The Independent,* 7 Nov

Human Rights Watch (1998) World Report

Human Rights Watch (2000) *Corporations and Human Rights* – Corporate Social Responsibility July 28 Letter to Secretary-General Kofi Annan

Human Rights Watch (2001) World Report

Independent Online (2007) 'US cancels Sierra Leone's debt', June, accessed 27 June 2007

International Labour Office (2003) 'Working Out of Poverty' – Report of the Director General.

International Labour Conference 91ˢᵗ Session, Geneva

International Organization for Migration (2002) News http://www.iom.int

Jackson, R.H. & Rosberg, C.G. (1994), 'The political economy of African personal rule' in Apter, D. & Rosberg, C (eds) *Political Development* and the New Realism in Sub-Saharan Africa, Charlottesville: University of Virginia Press

Jackson, P. (2007) 'Reshuffling an old deck of cards? The politics of local government reform in Sierra Leone' *African Affairs* 106 (422): 95–111, in Maconachie, R. & Binns, T. (2007a) 'Beyond the resource curse? Diamond mining, development and post-conflict reconstruction in Sierra Leone' *Resources Policy* 32

Jones, J. (2003), Al-Qaeda 'traded blood diamonds' *BBC News Online* 20 February, www.bbc.co.uk, accessed 15 October 2007

Joseph, R. (ed.) (1999), *State, Conflict and Democracy in Africa,* Boulder: Lynne Rienner.

Kaldor, M. (1999) *New and Old Wars. Organized Violence in a Global Era,* Oxford: Polity Press

Kandeh, J.D. (1999) 'Ransoming the State: Elite Origins of Subaltern Terror in Sierra Leone', *ROAPE* Vol. 26, No 81

Kanfer S. (1993) *The Last Empire: De Beers, Diamonds and the World,* New York: Farrar Straus Giroux

Kaplan, R.D. (1994) *The Coming Anarchy: Shattering the Dreams of the Post Cold War,* Random House: New York

Keen, D. (2005) *Conflict & Collusion in Sierra Leone,* Oxford: James Currey

Keen, D. (2002) 'Incentives and Disincentives for Violence in Berdal, M. & Malone, D. (eds) *Greed and Grievance. Economic Agendas in Civil Wars,* Boulder: Lynne Rienner

Kenneth Scott Associates (Architects and Town Planners) (1970) *Development Proposals for central Kono, Sierra Leone.* Mimeo report, London, cited in Binns, J.A. (1982) 'The changing impact of diamond mining in Sierra Leone', *Research Papers in Geography* No: 9, University of Sussex: 24–25

Killick, A. (1994) Structural Adjustment and Poverty Alleviation: *United Nations Standing Committee on Poverty Alleviation.* UN

Kilson, M. (1966) *Political Change in a West African State,* Cambridge, MA: Harvard University Press

King, D. (1975) *Africana Research Bulletin,* Vol. 5: 4

Lawrence, S & Reisch, N. (2006), *The World Bank Group, the Extractive Industries Review (EIR) and Governance: Evaluating the Bank Group's implementation of its commitments,* Washington DC: Bank Information Center, January

Lenin. V.I. (1933) *Imperialism: The Highest Stage of Capitalism,* London

Levin, E.A. (2005) 'From Poverty and War to Prosperity and Peace? Sustainable Livelihoods and Innovation in Governance of Artisanal Diamond Mining in Kono District, Sierra Leone' *M.A. thesis,* University of British Columbia February

Lewis, P. (1996) 'From prebendalism to predation: the political economy of decline in Nigeria', *Journal of Modern African Studies* 34 (1): 79–103

Leys, C. (1994), 'Confronting the African Tragedy', *New Left Review* 204: 33–47

Lilly, D. (2000) 'The privatisation of security and peacebuilding: a framework for action', *International Alert*, cited in *Research Highlight*: 14 November 2003

Little, A. (2010) 'Can Britain lift Sierra Leone out of poverty?' *BBC News – Newsnight* 23 June

Maconachie, R. (2008) 'Diamonds, governance and "local" development in post-conflict Sierra Leone: Lessons for artisanal and small-scale mining in sub-Saharan Africa?', *Resources Policy,* doi:10.1016/j.resourpol. 2008.05.006

Maconachie, R. & Binns, T. (2007a) 'Beyond the resource curse? Diamond mining, development and post-conflict reconstruction in Sierra Leone', *Resources Policy* 32: 104–115

Maconachie, R. & Binns, T. (2007b) '"Farming miners" or "mining farmers"?: Diamond mining and rural development in post-conflict Sierra Leone'. *Journal of Rural Studies* 23: 367–380

Mazrui, Ali A. (1998) 'The Failed State and Political Collapse in Africa', in Otunnu, O.A. & Doyle, M.W. (eds) *Peacemaking and Peacekeeping for the New Century,* Maryland: Rowman & Littlefield Publishers

McConnell, T. (2009) China and India engaged in 21st century 'scramble for Africa', *The Times,* Nov 12

McGowan, P.J. (2003), 'African military coups d'etat, 1956–2001: frequency, trends and distribution', *Journal of Modern African Studies* 41, 3

Michael W. Doyle (eds): *Peacemaking and Peacekeeping for the New Century,* Lanham: Rowman & Littlefield

Mines and Communities (November 2003) http://wwwminesandcommunities.org/Action/press213.htm, accessed 18 October 2005

Mines and Communities Organisation (May 2004) 'Statement of the Africa Initiative on Mining, Environment and Society' (AIMES). Mining Communities Charter http://www.minesandcommunities.org/charter/aimsdec.htm, accessed 18 October 2005

Mitchell, G. (2005) 'Terrorists Prefer Diamonds' How Predation, State Collapse and Insurgence Have Fashioned the International Exploitation of Sierra Leone's War Economy', March, *Peace Studies Paper, Working Paper 8,* Fourth Series, University of Bradford

Mohan, G., Brown, E., Milward B., Zack-Williams, A.B., (2000) (eds) *Structural Adjustment: Theory, Practice and Impacts.* London: Routledge

Muana, P.K. (1997), 'The Kamajoi Militia: Civil War, Internal Displacement and the Politics of Counter-insurgency', *Africa Development,* Vol. 22 (3/4)

Munck, R. & Rolston, B. (1987) *Belfast in the Thirties,* Belfast: The Blackstaff Press

Musah, A.F. (2000) 'A Country Under Siege: State Decay and Corporate Military Intervention in Sierra Leone', in Musah, A.F. & Fayemi, J. (eds) *Mercenaries: an African security dilemma,* London: Pluto Press

Napoleoni, L. (2004) *Terror Inc,* London: Penguin

Naylor, R. T. (1995), 'Loose cannons: Covert commerce and underground finance in the modern arms black market', in *Crime, Law and Social Change*, 22: 1–57

Naylor, R.T. (2003) 'Predators, Parasites, or Free-Market Pioneers: Reflections on the Nature and Analysis of Profit-Driven Crime' in Beare, M.E. (ed.) *Critical Reflections on Transnational Organized Crime, Money Laundering, and Corruption*, Toronto: University of Toronto Press

Network Movement for Justice and Development, (2004) Press Statement 'Sierra Leone' 23 January: Mines and Communities website http://www.minesandcommunities.org

Nkrumah, K. (1968) *Neo-colonialism: the last stage of imperialism*, Heinemann: London

O. Brien, K. (2003) 'The Privatization of Security in Sub-Saharan Africa' *Africa South of the Sahara* 32nd Edition

Okigbo, P. (1993), 'The Future Haunted by the Past', in Adedeji, A. (ed.) *Africa within the World – Beyond Dispossession and Dependence*, London: Zed Books

Oliver, R. & Fage, J.D. (1988), *A Short History of Africa*, London: Penguin

Pallister, D. (2005) 'Africa: special report', *The Guardian*, 1 June.

Partnerhip Africa (2000) *The Heart of the Matter: Sierra Leone, Diamonds and Human Security*, Ian Smillie, Lansana Gberie, Ralph Hazleton

Pech, K. (1999) 'Executive Outcomes – A corporate conquest' in Cilliers, J. & Mason, P. (eds) *Peace, Profit or Plunder? The Privatisation of Security in War-Torn African Societies*, Institute for Security Studies: South Africa

Peel, M. (2004) 'Gem miners' labours earn few riches for Sierra Leone', *Financial Times* 9 July

Perez-Katz, (2002) 'The Role of Conflict Diamonds in Fueling Wars in Africa: the Case of Sierra Leone', *International Affairs Review* (Winter/Spring 2002)

Peters, K. & Richards, P. (1998) 'Why We Fight': Voices of Youth Combatants in Sierra Leone', *Africa* 68

Peters, K. & Richards, P. (2011) 'Rebellion and Agrarian Tensions in Sierra Leone', *Journal of Agrarian Change*, Vol. 11, Issue 3, July

Peters, K., (2011) *War and the Crisis of Youth in Sierra Leone*, Cambridge: Carmbridge University Press

Petras J. (1999) 'NGOs: In the Service of Imperialism', *Journal of Contemporary Asia* 29: 4

Plaut, M. (2002) '"Blood diamonds" polished off' BBC News Online www.news.bbc.co.uk, 5 November, accessed 6 November 2002

Plaut, M. (2003) 'Al-Qaeda's Africa gems' BBC News Online, www.news.bbc.co.uk, 17 April, accessed 15 October 2007

Reno, W. (1995) *Corruption and State Politics in Sierra Leone*, Cambridge: Cambridge University Press

Reno, W. (1998) *Warlord Politics and African States*, Boulder: Lynne Rienner

Reno, W. (2000) 'Shadow States and the Political Economy of Civil Wars', in Berdal, M. & Malone, D. (eds), *Greed and Grievance. Economic Agendas in Civil Wars,* Boulder: Lynne Rienner

Richards, P. (1996) *Fighting for the Rainforest: War, Youth and Resources in Sierra Leone,* Oxford: James Currey

Richards, P., Bah, K, & Vincent, J., (2004) 'Social Capital and Survival: prospects for community driven development in post-conflict Sierra Leone', Social Development Paper No. 12, World Bank: Washington DC, cited in Fanthorpe, R. & Maconachie, R. (2010) 'Beyond the "Crisis of Youth"? Mining, Farming and Civil Society in Post-War Sierra Leone', *African Affairs,* Vol. 109, No. 435, April

Peters, K., (2011) *War and the Crisis of Youth in Sierra Leone,* International African Institute Library Series, Cambridge: Camridge University Press

Riddell, J.B. (1974) 'Periodic markers in Sierra Leone', Annals of Association of American Geographers 64 (4) cited in Binns, J.A. (1982) 'The changing impact of diamond mining in Sierra Leone', *Research Papers in Geography* No: 9 University of Sussex: 49

Roberts, J (2003) *Glitter and Greed: the secret world of the diamond cartel,* New York: Disinformation Press

Robinson, R. & Gallagher, J. (1961) 'Egypt and the Partition of Africa', in O'Collins, R., McDoanlad Burns, J. & Ching, E.C. (eds) *Historical Problems of Imperial Africa,* Princeton: Markus Wiener Publishers

Rodney, W. (1982), *How Europe Underdeveloped Africa,* Washington DC: Howard University Press

Ross, M. (2001) 'Extractive Sectors and the Poor', *Oxfam America Report* October, Washington DC

Ross, M.L. (1999) 'The Political Economy of the Resource Curse', *World Politics* 51: 297–322

Roth, K. (2000) 'Precious Stones Don't Kill, Guns Do: Enforce Arms Embargoes', *Los Angeles Times,* 21 July

Royal African Society (2005) 'A Message to World Leaders: What About the Damage We Do to Africa?' June, London: SOAS

Rubin, E. (1999) 'Saving Sierra Leone, at a Price', *The New York Times,* 4 February

Rubin, E. (2007) 'Mercenaries' *Crimes of War* 2.0. November Crimes of War Project 1999–2003

Ruggiero, V. (2000) *Crime and Markets: essays in anti-criminology,* Oxford: Oxford University Press

Ruggiero, V. (2003) 'Global Markets and Crime' in Beare, M.E. (ed.) *Critical Reflections on Transnational Organized Crime, Money Laundering, and Corruption,* Toronto: University of Toronto Press

Seibureh, I. (2005) 'Sierra Leone rated High for Child Labour', *Concord Times* (Freetown) 11 February

Serewicz, L. (2002) 'Globalisation, Sovereignty and the Military Revolution: from mercenaries to private international security companies',

International Politics 39: 75–89

Shearer, D. (1998) 'Private Armies and Military Intervention', *Adelphi Paper* 316 IISS, Oxford: Oxford University Press

Sierra Leone Diamond Industry Annual Review (2004), The Diamonds and Human Security Project, Partnership Africa, (Ottawa, Canada) and Network Movement for Justice and Development, (Freetown, Sierra Leone)

Simmel, G. (1957) 'Fashion'. *American Journal of Sociology* LXII/6: 541–58

Simms, A. (2009) 'What's yours is mine', *New Statesman*, 15 October

Simon, D. et al. (eds) (1995) *Structurally Adjusted Africa: Poverty, Debt and Basic Needs*, London: Pluto Press

Skinner, D.E. & Skinner, M.B. (1971), 'African-British relations in northern Sierra Leone 1807–1896', Sierra Leone Symposium, University of Western Ontario, London, Ontario cited in Harrell-Bond, B.E., Howard, A.M & Skinner, D.E. (1978), *Community Leadership and the Transformation of Freetown* (1801–1976), The Hague: Mouton Publishers

Smillie, I, Gberie, L. & Hazleton, R. (2000) *The Heart of the Matter: Sierra Leone, Diamonds and Human Security*. January, Partnership Africa Canada

Smillie, I. (2000) 'Getting to the heart of the matter: Sierra Leone, diamonds and human security. *Social Justice* 27 (4)

Smillie, I. & Gberie, L. (2001) 'Dirty Diamonds and Civil Society', Partnership Africa Canada

Smith, A.M. (2003) 'Israeli connection doing well', *West Africa*, June

Spooner, B. (1986) 'Weavers and dealers: the authenticity of an oriental carpet', in Appadurai, A. (1986) *The Social Life of Things – commodities in cultural perspectives,* Cambridge: Cambridge University Press

Sunday Times (2005) 'Tory MP in £1.5m diamond mine row', 27 March

Su-Young Chang, et al. (2002) *The Global Diamond Industry Chazen Web Journal of International Business*, Fall, Columbia Business School

Swindell, K. (1973) *Labour Migration and Mining in Sierra Leone*, PhD thesis, London School of Economics and Political Science

Temple, P. (2005), 'Improving the effective use of the Diamond Area Community Development Fund' (DACDF). Report by the Integrated Diamond Management Program (IDMP) for Submission to the Government of Sierra Leone High Level Diamond Steering Committee (HLDSC). *Management Systems International*, Washington, DC cited in Maconachie, R. & Binns, T. (2007a) 'Beyond the resource curse? Diamond mining, development and post-conflict reconstruction in Sierra Leone', *Resources Policy* 32: 104–115

Thomas, C. & Wilkin, P. (eds) (1997) *Globalization and the South*, New York: St. Martin's Press

Tombs, S. & Whyte, D. (1998) 'Capital Fights Back: risk, regulation and profit in the UK offshore oil industry', *Studies in Political Economy* 57, Autumn

Transparency International Corruption Perception Index (PCI) for 2005

Turay, E.D. & Abraham, A. (1987), *The Sierra Leone Army: A Century of History*, Basingstoke: Macmillan

Ungpakorn, Ji Giles (2004) 'NGOs: enemies or allies'? *International Socialism*, Autumn 104

UN Development Fund for Women (undated) War and Peace 'Gender Profile of the Conflict in Sierra Leone', New York

UNDP(1991) *Human Development Report*, Oxford University Press: 2

UNDP (2003) *Human Development Report*, Oxford University Press

UNDP (2004) *Human Development Report*, New York and Geneva

UNDP (2006) *Human Development Report*, Oxford University Press: Oxford

UNDP (2007) *Development Report. Human Development Index* (HDI)

UNECE (2008) *Life Expectancy UK* 2006

UNECE (2008) *Infant Mortality Rate by Sex, Country and Year. Figures for UK 2006*

UN Expert Panel's report (2000) 'Report of the Panel of Experts on Violations of security Council Sanctions Against Unita'

UNHCHR (1998) 55th Session 'Report on the question of the use of mercenaries as a means of violating human rights and impeding the exercise of the right of peoples to self-determination, submitted by Mr.Enrique Bernales Ballesteros (Peru), Special Rapporteur pursuant to Commission resolution 1998/6'

UN (2007/2008) *Human Development Report for Sierra Leone*, New York and Geneva

UNODC (2009) 'Transnational Trafficking and the Rule of Law in West Africa: a Threat Assessment', July, New York

UN (2007) 'Report of the Peacebuilding Commission Mission to Sierra Leone, 19–25 March (A/61/901–S/2007/269, 14 May 2007)

UN Security Council (1997) 'Security Council Unanimously Approves Sanctions Regime Against Sierra Leone' Press Release SC/6425

UN Statistics (2011) Social Indicators – Life Expectancy Figures for 2010–2015

Van der Laan, H.L. (1965) *The Sierra Leone Diamonds – An economic Study covering the years 1952–1961*, Oxford: Oxford University Press

Vines, A. (1999) 'Gurkhas and the private security business in Africa', in Cilliers, J. & Mason, P. (eds) *Peace, Profit or Plunder? The Privatisation of Security in War-Torn African Societies*, Institute for Security Studies: South Africa

WHO (2007) *Maternal Mortality Rates*: Figures for Sub-Saharan Africa (2005) (Sierra Leone, Rwanda Liberia and Nigeria), UK and Ireland

Wilkinson, R. (ed.) (2005) *The Global Governance Reader*, London: Routledge

Whyte, D. (2003) 'Lethal Regulation: State-Corporate Crime and the United Kingdom Government's New Mercenaries', *Journal of Law and Society* Vol. 30, No. 4, December

Whyte, D. (2009) 'Paradoxes of Regulation' in Green, P. & MacKenzie, S. ed(s). *Regulating the Illicit Market in Antiquities*, London: Hart

World Bank (2001) *Sierra Leone data*, www.http://data.worldbank.org/country/sierra-leone, accessed June 2005

World Bank report (2003) *Sustainable Development in a Dynamic World: Transforming Institutions, Growth, and Quality of Life*

World Bank (2008) *Sierra Leone data*. www.http://data.worldbank.org/country/sierra-leone, accessed August 2009

World Bank (2012) *World Development Indicators, GDP Growth* (annual %) for Sierra Leone, www.http://data.worldbank.org/indicator, accessed February 2012

Yearsley, A. (2002) 'The Diamond Industry – Do they have a conflict diamond strategy at all? Press Release 5 October, Global Witness, www.globalwitness.org/press_releases/display

Zack-Williams, A.B. (1995), *Tributors, Supporters and Merchant Capital: Mining and Underdevelopment in Sierra Leone*, Aldershot: Avebury

Zack-Williams, A.B (1999), 'Sierra Leone: the political economy of civil war, 1991–1998', *Third World Quarterly* 20

Zack-Williams, A.B. et al. (eds) (2000) *Africa in Crisis: New Challenges and Possibilities*, London: Pluto Press

Reports and newsletters

Alluvial Diamond and Gold Mining Association (ADGMA).

Letter of Campaign and Cordial Notification that Concern the Unjust Mining in Kono District, 29 March 2000

Letter Campaign Against Child Miners in the Mining Industry, 26 September 2002

Kono Peace Diamond Alliance in Coalition with ADAGMAK for Just and Transparent Mining (no date).

Annual Reports of the Mines Department for the Years 1950, 1957, 1959, 1960 (Freetown)

Diamond Industry Annual Review, Sierra Leone 2004

International Institute for Environment and Development 2002

International Labour Organisation (2003) *Working out of Poverty – Views from Africa* Geneva

Movement of Concerned Kono Youth (MOCKY) – Aims and Objectives, April 2003

Newsletter NMJD Mines and Communities Website, March 2004.

Report – Mineral Resources of Sierra Leone 1981, Sierra Leone Collection, Fourah Bay College, Freetown.

Sierra Leone 1956 Annual Report of the Colonial Office

Sierra Leone Box, File on Regulations, Surveys, Inquiry, Annual Reports 1891–1987 (Freetown).

Statistics Sierra Leone, Sierra Leone 1985–2004

Sierra Leone Ministry of Mineral Resources February 2003

Report Mineral Resources of Sierra Leone 1981 SL Collection- Fourah Bay
College, Freetown
Ministry of Development and Economic Planning 1974
Mines Department Annual Report 1950, 1959, 1960

Newspaper and periodicals

Awoko (Freetown) 25 June 2004
BBC News Online 28 August 2003
Cocorioko International 16 October 2010
Concord Times (Freetown) 26 March 2004
Daily Mail 13 Feb, 11 July 1957
The Daily Express 5 October 1932
The Daily Telegraph 3 September 1932
The Economist 1957, 2000, 2007
The Economic Times 2010 Mumbai
For Di People 16 April 2003
The Guardian 24 March, 2000; 12 Oct 2002; 10 June 2005; 30 May 2012
The Independent 25 January 2007; 25 June 2009; 7 November 2009
The Mail 24 March 2000
The Manchester Guardian October 1953
Midweek Spark 8 February 2003
New Internationalist Vol 36, 7 May 2004
New York Times 22 August 2000
The News (Freetown) 14 April 2003
The New Citizen (Freetown) 6 April 2004
The New Storm (Freetown) 23 July 2002
The Observer 20 October 2002
Network Movement for Justice and Development, Press Statement 23 Jan
2004
Reuters 1 November 2007 'Sierra Leone to review mining contracts'
Sierra Leone Weekly News (Freetown) 6 July 1935
Standards Times Press News (Freetown) 16 March 2004; 28 November
2007. 'The Challenges in the Management of the Mining Sector in
Sierra Leone'
The Sunday Times 5 January 2003; 27 March 2005
The Times 20 February 2003; 12 November 2009
The Washington Post 1, 7 November 2001
World Gazetteer (Freetown) 2009
World Press Review 2002 June Vol. 49, No. 6
Western Catholic Reporter, (Edmonton) 22 October 2007, 'Constant
blasting for diamonds, low wages are one firm's legacy'

INDEX

50/50 Group, 116

ADMS. *See* Alluvial Diamond
   Mining Scheme
AFRC. *See* Armed Forces
   Revolutionary Council
All Peoples Congress (APC):
   alienates Kono opposition
   elements, 62; and abuse of
   power, 72, 101; and the
   deteriorating economy, 64;
   declares one party state, 64;
   Joseph Momoh appointed
   leader, 73; mentioned, 11, 59,
   60, 61, 74; partial
   nationalisation of the diamond
   industry, 57; wins election
   (1967), 39
Alluvial Diamond Mining Scheme
   (ADMS): introduced (1956),
   8, 37, 46, 60; mentioned, 9, 80,
   93
alluvial diamonds: difference in
   appearance, 147; discovery, 33;
   formation, 3; mentioned, 40,
   130, 136; mining methods, 80
al-Qaeda: infiltrated diamond
   trading networks, 165;
   mentioned, 150, 166, 172
APC. *See* All Peoples Congress
Armed Forces Revolutionary
   Council (AFRC): fighting with

militias, 75; fighting with RUF
   forces, 76; forced labour, 161;
   mentioned, 108, 154

Bafi River, 43
'bailing', 117
Baldry, Tony: misuse of political
   position, 171
Bangura, Zainab, 116
Benn, Hilary: former Secretary of
   State for International
   Development, 171, 178
Berlin Conference (1884-5), 28
Bio, Brigadier Julius, 159
blood diamonds, 1, 125, 161, 169,
   176, 177, 179; in newspaper
   headline, 188
Bo District, 33, 36, 37, 43, 46, 53,
   102
Bo, town of, 50, 55
'boundaries of permission', 167
Bout, Victor, 164, 171
Branch Energy: and Kimberlite
   mining, 110, 112, 127, 146;
   concerns over use of explosives,
   89; connections with Executive
   Outcomes (EO), 156, 162, 163;
   mentioned, 3, 85, 91, 92, 108,
   131, 159, 189; receives mining
   concessions, 161
Brima, Abu A. NMJD national
   coordinator, 111